AF505969

Imagining Globalization

ADVANCE PRAISE FOR *IMAGINING GLOBALIZATION*

"This volume adds new spark and spice to how we perceive and conceive globalization in all its hues and nuance. Rather than examining language, identity, and boundary in broad and abstract cultural and discourse terms, the essays address these thematic topics through multiple disciplinary lenses in concrete places where globalization 'touches down.' The book will stand as a fresh and special contribution to globalization research."

—Xiangming Chen
Dean and Director and Paul Raether
Distinguished Professor of Sociology and International Studies
Center for Urban and Global Studies, Trinity College

Imagining Globalization
Language, Identities, and Boundaries

Edited by Ho Hon Leung, Matthew Hendley,
Robert W. Compton, and Brian D. Haley

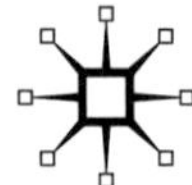

IMAGING GLOBALIZATION

Copyright © Ho Hon Leung, Matthew Hendley, Robert W. Compton, and Brian D. Haley, 2009

First published in 2009 by
PALGRAVE MACMILLAN®
in the United States – a division of St. Martin's Press LLC,
175 Fifth Avenue, New York, NY 10010.

Where this book is distributed in the UK, Europe and the rest of the world, this is by Palgrave Macmillan, a division of Macmillan Publishers Limited, registered in England, company number 785998, of Houndmills, Basingstoke, Hampshire RG21 6XS.

Palgrave Macmillan is the global academic imprint of the above companies and has companies and representatives throughout the world.

Palgrave® and Macmillan® are registered trademarks in the United States, the United Kingdom, Europe and other countries.

ISBN: 978-0-230-60963-1

Library of Congress Cataloging-in-Publication Data

Imagining globalization: language, identities, and boundaries/edited by Ho Hon Leung ... [et al.].
   p. cm.
  Includes bibliographical references and index.
  ISBN-13: 978-0-230-60963-1
  ISBN-10: 0-230-60963-5
 1. Culture and globalization. 2. Anthropological linguistics.
3. Group identity. I. Leung, Ho Hon, 1961—

HM621.I43 2009
306.44'6—dc22   2009024059

A catalogue record of the book is available from the British Library.

Design by Macmillan Publishing Solutions

First edition: December 2009

10 9 8 7 6 5 4 3 2 1

Printed in the United States of America.

Contents

I Language

II Identities

III Boundaries

List of Figures

List of Tables

Acknowledgments

The chapters in this volume came from three different conferences organized by the Center for Social Science Research at the State University of New York (SUNY) College at Oneonta. The editors would like to thank the grant support from the SUNY Conversation in Disciplines program for one of the conferences, Language and Globalization. The success of this conference was indebted to the Grant Office at the College at Oneonta, and the President's Office. Thanks should also be extended to the Teaching, Learning and Technology Center that helped to organize the conference, broadcast it through satellite, and make the conference program available on DVDs for library use. None of the editors has a broad knowledge in all the fields covered in this volume. Thus, we are particularly grateful to the contributors' patience and understanding of the challenging editorial process. Finally, thanks also to Samantha Hasey and the editorial assistants at Palgrave Macmillan. Their professional advice and support made the process of editing smooth and straightforward.

Imagining Globalization through Changes in Place

Ho Hon Leung and Matthew Hendley

Globalization is a fact of life. Perhaps, this statement may appear too bold to many people. Some might even argue that globalization is only a matter of rhetoric (see Hirst and Thompson 1996) and question its veracity. However, globalization is very real, particularly in this millennium. The 2008 global financial crisis, or tsunami, as some Asian countries call it, is a good example. Economists, politicians, financial advisers, journalists, and other experts have been trying to comprehend how it happened and how to solve this problem through global collaboration. "This is a global crisis and it needs global solutions," said a statement released after the meeting between the German chancellor, Angela Merkel, and the heads of the International Monetary Fund, the World Bank, the World Trade Organization, the International Labour Organization, and the Organization for Economic Cooperation and Development at a summit in Germany (Deutsche Welle February 5, 2009). Even though some small investors outside the United States may not consciously understand this crisis from a global perspective, the collapse of Lehman Brothers Inc., one of Wall Street's investment giants, had a deep impact on their lives. Many other crises also altered our consciousness of interconnectedness in our world. The outbreak of Severe Acute Respiratory Syndrome, 9/11, energy shortage, and global warming are good examples. However, crises are not essential to spark an awareness of globalization at work. The global culture of consumerism promoted by transnational corporations (Chiang and Mi in this volume) has reached different corners of the world. The consumption of the Internet, mobile phones, fast food, fashion, and music is increasing rapidly every day. If modernization, a concept that described the previous phase of world development, was so widespread that no part in the world was left untouched, the effect of the forces of globalization on the world are even more far-reaching, both quantitatively and qualitatively.

What Is Globalization and How Does It Affect Everyday Life?

In spite of consensus (see Guillén 2001; Pieterse 2004, 8) on several general observations on globalization that include (1) the driving force of globalization is technological change (Levy 1997; Gabel and Bruner 2003) that compresses time and space (Harvey 1989), (2) globalization destabilizes (Cox 1996) and delegitimizes (see Suáraz-Orozco and Sommer 2002; Compton in this volume) the nation-state, (3) globalization moves in tandem with regionalization (Morrison et al. 1991; Ruigrok and van Tulder 1995, cited in Pieterse 2004), and (4) its development is uneven (Hedley 2002, 375; McMichael 2007), the ontological question, "What is globalization?" remains controversial and contested. Globalization means different things to different people in different places. Various social science disciplines define globalization according to their schools of thought (see Guillén 2001; Pieterse 2004, 8). Scholars have also developed several perspectives on globalization, including its examination as a process, as projects, as a system, as discourse (Pieterse 2004, 18), and as ideology, good and bad (Taylor et al. 2002, 13; Legrain 2002; Urry 2003).

The challenge of finding globalization in a "flat" world, using Friedman's term (2007), is not an easy undertaking. However, this task does not intimidate those who are concerned about every form of life and the happenings in the world that are shaped by the forces of globalization. The discourse of this finding has taken some promising directions. Some scholars (Suáraz-Orozco and Qin-Hillard 2004; Kenway and Fahey 2009) argue that the relevance of globalization, as confined to free markets, free capital flows, and a neoliberal economic system, should not be dismissed, but this argument is too narrow. Also, research and books on globalization that "tend to confine themselves to disciplinary domains and perspectives" (Pieterse 2004, 15) are fragmented and exclusive rather than holistic and inclusive. Given the nature of globalization, which intersects political, economic, social, cultural, and environmental domains in everyday life, the investigation of globalization requires a multi- and interdisciplinary approach (Pieterse 2004, 15; Gardner 2004; Kenway and Fahey 2009). Furthermore, instead of examining globalization at high levels of generalization and abstraction with its empirical emptiness, Kenway and Fahey (2009, 18) quote an interview of Doreen Massey's view on globalization that "isn't up in the air, it's always produced in places." It also involves "real world linkages between places" and "quite mundane, quotidian practices in relation." In other words, the finding of globalization should be guided by the dialogue between theoretical and empirical imagination (Kenway and Fahey 2009) that is place-based, multi- and interdisciplinary, open, and inclusive.

It is in this spirit that our project commenced, developed, and finally concluded. This book is not an attempt to define globalization. Rather, it creates a platform where individual contributors and readers are invited to participate in imagining what globalization is and its effect on everyday life. The conceptualization of the book came from a series of conferences hosted by the Center for Social Science Research at the State University of New York (SUNY) College at Oneonta. Through formal and informal communications with different scholars in the college, we realized that a few of us shared a major research interest: how peoples and cultures could be bound together through globalization. We agreed with many theoretical points made in the literature reviewed above. In particular, globalization is more than just an economic entity that, no doubt, has a fundamental impact on political, social, and cultural life. The research agenda on globalization should be multi- and interdisciplinary. The platform should be as inclusive as possible. Thus, this volume includes perspectives from the sciences, humanities, social sciences, and the arts. The account on globalization and its effect is represented by a wide range of perspectives from personal lived experience (chapters 1, 2, and the Epilogue, in particular) to different theoretical approaches. The chapters provide rich empirical documentation about everyday life experiences of globalization, and the analyses are framed by the contributors' own theoretical orientations.

Language, Identity, and Boundaries in Place

The subjects of language, identity, and boundaries can be studied independently in their own domains: language in linguistics and communication arts, identity in gender and ethnic studies, boundaries in geography and political science, just to name a few. The possible and multiple horizons of investigation in each field are already infinite. When a lacuna of one field overlaps with that of another in the study of globalization, the complexities take on an even higher level. Yet the gravity of the multilevel and complex issues impacted by the forces of globalization represented in this volume is always anchored to a singular space: place. However, this place is not "the timelessness of space" (Dirlik 2001, 18) that does not have history, actors, and dynamics. In other words, places offer "a way to recenter people in full recognition of the nondivisibility of humans and nonhumans" (Dirlik 2001, 42).

Dirlik observes, "It is difficult to imagine life without places; so that it is necessary to keep the idea of place alive" (2001, 35).

In this light, instead of imagining globalization in a vacuum or theoretical abstraction, this volume contextualizes globalization with reference to the everyday practice of language, identity, and boundaries. A simple, problematic, and even faulty relationship among these three elements catalyzes an investigation of their complex connection to globalization. A romanticized (Gellner 1987) or imagined (Anderson 1991) scenario can involve a people who speak a language and live in a community (a nation) located inside a geographical boundary. Yet, much literature (Levy 1997; Urry 2003; Dürrschmidt and Taylor 2007) has already indicated that the process of globalization has deterritorialized the community by ways of "foreign/ outside" ideologies, values, commodities intruding into the heartland, and in-and-out human migration for various economic, political, social, and natural reasons, thus interrupting the harmony of a place. The (national) boundaries become borderless, and the communities become ethnically and linguistically diverse. Any vigorous and tight security at the border cannot be immune to the flow of information, images, and messages through advanced information technology completely (Castells 2000). Even though such a "nostalgic" community existed at one point of human history, it has become an illusion in the age of globalization.

In reality, notions of place, community, and locality, which used to conventionally and conveniently distinguish "us"/"insiders" and "them"/ "outsiders," are, in fact, a product (Dirlik 2001) of interrelation and interaction between the inside and the outside, and the local and the other (Massey 1994). Massey's case study (1994) on the Docklands of East London is a case in point. The "local working class" community of Docklands defended its place from the "invading yuppies" and their investment houses. On the surface, the conflict was about the locals who wanted to preserve the essence, the traditions, and the past of the place, which they had always been familiar with, against newcomers who were going to change the lifestyle and the landscape of the community. But a further analysis of the conflict reveals the complexity of place identity. Interestingly, the "locals," who were attracted by the demand of labor, had earlier displaced the settlements and lifestyles of an already-established rural existence, and had been settled there for only a couple of centuries. The essence, traditions, and the past of this place that the locals wanted to preserve could only be referenced back to a particular moment in history. Race, gender, and social class added other levels of complication in the identity of the place. The white working-class locals defended their community against the white yuppies. Moreover, the town's delineation of its past was basically a male interpretation of the place that included football, pubs, and the docks. Massey argues that women's views on the geography of the place and in the recounted activities and social relations would most likely be different. Furthermore, some areas in the larger Docklands regions had been the most active in the country in trying to exclude immigrants of color. The locals' sentimental characterization of the place was as historically "our place," belonging to "our kind of people," in the battle against the encroaching yuppies, Massey observes. In the midst of this multilevel conflict in defending the identity of a place and a community, Massey argues, "There is no single 'past' to point to anyway" (1994, 113), and "There is no single simple 'authenticity'" (1994, 119). Massey also says, "The identity of a place is formed out of social interrelations, and a proportion of those interrelations—larger or smaller, depending on the time and on the place—will stretch beyond that 'place' itself" (1994, 115). In other words, the formation of the characteristics of the Docklands at the time must be understood from the point of economic spatial division of labor between the region and the rest of Britain and the politics of conceptualizing the nature of places. This perspective can be applied to the study of place identity in local and global relations. Massey sums up, "The attempt to align 'us' and 'them' with the geographical concept of 'local' and 'global' is always deeply problematic. For in the historical and geographical construction of places, the 'other' in general terms is already within. The global is everywhere and already, in one way or another, implicated in the local" (1994, 120). Simply put, "the global [is] in the core of the local" (interview with Fazal Rizvi in Kenway and Fahey 2009, 30).

Massey's study challenges the linear relation between place identity and boundaries. What complicates the research agenda on globalization is the notion that place, boundary, and community are amorphous and their interconnection is complex. First of all, the scale of the research units can be stretched from structures or buildings (Leung and Lau in this volume), to neighborhoods, mining communities, transnational child adoption groups, organized sports for children, diaspora communities (see Amit 2002), communities in cyberspace (Nakamura 2002), and a nation (Anderson 1991), to list just a few. To make the matter worse, people build a sense of community beyond any physical boundary. Gray (2002) categorized this phenomenon as "place without community." Instead of making place inside a confined boundary, some people make their communities on the basis of what they see as its core meaning, institution, occupation, and/or activity, the latter of which can be found in the practice of capoeira, a cultural African expression that originated in Brazil (Rosenthal in this volume).

Research on place identity also requires taking into account the construction of the members' identity, for place identity is closely related to the identity of the actors in that place. Massey conceptualizes this relation as "double articulation" of place identity and the identity of the people (1994, 118). They are both articulated through memories, imagination, and sentiment from a particular point in history.

Basso's short but rich account (1996) on Cibecue's place-making by the Western Apache, Arizona, reveals the symbiotic relationship between place identity and the identity of a people. Basso was hired to make Apache maps, not the usual maps of the white men (1996, xv), with Apache places and names. In the making, he discovered that the Apache construction of place was a form of cultural activity that included "conceptions of wisdom, notions of morality, politeness and tact in forms of spoken discourse, and certain conventional ways of imagining and interpreting the Apache tribal past" (1996, xv). He observed that "what people make of their places is closely connected to what they make of themselves as members of society and inhabitants of the earth, and while the two activities may be separable in principle, they are deeply joined in practice" (1996, 7). This ethnography also reveals the importance of language in Cibecue in relation to place identity and collective identity that is manifested in storytelling and naming places.

Identity is inseparable from place, as is language. The relationship between language and place is no less fluid than that between identity and place. Simple statistics show the challenge immediately that "there are only about two hundred countries in the world, but there are over five thousand-languages" (Dorian 1999, 26). When a language refers to a people, the category of the people is usually defined by ethnic or national origin. De Vos argues, "Language is often cited as a major component in the maintenance of a separate ethnic identity, and language undoubtedly constitutes the single most characteristic feature of ethnic identity" (2006, 9). Theories also assert that another major component in the maintenance of a separate ethnic identity is boundary (Barth 1969) or territory (Hutchinson and Smith 1996). In theory, it is simple to conceptualize the interconnectedness of language, identity, and boundaries within a place. Yet, the interplay and incongruity of language, identity, and boundaries in the human practice of place-making yield unequal consequences particularly in the age of globalization (see Kempny and Jawlowska 2002), where rapid development in technology and the neoliberal economic and political practice distend, hybridize, crisscross, crack, and disjoint (see Levy 1997, 137) every basic component of life. Who are we in the age of globalization? The answer lies in human practice that requires documentation through empirical research.

Overview of the Book

This volume is a collection of thirteen essays that examine identity formation, maintenance, and transformation through time and space. It examines how the conceptualization of the "other" impacts the contours of identity of specific communities (e.g., ethnic groups, scientific communities, and national identity). This book is organized along three issue areas: Language, Identities, and Boundaries. The theoretical nexus of this book juxtaposes the integrative, mutative, and disintegrative impact of globalization on identity formation, expression, and maintenance and change. Collectively, the chapters address how communities (e.g., national communities, academic communities, minority groups, and locales) shape and are shaped by the globalization process. The case studies selected seek to add to the empirical and theoretical literature on globalization by exploring some of its dominant manifestations as well as those not so readily apparent, yet equally important ones, which are revealed through an interdisciplinary and multidisciplinary lens. Perhaps the platform of our book should be thought of more as a "flatform" in homage to Thomas Friedman's concept of a "flat world." This "flatform" brings together the natural and social sciences and the humanities to explore the impact of globalization. One of the salient approaches to the topics in this book is to stretch the timeframe of globalization from the early existence of the human race (Horvath in this volume) to the contemporary world. The theoretical reason behind this, as Robertson clearly states, is: "Today we tend to regard [the interconnectivity of human communities] as a feature of contemporary globalization only, but the record of the past clearly demonstrates its centrality as a motor for human change" (2003, 74).

This edited volume is divided into three sections as the subtitle of the book suggests. The first section on Language is comprised of three chapters that examine the influence of English as a language across the globe in scientific and literary communities and the work of global brand name transposition in the global market. Using a first-person perspective to examine the shift of languages in the field of sciences that is trying to reach all peoples in the world, Chiang (Chapter 1) studies how English has become the lingua franca of the contemporary world of sciences. Xi Xu (Chapter 2) questions whether "global English" exists in literature or if it is an oxymoron among many Asian writers and whether the fiction is produced as "national" or "Asian" if the language is "global" or whether it is a "universal" literary expression. Chiang and Mi (Chapter 3) examine the use of language in the transposition of global brand names in China and argue that such practice is a "glocal" process in which the global value and the local value interact with each other.

The section on Identity explores how race, ethnic, and gender identities change when different groups experience intergroup (global) and intragroup (local, community group) interconnectedness in different waves of globalization. Echoing the chapters dealing with issues in language, Montoya (Chapter 4) explores how a group of second-generation Hispanic college students in New York State constructs its identity that emphasizes greater cosmopolitanism with adherence to a strong ethnic and linguistic identity base. Little (Chapter 5) uses the ethnographic and linguistic composition of the tourism handicrafts market in Antigua, Guatemala, to discuss the interrelationship between language and economics. He observes that global tourism can have positive effects on the maintenance and promotion of indigenous languages. Leung and Lau (Chapter 6) investigate how a Chinese community in Markham (a suburb of Toronto), Ontario, Canada, transforms and maintains its ethnic identity and pride through a Chinese iconic shopping mall, Pacific Mall, realized by a non-Chinese developer. Hendley (Chapter 7) examines changes in the British Conservative Party's conceptualization of the typical female voter in Conservative political propaganda in two world wars. He argues that the shift in portraying female voters as citizens in the First World War to consumers in the Second World War is a result of Britain's changing position in the world due to the forces of globalization. He also argues that the political success of the British Conservative Party in the twentieth century is linked to its adeptness at adapting to such changes.

The section on Boundaries includes five chapters that scrutinize how de/re/construction of race, ethnic, and national boundaries and territories impact the transformation of their identities, and how the transborder movement of humans deterritorializes "natural" boundaries of species. Rosenthal (Chapter 8) uses a participatory research approach (participating in the practice of capoeria while conducting research of the activity at the same time), to examine how historical memory and origins are represented on Web sites about the practice of capoeira, the Afro-Brazilian cultural form often described as an improvised mix of martial arts and dance. The spread of capoeira's popularity beyond the contested origin(s) of the art deserves inquiry into the way that globalization has opened new public spaces for redefining identities. This inquiry is not only across international borders but across long-standing categories involving nations, ethnicity, and cultural practice. Haley (Chapter 9) challenges the conventional wisdom that people in the United States whose family histories trace back to Mexico would share a common ethnic identity as Mexican Americans. Evidence indicates that such people, individuals, and communities occupying different social positions and identifying themselves variously as

Spanish, Native American, Mexican American or Chicano, and Mexican are a result of complex migration experiences, changes in the nature of political and economic relationships with other groups, and the shift of cultural associations attributed to various social positions within a multiethnic, globalized, class-based society. Compton's comparative analysis (Chapter 10) traces the sources of legitimacy of regimes in Japan and South Africa, over time, from their respective inception (i.e., Japan in 1868 and South Africa in 1948) and notes the similarities and differences in the construction of state legitimacy. He argues that the pressures resulting from globalization and internal political changes destroyed the old system and created the bases for new sources of state legitimacy in the late twentieth century. In the twenty-first century, both Japanese and South African political elites will increasingly rely on divergent approaches to constructing state legitimacy despite striking past similarities. Legname (Chapter 11) raises a question similar to the one in Xu Xi's chapter. He asks whether music, as a system of sound signs or a language, is semantic or universalistic in nature. He demonstrates that music, like Xu Xi's concept of "global English" (Chapter 2), can become a universalistic language, by comparing how Brazil advocated nationalism through its music in the beginning of the twentieth century and how Japan incorporates western music with its ancient cultural elements in the search of its identity in contemporary music. Horvath (Chapter 12) looks at how natural borders of nonhuman species are becoming less and less meaningful. The nonhuman species' movement from their natural surroundings is the result of human activities, the speed and intensity of which have increased rapidly during the contemporary period of globalization.

The Epilogue, written by Thomás Sakoulas, is a very short but intriguing narrative. Like Joseph Chiang's chapter, it is written from the first-person point of view. Sakoulas was invited to give a talk about his artwork at the Symposium on Greece hosted by the Center for Social Science Research at our college in October 2008 and we subsequently invited him to write a short piece for this book. There is a striking similarity between his art theory and the substance of this book. His imagination of the motif—an arc—is echoed in a number of cultures from ancient to modern times. His repetition of a simple arc in the form of geometric ideals across different material surfaces creates "more complex, independent forms free from their source but without ever denying their origin" (Sakoulas in the volume). Language, identity, and boundaries are simple arcs of human social, cultural, and political constructions that exist in ideal forms. The lived human experience across time and space is the artwork in place.

References

Amit, Vered, ed. 2002. *Realizing Community, Social Relationships and Sentiments.* New York: Routledge.

Anderson, Benedict. 1991. *Imagined Communities.* New York: Verso.

Barth, Fredrik. 1969. Introduction. In *Ethnic Groups and Boundaries: The Social Organization of Culture Difference,* ed. Barth, 9–38. Boston: Little, Brown.

Basso, Keith H. 1996. *Wisdom Sits in Places: Landscape and Language Among the Western Apache.* Albuquerque: University of New Mexico Press.

Castells, Manuel. 2000. *The Rise of the Network Society,* 2nd edition. Oxford: Blackwell.

Cox, R. W. 1996. A Perspective on Globalization. In *Globalization: Critical Reflections,* ed. J. H. Mittelman, 21–30. Boulder, Colorado: Lynne Rienner.

De Vos, George A. 2006. Introduction: Ethnic Pluralism: Conflict and Accommodation, The Role of Ethnicity in Social History. In *Ethnic Identity: Problems and Prospects for the Twenty-First Century,* 4th edition, ed. Romanucci-Ross, Lola, George A. De Vos, Takeyuki Tsuda, 1–36. New York: Altamira.

Deutsche Welle. Global Call to Fight Financial Crisis at German Summit. February 5, 2009. http://www.dw-world.de/dw/article/0,,4005466,00.html (accessed February 6, 2009).

Dirlik, Arif. 2001. Place-Based Imagination: Globalism and the Politics of Place. In *Places and Politics in an Age of Globalization,* ed. Roxann Prazniak and Arif Dirlik, 15–52. New York: Rowman & Littlefield.

Dorian, Nancy C. 1999. Linguistic and Ethnographic Fieldwork. In *Language & Ethnic Identity,* ed. Joshua A. Fishman, 25–41. Oxford: Oxford University Press.

Dürrschmidt, Jörg, and Graham Taylor. 2007. *Globalization, Modernity & Social Change: Hotspots of Transition.* New York: Palgrave Macmillan.

Friedman, Thomas L. 2007. *The World Is Flat: A Brief History of the Twenty-First Century.* New York: Picador / Farrar, Straus and Giroux.

Gabel, Medard, and Henry Bruner. 2003. *Globalinc.: An Atlas of the Multinational Corporation.* New York: The New Press.

Gardner, Howard. 2004. How Education Changes: Considerations of History, Science, and Values. In *Globalization: Culture And Education in the New Millennium,* ed. M. Suáraz-Orozco and D. B. Qin-Hilliard, 235–59. Los Angeles: University of California Press.

Gellner, Ernest. 1987. *Culture, Identity and Politics.* Cambridge: Cambridge University Press.

Gray, John. 2001. Community as Place-Making Ram Auctions in the Scottish Borderland. In *Realizing Community: Concepts, Social Relationships and Sentiments,* ed. Vered Amit, 38–59. New York: Routledge.

Guillén, Mauro F. 2001. Is Globalization Civilizing, Destructive or Feeble? A Critique of Five Key Debates in the Social Science Literature. *Annual Review of Sociology* 27: 235–60.

Harvey, David. 1989. *The Condition of Postmodernity.* Oxford: Blackwell.

Hedley, R. Alan. 2002. Running Out of Control: Understanding Globalization. In *Contemporary Sociological Thoughts: Themes and Theories,* ed. Sean P. Hier, 375–92. Toronto: Canadian Scholars' Press.

Hirst, Paul Q., and Grahame Thompson. 1996. *Globalization in Question.* Cambridge: Polity.

Hutchinson, John, and Anthony D. Smith. 1996. Introduction. In *Ethnicity,* ed. John Hutchinson and Anthony D. Smith, 3–14. Oxford: Oxford University Press.

Kempny, Marian, and Aldona Jawlowska, eds. 2002. *Identity in Transformation: Postmodernity, Postcommunism, and Globalization.* Westport: Praeger.

Kenway, Jane, and Johannah Fahey. 2009. *Globalizing the Research Imagination.* New York: Routledge.

Legrain, Philippe. 2002. *Open World: The Truth about Globalisation.* London: Abacus.

Levy, Pierre. 1997. *Collective Intelligence: Mankind's Emerging World in Cyberspace.* Trans. Robert Bobonno. Cambridge, MA: Perseus.

Massey, Doreen. 1994. Double Articulation: A Place in the World. In *Displacements: Cultural Identities in Question,* ed. Angelika Bammer, 110–21. Bloomington and Indianapolis: Indiana University Press.

McMichael, Philip David. 2007. *Development and Social Change: A Global Perspective,* 4th edition. New York: Pine Forge.

Morrison, A.J., D.A. Ricks, and K. Roth. 1991. Globalization versus Regionalization: Which Way for the Multinational?" *Organizational Dynamics* 19(3): 17–29.

Nakamura, Lisa. 2002. *Cybertypes: Race, Ethnicity, and Identity on the Internet.* New York: Routledge.

Pieterse, Jan Nederveen. 2004. *Globalization & Culture: Global Mélange.* New York: Rowman & Littlefield.

Robertson, Robbie. 2003. *The Three Waves of Globalization: A History of a Developing Global Consciousness.* New York: Zed Books.

Sassen, Saskia. 2007. *A Sociology of Globalization.* New York: W.W. Norton.

Suáraz-Orozco, M., and Desire Baolian Qin-Hilliard. 2004. *Globalization: Culture and Education in the New Millennium.* Los Angeles: University of California Press.

Suáraz-Orozco, M., and D. Sommer. 2002. *Globalization, Immigration, and Transculturation.* Unpublished Manuscript. Cambridge, MA: Harvard University.

Taylor, Peter, Michael J. Watts, and R. J. Johnston. 2002. Geography/Globalization. In *Geographies of Global Change: Remapping the World,* ed. R. J. Johnston et al., 1–18. Malden, MA: Blackwell.

Urry, John. 2003. *Global Complexity.* Cambridge: Polity.

PART I

Language

CHAPTER 1

English: A Globalized Language in Science and Technology*

Joseph F. Chiang

As a chemist specializing in nanotechnology, I have observed the increasing use of English as the lingua franca of the science world. This chapter provides a non-social-science perspective regarding the implications of the globalization of English in the sciences. Over the years, I have witnessed a major shift of language use in my fields from Latin, German, and Russian to English. When I entered Tunghai University, a Christian university, in Taiwan as an undergraduate, I realized the importance of English as the most "popular" tool for science and technology. This newly established Christian university was created by the United Board for Christian Higher Education in Asia in the late 1950s. Its origins date back to the late nineteenth century when seven European countries and the United States invaded China during the Qing dynasty era. They won the war and forced the Qing government to pay reparations. All seven European countries kept the monetary payment except the United States. The United States used the reparation payment they received from the Qing government to establish the Tsinghua Preparatory School to prepare high school graduates for entering universities in the United States. These Chinese students returned to China after finishing their education. All of them had a major impact on education, political reform, culture, and even literature. At this time, in 1922, the United Board for Christian Higher Education in Asia was established in New York City. Many Christian churches joined the United Board to send priests, educators, and scientists to China. Thirteen universities were founded during this period; however, due to the Communist Revolution in China, all of them were closed. From 1951 on, the United Board established several universities in Japan, Hong Kong, Korea, and Taiwan. Tunghai University, located in Taiwan, emphasizes the use of English, especially in formal instruction. I had full exposure to English during all four years of my undergraduate education. Upon graduation, I was awarded a full scholarship to enroll in graduate school at Cornell. After receiving my PhD in chemistry, I joined the State University of New York College at Oneonta, where I have been teaching chemistry for over thirty years. All my research results have been published in English, and all my presentations of my research work at various national and international conferences/meetings are in that language. Although I have been using English in my work for a long time, I did not seriously think about it until my last visit to the prestigious Tsinghua University in Beijing, which made me ponder on the language shift that occurred in the post–World War II era. At Tsinghua's invitation, I made contacts with graduate and undergraduate students.

One of the assignments at Tsinghua consisted of helping to teach, as part of a team, a course for undergraduate students majoring in arts, social sciences, business, and engineering. The title of the course was "Chemistry and Society." It taught students the basic concepts in a nontraditional way to explain the importance of chemistry in our daily life, the way chemistry improves our health, our environments, etc. At the university's request, I was the only instructor who used English for lecturing. In order to increase students' interest in reading English, I purposely selected John Grisham's novel *Skipping Christmas*. I chose this novel because the story requires very little knowledge of American culture on the part of readers in comparison to Grisham's other novels. For example, *The Chamber* requires some knowledge of the American judicial system, while *Bleachers* assumes familiarity with American football. *Skipping Christmas*, on the other hand, requires only a minimal familiarity with Christmas traditions.

To me, searching for new knowledge is the goal of science and technology. The results aim to improve the quality of human life by prolonging life span and reducing the damage suffered by human beings due to exposure to all types of pollution. However, new knowledge becomes useless unless it can be communicated. The communication technique must be efficient and functional.

While scientists disseminate their research results in several ways, there are two major vehicles for dissemination: publication of the results, and formal and informal interactions at technical meetings and conferences. The English language has played the most important role in these cases in recent decades. English has become the general tool for scientific presentations, and we may categorize it as the lingua franca of the contemporary world of sciences.

The 'Global English' Phenomenon

English did not become the lingua franca overnight. Meierkord (2006) documents in detail the changes in lingua franca communication from ancient Greece to the present. Here I offer my own experience. Thirty years of academic life as a chemist have allowed me to witness this change. I began my career in research and teaching as a structural chemist who investigated molecular structures by electron diffraction and microwave spectroscopy. Later in my research, I was involved with new ceramics and received two U.S. patents for the properties and processing of new glass ceramics. During the same period, I spent time studying the 123 ceramic superconductors. Moving ahead, I began research in nanotechnology, especially in nanotherapeutic devices. Just like other scholars in all fields, I am required to present my research at national and international conferences.

At the many national scientific meetings in the United States and international meetings in China, Germany, Japan, Hungary, and Singapore, including the International Conference on NanoTech, the United States–China Materials Conference, and the International Union of Pure and Applied Chemistry Conference, English is always the main conference language. Even the smaller meetings such as the American Chemical Society–China meeting, the meetings of the Royal Society of Britain, and the German-China Chemical Societies meetings also use English as the official conference language. Furthermore, scientists and researchers communicate verbally in English more often today than they did thirty years ago. In the global tower of Babel, English is the most commonly understood language and the most efficient tool for scientists and engineers for sharing their research results.

Why and how has this shift taken place? What are the ramifications for researchers who now rely on English as the medium of communication? I am going to use two phenomena to illustrate this language shift. The first examines the languages used by scientists to disseminate knowledge among themselves. The second discusses the high demand for scientific English in contemporary China.

Language Use in Dissemination of Scientific Findings

Language plays an important role in disseminating research findings to a wide scientific and nonscientific audience. In science, English is increasingly a prerequisite for professional networking and delivery of findings. Lack of English facility limits a researcher's information market, in terms of both delivery and consumption of new findings in the field.

The use of English as an international or global language has gained acceptance all over the world. Many scientists in other regions, such as Africa,

Asia, Latin America, and parts of Europe, do publish their results in their own languages, but the accessibility of their results is limited to the audience well versed in these languages. However, if these publications were in English, the results would have wider reach since most people in the world use this language as part of their work. Major international journals are published in English and, occasionally, in other languages, such as French. However, the use of French in the larger scientific community is more limited than the use of English. Most scientific training, as I observed in China, also takes place in English.

Phillipson (2008, 250) articulates several "special purposes" of English: *lingua economica*, *lingua emotiva* (the imaginary of Hollywood, popular music, consumerism, and hedonism), *lingua academica*, and *lingua cultura*. More and more non-English native speakers use English to communicate with each other (Li 2003, 33–4). Pope John Paul II used English to address Christians, Muslims, and Jews in the Middle East, but not Latin, Arabic, Hebrew, nor even his native Polish.

Of the sixteen living Nobel Prize laureates in literature who write in their native languages, only nine use English (Meneghini and Packer 2007, 112–116). Many of their non-English works have been translated into English for a larger audience. On the other hand, most Nobel laureates in the sciences deliver their findings in English. Many non-English-speaking scientists I have talked to, including Chinese, Koreans, Japanese, Germans, Spanish, and others, believe that they should use English for their research reports in order to access a larger readership. The communication of important findings published in a scientist's native language that is other than English may never be noticed. An example is a non-English communication published in German in the 1930s that showed a connection between smoking and lung cancer (Proctor 1999, 173). But this report was ignored until the 1960s when American and British scientists rediscovered the link.

Before 1660, science was considered an avocation. Latin, French, German, Spanish, and Russian were used for science communication. However, from the beginning of the twentieth century, English became recognized as the most popular tool to disseminate results. In the mid-1960s, most Russian scientific journals were translated into English in the United States with U.S. government funding. There were changes in foreign language requirements for PhD candidates in the country. They were required to be proficient in at least two of the following languages: German, French, or Russian. However, current PhD programs no longer require foreign languages as a research tool. In Russia today, most German, French, and Russian scientific publications are translated into English.

Table 1.1 provides a very interesting survey on the distribution of scientific articles published in various languages in the nineteenth and twentieth centuries. An examination of *Chemical Abstracts* shows that while publications on chemistry in English rose from 50.5 percent to 54 percent between 1958 and 1979, publications in German dropped from 9.7 percent to 4.2 percent. Similarly, an examination of the medical *Index Medicus* shows that publications about medical science in English increased from 42 percent in 1879 to 66.4 percent in 1973, and publications in French dropped from 23 percent to 4.3 percent during the same period.

Table 1.2 tells the same phenomenon about the popular use of English in science (also see Taavitsainen 2006). More than half of the scientific literature

Table 1.1 Distribution of scientific articles by language in *Chemical Abstracts* (percent of total) and in *Index Medicus* (percent of total)

Language	1958[a]	1965[b]	1979[c]	1879[d]	1965[h]	1973[d]
Chinese	–	0.5	0.4	–	0.4	
English	50.5	50.3	54.0	42	51.2	66.4
French	5.5	7.3	2.2	23	8.6	4.3
German	9.7	6.4	4.2	20	17.2	8.9
Italian	–	–	0.8	6	–	1.4
Japanese	6.1	3.6	4.7	–	0.9	2.5
Polish	–	–	0.2	–	–	2.1
Russian	16.8	23.4	18.0	–	5.6	7.6
Spanish	1.0	–	0.7	3.5	–	1.1

[a] I. L. Kosin, "The Growing Importance of Russian as a Language of Science," *Bioscience* 22 (1972): 723–24.
[b] D. N. Wood, *Chemistry in Britain* 2 (1966): 346.
[c] Letter from R. J. Rowlett, Jr., to the author, October 22, 1980.
[d] Mary E. Corning and Martin M. Cummings, "Biomedical Communications," in *Advances in American Medicine: Essays at the Bicentennial*, vol. 2, (New York: Josiah Macy Jr. Foundation, 1976), 722–73.

Table 1.2 Distribution of language of scientific literature holdings in the National Library of Medicine (1973)

Language	Serials (Percent)	Monographs (Percent)
Chinese	0.3	0.7
English	55.8	55.7
French	8.7	6.1
German	9.3	9.7
Italian	3.8	3.8
Japanese	3.3	3.9
Portuguese	1.7	0.7
Russian	4.2	8.4
Spanish	5.5	2.4

holdings in the National Library of Medicine are in English. The next highest share goes to German, 9.3 percent in serials and 9.7 percent in monographs. There is a roughly 40 percent difference between the number of books in the two languages.

Other current statistics on the rise of the number of scientific journals published in English are illustrative. In the United States, 4,175 journals were published in English in 1975, and the number rose to 6,770 in 1995. This fact is not surprising. In 1978, 8,062 science journals were published worldwide, but in 1988, the number rose to 37,683. As of 2004, 80 percent of science journals were published in English worldwide. In my investigation, I found that there are a total of 11,731 journals listed in *Chemical Abstracts*. Of these, 9,221 periodicals are published in English; in other words, 79 percent of the listed scientific journals are published in English.

The Impact on and of China

The demand for the use of English in science in contemporary China has definitely accelerated the momentum of English as the language of science. China has changed the way of publishing science and technology journals in English and the translation of Chinese articles into English. Comments by two scholars, reported in a newspaper article titled "Chinese Science Journals Go Global" in *People's Daily* (April 12, 2006), which is among the most influential and authoritative newspapers in China, help to highlight this demand. In this article, Dr. Zhaohui Peng has made some comments regarding his gene therapy company, Shenzhen Sibiono Genetech. Much of his research and clinical data have been published in Chinese, but most of these data are inaccessible to foreign researchers. Thus, attempts have been made to publish his findings in English. Such publications receive a larger readership than do publications in Chinese, German, French, or Spanish. Dr. Tongbin Chen, a biologist from the Institute of Geological Sciences and Natural Resources Research of the Chinese Academy of Sciences, indicated in the article that the international science community suffered from a lack of access to Chinese research results.

Many Chinese scientists prefer to have their research results published in English journals, and most editors require strong English language skills in all submitted manuscripts. More than 1,800 Chinese university journals have their articles translated into English. Japanese, Czech, Hungarian, and South Korean journals have article indices in English. Such a change has also happened in two other important German journals on chemistry, *Liebigs Annalen* and *Chemische Berichte,* which started publishing in English in 1997. A third German journal, *Angewandte Chemie*, international edition, has been published since 1962 in English.

The Reason for English Being a Lingua Franca

The use and survival of a language depends on a wide range of social, economic, political, and cultural factors. Some historians such as Niall Ferguson have argued that the worldwide use of English is a legacy of British hegemony in Protestantism, capitalism, and sports (Ferguson 2002, xxv). Clearly, the expansion of the British Empire, especially after 1750, into large parts of Asia and, later, Africa greatly facilitated the reach of English. In some areas of the Empire, like India, the multiplicity of "native" languages often made it easier for Indians from various regions, even after independence, to speak English to each other for mutual comprehension (Lloyd 1996, 384–385). During the nineteenth century, British influence spread beyond the formal confines of its Empire through the globalization of trade. Britain was the predominant trading nation in the world and rigidly followed the doctrines of free trade between 1846 and 1932. Free trade sent British products and the English language everywhere, even into areas that were not formally part of the British Empire—Japan, South America, and Turkey (Ferguson 2002, 242–244). Within the Empire, there developed a proliferation of culture, both high (Shakespeare) and low (the popular boys' adventure stories of the late Victorian writer G. A. Henty), as well as advertising that spread English (Mackenzie 1986). After 1945, Britain lost its empire, and the United States replaced it as a worldwide power. The United States is a military superpower that is far larger than Britain ever was (Ferguson 2004). American servicemen can be found on every continent (including Antarctica), and large numbers of U.S. armed forces, traverse the world speaking American English and "spreading democracy" (Ferguson 2004).

However, the United States does not control an empire on the same scale as the British did; it has spread English through more indirect than direct means. Like the British before them, the United States has embraced global free trade. Consequently, American products, ranging from automobiles to computer software to agricultural goods, span the globe. Perhaps even more importantly, American popular culture, in the form of Hollywood films, fast food, and popular music, has put American English on movie screens, televisions, computers, and ipods everywhere (Lloyd 1996, 385). There is no corner of the world that is immune to McDonald's, Walt Disney, and hip-hop music.

Other than the expansion of British colonial power and the recent Americanization of the global economy that have helped spread the acceptance and popularity of the English language, the natural structure of the language might also be aiding its promotion. Gannon (2004, 384–5) compares the nature of the Chinese, Japanese, and English languages and observes that the Chinese and Japanese languages are considered high-context languages, while English is considered a low-context language. First of all, there are numerous Chinese dialects that are mutually unintelligible, although there is a unified and standardized written form. Roughly, there are about 50,000 characters in the language, each of which stands for different words. It requires an amazing feat of memory to master the language well. Gannon states, "[B]oth the Chinese language and the Japanese language are high context, and the writer must choose words carefully, as there are complex meanings that can be inferred from the context in which they are spoken and written" (2004, 385). However, the English language, which "employs only 26 letters to represent all spoken sounds and written words … is direct and understandable, and this has facilitated the use of English worldwide …" (Gannon 2004, 384).

There is one final point to consider: China's strategic embrace of the English language as a means for international advancement. The Chinese are eager to expand their global influence through trade and scientific discovery. English is their language of choice. Many undergraduates can read English texts in their fields of study, but do not have the capability to write good and clear articles in English to represent their research at the graduate research level. Many students want to learn English well to further their studies in some English-speaking countries like the United States. In the science and engineering fields, a large number of foreign graduates have sought advanced studies in the United States for the past fifty years.

Conclusion

My conclusion is that English is a global language for science and technology. This conclusion is based on my own observations and personal experiences. The historical legacy of the British Empire and the present global power of the United States have contributed to this shift. It is further buttressed by the scientific and technological advancement during and after World War II. In this period, many scientists from Europe and elsewhere joined the American scientific community for the purpose of research. Scientists realize that a general communication tool must be transnational and widely used. English has become the default language due to the historical development of globalization. I personally support the use of English in scientific professional life, as evidenced by my scientific publications and conferences/meetings, as noted earlier.

Note

* The author would like to thank the staff of Milne Library at the State University of New York College at Oneonta for their help in collecting some data for this chapter. The help from Professors Matthew Hendley and Ho Hon Leung is also appreciated.

References

Corning, Mary E., and Martin M. Cummings. 1976. Biomedical Communications. *Advances in American Medicine: Essays at the Bicentennial, vol. 2.,* 722–73. New York: Josiah Macy Jr. Foundation.

Ferguson, Niall. 2002. *Empire: The Rise and Demise of the British World Order and the Lessons for Global Power.* New York: Basic Books.

———. 2004. *Colossus: The Rise and Fall of the American Empire.* New York: Penguin.

Gannon, M. J. 2004. *Understanding Global Cultures. Metaphorical Journeys through 28 Nations, Clusters of Nations, and Continents,* 3rd ed. London: SAGE.

Kosin, L. 1972. The Growing Importance of Russian as a Language of Science. *Bioscience* 22: 723–24.

Li, D. C. S. 2003. Between English and Esperanto: What Does It Take to Be a World Language? *International Journal of Sociology of Language* 164: 33–63.

Lloyd, T. O. 1996. *The British Empire 1558–1995,* 2nd ed. Oxford: Oxford University Press.

Mackenzie, John M. 1986. *Propaganda and Empire: The Manipulation of British Public Opinion 1880–1960.* Manchester and New York: Manchester University Press.

Meierkord, Christiane. 2006. Lingua Franca Communication Past and Present. *International Journal of Sociology of Language* 177: 9–30.

Meneghini, R., and A. L. Packer. 2007. Is There Science beyond English? *European Molecular Biology Organization* 8(2): 112–16.

National Library of Medicine of United States. 1973. *Advances in American Medicine: Essays at the Bicentennial.* Bethesda, MD: National Institutes of Health.

People's Daily. English online version. Chinese Science Journals Go Global. http://english.peopledaily.com.cn/200604/12/eng20060412_257794.html (accessed on November 20, 2008).

Phillipson, R. 2008. Lingua Franca or Lingua Frankensteinia? English in European Integration and Globalization. *World Englishes* 27(2): 250–67.

Proctor, R. N. 1999. *The Nazi War on Cancer.* Princeton, NJ: Princeton University Press.

Rowlett, R. J., Jr. 1980. Letter to Joseph Chiang, October 22.

Taavitsainen, I. 2006. *Encyclopedia of Language & Linguistics,* 2nd ed. MO: Elsevier.

Wood, D. N. 1966. Chemical Literature and the Foreign Language Problem. *Chemistry in Britain* 2: 346–50.

CHAPTER 2

Global English in Asian Fiction: Some Thoughts on Writing Contemporary Fiction from and of Asia in English

Xu Xi

So here I am, an English language fiction writer who happens to be from Asia, Hong Kong specifically, who is of Chinese-Indonesian ethnicity, and who, despite my U.S. passport (for which I exchanged my former Indonesian one) still writes fiction of my birth city, one that is hard to leave behind entirely. Of course, I am also eternally a "resident" of Hong Kong, where I have the right of "permanent abode" if permanence can indeed be ascribed to this former British colony that is now a Special Administrative Region of China, at least until the year 2046. So if you are somewhat like me, culturally and politically confused, with an ambivalent sense of identity, writing contemporary fiction from and of Asia in English, questions do arise for the practice of your art for which real and satisfactory answers are difficult to come by. One particularly troublesome one is the presumption that our lingua franca, English, is in fact a kind of "global language" that transcends culture, race, nationality, country, the "authentic" language of place, allowing you, the writer, to write fiction of that culture, race, etc., that "authentically" voices the human condition. This chapter offers a few thoughts from my perspective as such a "global fiction writer."

There are three principal questions that inform this investigation. First, does a *global language for literature*, meaning English, really exist? Second, in examining representative contemporary examples of fiction from Asia in English, how should we define the sensibility of such work? Hong Kong's attempt to define a "native" English-language literature provides an example. But is there a guiding perspective common to such fiction that diverges from or dovetails into contemporary English language fiction as practiced elsewhere, especially in nations where English is the primary language of its literature? Finally, if this fiction is in English, can we really call it "Asian" fiction or even "fiction from Asia," or is it something else entirely, a kind of "global fiction" perhaps? The overriding concern in all these questions regarding such literature is whether or not it can achieve *universality*, an effect that literature, at least in the Western tradition, is presumed to embrace, and that writers of fiction seek to create on their particular canvases depicting the human condition.

Beginning First of All with the Idea of a "Global Language," Is This, in Fact, an *Oxymoron*?

Can language really be uprooted from its cultural and national origins in literature? Literature is supposed to tap into the soul of our common humanity. As writers, and certainly in teaching creative writing at the master of fine arts (MFA) level, we presume this, perhaps overly so, and expect the next generations of writers will embrace this same perspective. In fiction particularly, we read for the specific stories of person, place, or thing, to enter into an alternate universe and sensibility, to gain perspective from the large or intimate canvases of society an author selects for display. While prose does not always have the deep emotional power of poetry, literary prose is a close cousin. Consequently, when we think of the great novels or stories of nations, we expect them to deliver something of the soul of those national cultures. Dostoyevsky and Tolstoy are those writers who represent "Russia" in the study of literature, just as Flaubert or Maupassant have become "France." In the nations for which English is the mother tongue, Charles Dickens is as English as Mark Twain is American; Henry James, on the other hand, straddled the old and new worlds in his sensibility, but is indisputably a writer who could use no other language but English in his work. Hailing from what is still referred to as the "Far East," despite the contemporary, politically correct preference for "Asia," Cao Xueqin, the author of the classic novel *Dreams of Red Chambers,* is undeniably Chinese. The literary tradition assumes fiction from various nations to be written in the native tongue, the national language, and yet to resonate universally as good fiction is supposed to do. The only barrier would be how well or badly the translator has rendered the original prose.

What then should we call English, in the context of a language for fiction from Asia? Even if that language is entirely recognizable as

"English as she is writ," does it somehow transform into what we might term "global English"? Further, is it truly a *language* or simply our lingua franca? If we think about commerce, which is nothing if not the engine that drives globalization, English functions today as the lingua franca, and few would dispute its currency. In Asia especially, where the brand of multilingualism common in Europe does not have a true parallel, English is more often than not the means of communication between, say, a Korean and a Malaysian, or even two Chinese who speak different dialects, as is the case in Hong Kong for Putonghua (Mandarin) and Cantonese speakers.

The Oxford English Dictionary defines lingua franca as "any mixed *jargon* formed as a *medium of intercourse* between people speaking different languages." Note the distinction: a jargon, not a language. Jargon is, at worst, a debased form of language or at best, a medium of discourse peculiar to a specific group or profession that might be incomprehensible to any outsider. The key notion behind a lingua franca, however, is that it aids discourse among those who speak a variety of native tongues. Hence it is considered a medley, a Babel of sounds.

Historically, the Use of English in Asian Fiction Falls Primarily into Two Categories

The first is writing by early-generation immigrants in the West using their "adopted" English; C. Y. Lee, the Chinese author of *The Flower Drum Song*, and Younghill Kang, the Korean who penned *East Goes West*, are two examples in America. We need to distinguish such fiction from the work by Asian-Americans (or other Asian hyphenations) of later generations because for such writers, English is often a native, if not the only, language; they write from a space where English is the primary language. Contrast that to the world depicted in *The Flower Drum Song*—San Francisco's Chinatown of the 1950s—which is a Chinese language space for the protagonist and most of the characters.

The second group arises from the postcolonial or postwar and transnational or globalized experiences rendered by writers from postcolonial countries such as India, Pakistan, Singapore, Malaysia, the Philippines, all of which by now have a significant literature in English. The British Empire ensured that at least a local elite in these nations would be as literate in English as in their native languages. For several contemporary writers, English would prove to be their only language for literary expression: one famous example is the Indian writer Salman Rushdie, whose fourth novel, *The Satanic Verses*, earned him a fatwa in 1989 that sent him into hiding for approximately a decade. In the case of the Philippines, American colonization diminished an earlier literacy in Spanish,

from America's superpower stature today creates a political or commercial "neo-empire" that often resembles the older British one. Consequently, a certain *linguistic defiance* characterizes the literary language if a writer wishes to do more than to merely ape or submit to the tradition of the colonizer. The result can be simultaneously cacophonous or harmonious, depending on how your ear is attuned.

Evelyn Ch'ien describes such literary language as "weird Englishes" in her book of that name. She argues that we increasingly encounter unorthodox uses of English that combine one or more languages in literature. Her analysis explores fiction by transnational writers, some with Asian roots, such as Arundhati Roy, the Indian writer who won the 1997 Booker prize for her first novel, *The God of Small Things,* or Maxine Hong Kingston, the highly acclaimed Chinese-American author who penned, among many other works, *The Woman Warrior,* her first book published in 1976 that was transformative for Asian-American literature and helped shape its literary canon. "Weird English," she says, "wants to do more with English than communicate *what* the subject is; it also wants to show *who* the speaker is and *how* the speaker can *appropriate the language*" (italics, mine; see Ch'ien 2004, 8).

Appropriation of a language seems the natural route for any writer bent on using a tongue that is "foreign" or "non-mother" tongue to the culture from which she emerges, regardless of the primary language of the space in which she writes. Kingston, for example, being Chinese-American, would use English as a natural literary language, but the immigrant world she renders "babbles" in Cantonese. It is a babble, because the author's own comprehension of Cantonese is limited, but she depicts, through cultural context and the appropriation of Cantonese into English, the feelings and sensations of such an immigrant space.

Ch'ien's study is confined to writers who are already well established internationally, particularly in Anglo-American literature. The language, and arguably the effect of the work, is often guided, or at least critically interpreted, by an Anglo-American perspective. Like Kingston, Roy and Junot Diaz, two other authors examined by Chien, write what could be described as thinly veiled autobiography. While most fiction is to some extent autobiographical, the Anglo-American critical eye for such "weird English" fiction focuses more readily on expected and predictable narrative lines. In the first instance, it is that of the immigrant experience, as in the works by Kingston and Diaz. Perhaps more troubling is the literary perspective that we might call politically correct or, at least, palatable from a Western standpoint, as in Roy's only novel to date, which presents its Indian world as "weirdly" other, both in terms of her linguistic wordplay and in the controversial sexual subject matter of incest, or, in other words, exotica. The *sensibility* or perspective of such fiction therefore arises from what is understood in an English language space, which is that of the "other"—foreign, exotic, even Orientalist—and not mainstream culture.

"Weirder," or arguably, more intriguing English will, however, be found in fiction from Asia that is not as widely known in the West, and which remains relatively unknown because it exists in what is still a marginal space of "globalized English." Even though such literature is arguably "exotic," what is notably different is the sensibility: such Asian fiction details contemporary Asia as it is, through the transformative power of fiction, and not Asia as the West might imagine it, where the exotic is more acceptably "real" than what actually is. For example, here is a brief passage from Ming Cher's novel *Spider Boys,* written in street-slang Singapore English (*a.k.a.* "Singlish") about street gangs who raise and bet on fighting spiders.

> More months have passed. Spider fames from Kwang spread further to other corners of Singapore. He catch more spiders. Everywhere he go, he wins, his income and his followers multiply. His house without mother rule turn into community center for more spider boys hanging around to court friendship … A temple has emerge on his throat to make his voice change. "Always wins!" he boast to Kim.
>
> (Cher 1995, Ch. 7, 64)

Such linguistic wordplay is derived from an actual form of English, as opposed to Roy's linguistic wordplay, which is principally a linguistic aesthetic, and not necessarily reflective of the way anyone in Asia would speak.

Less "weird" but just as clear a signal of a non-English sensibility from Singapore is Gopal Baratham's novel titled *Sayang,* a term the novel's protagonist calls

> a truly Southeast Asian word, soft as its people and well-understood from Marang to Manila, Surabaya to Sulawesi, Kuala Lumpur to Kota Kinabalu. It describes a love bound to sadness, a tenderness trembling on the edge of tears, a passion from which pity could not be detached …
>
> (Baratham 1991, Ch. 3, 47)

Although the word *sayang* is not English per se, it is transformed by the novelist into an intra-Asian lingua franca, articulated via a kind of "global English," in order to capture *a sensibility beyond the established Anglo-American register.* In that respect, it is no different from European words that have become acceptable as a kind of English, for example, cul de sac or sushi (from Japan), because the meanings of these terms are readily understood in an all-English context. Were Baratham's fiction exposed to a wider literary readership, it is conceivable that *sayang* could evolve into a kind of "global English" in much the same way.

A term that comes to mind to describe this sensibility is "friction-fiction."[3] Friction-fiction achieves its unique sensibility through language as well as content and in that regard, fulfills Ch'ien's observation that weird English fiction wishes "to show *who* the speaker is" and not just what the story is about. In her short story "Now That I Am Dead," the globalized Filipino writer Reine Arcache Melvin describes a man who is shot by "the dictator" and whose family has brought him out of the Philippines for Western medical care. The political situation at home is unstable. The man dies, despite both the Filipino psychic healer and Western medical treatment. Here is a scene following the wake.

> When the ceremony was over, Miguel invited the doctor to join the family for dinner … Over coffee, Marilen said: "We're going back to Manila."
>
> Lisa stirred a sugar cube into the black liquid, crushing it against the side of the cup.
>
> The doctor, the only American in the group, was the only one who thought it necessary to respond. "Is it safe to go back?"
>
> (Melvin 1999, 11)

The American perspective in this story is that of the "nonbelonger," even though the language "belongs" to America; he is the only one who separates the idea of safety from home for the exile, because it *is* always somehow "safer" at home for a "belonger," even when conditions are obviously unsafe. "Weird" is "normal" in such friction-fiction from Asia in English, because things are only "weird" inside the original cultures of the English language. As Ch'ien suggests, the author posits a worldview in this linguistic appropriation and declares: *this is who we are, which is not "you," the ones who used to "own" the language.* In this way, such writers transform English, globalizing it in their fiction, in order to articulate what they know to be true of their fictional "space."

But then we should ask, "Who's Asian?" in this globalized English landscape? Can we really talk about "Asian" fiction in English? Earlier in this "global conversation," I felt compelled to identify Cao Xueqin, but not Dickens, Twain or James, or, for that matter, the Europeans such as Dostoyevsky, Tolstoy, Maupassant, or Flaubert. When we articulate literature under the auspices of "globalization," we are assured of some common—dare we call it "universal"?—knowledge, but not of other knowledge that might be considered "universal" in a non-English literary landscape. Barring specialists in a specific discipline, we can almost always point to the dominant "general knowledge" perpetuated by the English language and its associated cultures. *Oliver Twist,* after all, is a musical on stage and in film that is seen around the world, originating from Dickens' novel of the same name, and even in countries where Christmas does not inform the cultural heritage, people know of Dickens' Scrooge; the rash of Jamesian novels such as *The Wings of the Dove* or *The Bostonians,* adapted for film, is comparable. Twain may have less currency in non-American cultures, but among educated English speakers, he is a known quantity, even to someone who has never read *Huckleberry Finn* or *Tom Sawyer.* As for the Russian and French authors noted above, their widely translated works in most languages, but especially in English, assure a general recognition of their importance in their respective national (and world) literatures.

However, China's fictional masterpiece *Dreams of Red Chambers,* although widely translated, is rarely read or mentioned outside specialist studies in Asian or Chinese literature and culture, even though it is clearly a significant contribution to world literature. What would it take to raise awareness of such literature? A Hollywood movie version of the novel, if it were as successful as Ang Lee's Academy Award–winning Chinese language feature film, *Crouching Tiger Hidden Dragon,* would probably be required.

Inevitably, the process takes us back again to the possible oxymoron and we are compelled to ask, can a "language," the thing that articulates national identity, culture, and experience in literary expression, really be global? In thinking about English, the most popular "foreign" language studied and used by the world today—evidenced especially by the explosion of English language studies in China, which is not linguistically postcolonial in the way India, that other major global player, is—should we say instead that it is merely a lingua franca used for some Asian fiction in our present era, something *globalized* to suit this world, which crosses borders and has, perhaps, already begun to transform our notions of native tongues, nationality, ethnicity, and cultural heritage? If where one is born is not necessarily where one grows up or lives and works, will "globalization" become the norm, as it increasingly threatens to do? If so, the troublesome prospect of a lingua franca, when applied to fiction from Asia in English, means that at best, such writers only have available a debased form of language, a mere aid to discourse, with which to write their fiction. Logically, debased language can only produce debased fiction, if we accept the Greeks and their linear approach to logical thought. Aristotle's *Poetics* is still one of the guiding texts for English language creative writing students of fiction in terms of a structure for a linear narrative's development of exposition, conflict, and denouement, one that is fundamental to much Western fiction. However, the historical center of culture in Asia has nothing to do with Athens, or Aristotle, or all those Greeks we revere in the study of literature. From a writer's perspective, surely there has to be a better answer?

The author Gish Jen poses the question "Who's Irish?" in the title story of her collection of that same name. Jen is second-generation ethnic Chinese but chooses to refer to herself not as an Asian-American writer, but as an American one. Her inclusion in *Best American Short Stories of the Century,* selected by the celebrated American author-editor John Updike, ensures that at least in some quarters, her self-classification stands. In her story collection, Jen chronicles the family comedy that arises from an interracial marriage between an Irish-American and a Chinese-American. Her other works address similar cross-cultural issues. America's history of melting-pot immigration can today demand that such fiction be considered a part of the national literature, in American English. Whether we read it as Asian-American or American is irrelevant to its clearly defined national identity, linking it, without question, to the American literary landscape and the primary language of that space.

But Asian fiction in English, or "global English," is a distinctly different form of literary expression than such Asian hyphenated work, one that has risen like a tower of Babel. We can no more easily define what "Asian" fiction is than we can name someone an "Asian writer." All the three examples cited above detail specific national and transnational lives with Asian characteristics in their brand of "global English" fiction. The resonance with common humanity is undeniable, whether in Cher's Singaporean street life, Baratham's Southeast Asian "kind of love blues," or Melvin's sense of exile and home.

Pico Iyer argues for the notion of a "global soul" in his book of that name, citing Emerson, who asks, "What is man but a congress of nations?" In one of the essays in the book "The Burning House," Iyer says:

> Our shrinking world gave more and more of us a chance to see, in palpable, unanswerable ways, how much we had in common, and how much we could live, in the grand Emersonian way, beyond petty allegiances and labels, outside the reach of nation states.
>
> (Iyer 2000, 13)

He refers to himself as "homeless," and a "permanent alien," an Indian born in England who moved to California as a boy and has been rooted for a while in Japan. His experience is paralleled in various ways by Cher, who emigrated to Australia, by Baratham who is a Western medical doctor, and by Melvin, who lives between Paris and Manila. Yet he admits that this global soul might live in "the metaphorical equivalent of international airspace" with air miles as currency and memories set in airports that increasingly resemble transnational cities, and who, "lacking a binding sense of 'we' … [might] remain fiercely loyal to a single airline" (Iyer 2000, 13). Certainly, I can testify to my own propensity to hoard miles on either the Star Alliance network or the Continental and Northwest congress of airlines; it is as if my ability to remain in airspace will somehow create a place that is congruent with an ambivalent, uncertain identity, providing this "Asian writer" a "home" for her fiction.

The language base for writing has expanded. And that language has transcended or expanded its structure and meanings of words. Therefore, that language has become a "global" language that evolves, reflects, and consumes. If standard British or American English is not well equipped to express what Asian writers need, they invent and modify its nature and use it to suit their needs. Their English has changed from British to American to "global."

Yet Asian writers do not necessarily abandon "home" in their fiction, whether it be an Asian street, town, or city; a nation state; a pre- *cum* postcolonial or pre- *cum* post-emigrant sense of being. Instead, home has been redefined in a global context as a kind of metaphoric airspace, elevating the author somewhere between a remembered space and the present, between a felt space and its reality. Alex Kuo is an author who has spent the greater part of his adult life in the United States, but returns to the China of his youth, and even Hong Kong, where he attended high school in the 1950s, in his story collection *Lipstick*, which won the American Book Award. His satirical take on Mao and the Cultural Revolution is unique in Chinese-American fiction. Here, for example, is the opening paragraph from the story "The Connoisseur of Chaos," which appears in the collection:

> Mao Zedong had been in this library before, maybe seventy-one years ago exactly, here, looking at the same history books that he was to have shelved yesterday, not reading them but knowing what they promise for his imagina-tion, looking out the dusty window to the sun setting on farmers seeding in the fields in another March or this March or not March at all, but April or May in 1918.
>
> (Kuo 2001, 71)

Significantly, the epigraph to the story is a quote from the American poet Wallace Stevens, "*And of ourselves and of our origins / In ghostlier demarcations, keener sounds,*" which speaks to the subject of this chapter.

Kuo "channels" Chinese culture in the form of Chairman Mao, but with a deliberate imprecision and blurring of actual history in these opening lines, to render "keener sounds" in his fiction of China.

Likewise, the Malaysian-Chinese-American writer Shirley Geok-lin Lim details her birth country in her novel *Joss and Gold* (2001); she grew up in Malaysia, where she completed a first degree before coming to the United States. Most Asian hyphenated writers borrow from their ethnic cultures in fiction, but their fictional locales are often either in the West or historically based in the "homeland"—Amy Tan is an internationally known writer of popular fiction in this vein—since their sense of self may often have little to do with Asia as it is today. In that respect, both Kuo and Lim are a departure from the Tan style of Asian-American fiction, even though both authors can readily be classified as Asian-American writers.

The Key Perhaps Is Not Where You End up But Where You Find Echoes of Your Global Self

Lim, who is an English department professor at the University of California, Santa Barbara, has also taught creative writing at the University of Hong Kong, where she held the chair in English from 1999 to 2001. Among her many accomplishments as chair was to establish the journal *Yuan Yang*, which continues today as a space for "Hong Kong and international writers," and is one of only two English language literary journals that specifically highlights Hong Kong writers[4]; she is also one of the supporters of the original Hong Kong International Literary Festival launched in 2001 by the writers Nury Vittachi and Jane Camens, which aimed to bring in writers whose work focused on Asia to the city for panels, readings, book launches, and workshops. The annual festival has expanded over the years to include international writers, regardless of the focus of their work, although the majority is in some ways connected to Asia. It is now called the Man Hong Kong International Literary Festival, reflecting its main financial sponsor, the Man Group, which also supports the Booker Prize. For example, the 2008 festival featured some sixty authors over a month-long period, which is approximately twice as long as the first festival.

Kuo precedes Lim in a similar global echo. In 1997, as the Lingnan scholar at Baptist University in Hong Kong, he organized the first significant conference of Hong Kong writing in English.[5] The presence of these two global Asian writers in English in my home city was instrumental in advancing the idea of an Anglophone literature in Hong Kong. Local conventional wisdom had long disdained the idea of writing from Hong Kong in English, relegating such work to the kind of debased literature that a lingua franca might produce. An earlier conference in 1992 on Asian Writing in English held at the University of Hong Kong excluded Hong Kong writers in the conference publications[6]; arguably, since the city was not yet "postcolonial" then, except perhaps in spirit—the term "colony" was no longer officially used for the territory by then—writing in English perhaps still remained the province of Empire. In *Prizewinning Asian Fiction,* published a year earlier, the editor Leon Comber offered the following opinion in his preface on why no indigenous writers from Hong Kong were included[7]:

> [I]t would seem that creative writers in English are not yet ready to emerge, although there is no shortage of skilled speakers of the language. There is perhaps a further reason for their present "writing block", apart from the language not being their own. It is that Hong Kong is reverting to Chinese suzerainty in 1997 and there is a move towards learning *Putonghua,* the national language of China.
>
> (Comber 1991, 6)

Comber may have been overly pessimistic, as the 1990s saw a spurt of creativity in the arts, which included publication of English poetry and prose by several Hong Kong writers. Since the handover to China, the number of local English publishers has increased, as has the teaching of creative writing at Hong Kong universities. However, there is concurrently a decline in the interest in the English language generally as attention has turned to the learning of Putonghua.

In 2003, Hong Kong University Press published the first comprehensive anthology of Hong Kong writing in English, which I was privileged to compile and coedit with Mike Ingham, who teaches literature at Lingnan University (*City Voices* 2003). Interestingly, one reason the press proposed the editorial collaboration is that Ingham teaches a course called "Asian Voices," covering the kinds of writing discussed here, including some Hong Kong Anglophone writing; admittedly, he is something of a pioneer in my home city in this regard, although the reading syllabus at the university level generally is changing, albeit slowly, to include contemporary local and Asian writers. This is an emergent literature, one that has grown, surprisingly, like Topsy, and continues to do so in this new era of our city as a Special Administrative Region of China, since the handover of sovereignty by Britain in 1997. Among the catalysts for the emergence were the two "global Asian" writers described above, who, in their way, helped to extend this growing literary evolution from which both were also born.

It is somewhat ironic that Anglophone literature, as well as the attention to creative writing in English at the universities, would experience growth in this posthandover era. As of this writing, three English departments in Hong Kong, namely, the University of Hong Kong, Chinese University, and Lingnan University publish an annual journal of creative work by students, and a limited amount of creative writing is taught at the undergraduate level. In 2008, Lingnan introduced a "writer-in-residence" in the English department, who complements the Chinese department's resident writer. In 2005, the University of Hong Kong established a two-year postgraduate diploma in creative writing, the majority of students being fiction writers. In 2004, Baptist University established its International Writers Workshop to bring in several international writers each year as resident writers for approximately a month. The number of local commercial publishers has also increased; from only one in the early 1990s, there are today at least six houses that regularly publish English language literary work by local and Asian writers.[8]

So is it globalized or "glocalized" English that we write? The Ghanaian philosopher Kwame Anthony Appiah posits the notion of a "rooted cosmopolitanism" in his two volumes, *The Ethics of Identity* (2005) and *Cosmopolitanism* (2006). His multidisciplinary approach is useful in our conversation, and aids this examination of "Asian" fiction. He calls the version of cosmopolitanism he defends

> wishy washy [because it] does not seek to destroy patriotism, or separate out "real" from "unreal" loyalties ... [he resists] the sharp distinction that is sometimes made between "moral" and "cultural" cosmopolitanism, where the former comprises those principles of moral universalism and impartialism, and the latter comprises the values of the world traveler, who takes pleasure in conversation with exotic strangers ... [that] a form of cosmopolitanism worth pursuing need not reflexively celebrate human difference; *but it cannot be indifferent to the challenge of engaging with it ...* [it is] cosmopolitanism with prospects [that] must reconcile a kind of universalism with the legitimacy of at least some forms of partiality.
>
> (italics, mine; Appiah 2005, Ch. 6, 222–23)

The Hong Kong that informs my fiction, experienced from an inside-outsider's perspective, bears only a passing resemblance to the capitalist enclave depicted in much of the English language fiction of the city, in which mythical dragons, triads, gangsters, and slant-eyed maidens sub-servient to foreign men prevail. Instead, I attempt to transform Hong Kong, through fiction, into a kind of contemporary cosmopolitan space, with primarily Chinese characteristics. From that perspective, it would be gratifying if Appiah's "wishy washy" cosmopolitan form of universalism could be applied to the result.

The echoes of our global selves are, by definition, beyond the confines of "authentic" national culture, as such echoes are found between cultures and in a variety of real and imagined spaces. Perhaps it is time, as the Australian writer and critic Jane Camens observes of globalized English Asian fiction, to redefine the universal space. In her essay on "literary contamination"—the term derives from Appiah's "cultural contamination"—with respect to fiction from Asia, she notes:

> These authors, who flip between cultures like mental trapeze artists, catch us up in their space between realities, reach out to let us grasp their meaning, and take us for the ride. I question whether any emotionally honest narrative, closely perceived, can be *in*authentic. Perhaps we are talking here about a *new* authenticity—the authentic globalised world.
>
> (Camens 2007)

Perhaps this is akin to the "ghostlier demarcation," where Stevens hears a "keener" sound.

We Return Then to Content in Our Fiction, through the Medium of English, and Remain, Necessarily, Ambivalent

The politics of globalized publishing favors the English language and publication by a "major" publisher, which generally means a U.S. or to a lesser extent, British house, the ones that pay the largest advances. It is worth noting that translation rights are more readily sold if one has backing by a major Anglo-American publisher. Consequently, you will find Gish Jen or Amy Tan or Pico Iyer in several languages, billed as "Asian writing." But few of the examples cited from Asia, all of whom have reasonable literary reputations globally, can compare against that larger, "globalized" literary world. In fact, many of those writers, myself included, are published "offshore," in Malaysia, Singapore, Hong Kong, the Philippines, or Australia (which is offshore by Anglo-American globalized publishing standards). What then is an Asian fiction writer in English to do?

One clearly friction-fictional answer is to be found in the relatively new phenomenon of Chinese writers from the Mainland choosing, or switching to, English for their fiction. Perhaps the most successful to date is Ha Jin, who penned the novel *Waiting* (1999), which won the National Book Award in the United States. Jin emigrated to the United States as an adult, but is steeped in the Western literary tradition; his literary ancestors are the likes of Chekhov and Nabokov to whom his fiction pays homage. However, he did not grow up bilingual, and despite a startling and admirable literary fluency in English, he speaks with an expected second-language accent. In that respect he is unusual as a Chinese-American fiction writer. Unlike Jen and a host of later-generation Asian-American authors, he seems far less American. For one thing, the setting for the vast majority of his fiction is China, mostly during the Cultural Revolution era, with primarily Chinese characters, although that world is rendered entirely in a kind of global English. In his acceptance speech for the 2001 Asian American Writers Workshop award for his collection The *Bridegroom: Stories,*[9] he expressed pleasure at that particular award, because it signaled, for him, an important acceptance in the space he has chosen to write in. He noted that after all, he no longer really could be considered a Chinese writer, since he did not engage in contemporary China. Jin, notably, writes *only* in English.

Since Jin's success, there has been a small but growing number of writers who straddle an even more controversial friction-fictional, Sino-global space. Two notable examples are Guo Xiaolu and Geling Yan, both of whom initially published fiction in Chinese that was translated into English; their translated works received only moderate critical attention. Both authors have each since penned a novel in English: Guo's *A Concise Chinese-English Dictionary for Lovers* and Yan's *The Banquet Bug* (2007 American title; *The Uninvited* is the British title). Both these English language novels have received wider critical attention than their previous books (Guo's novel was shortlisted for the 2007 Orange Prize; Yan's novel, originally published in Britain, crossed the transatlantic divide to an American publication). The politics of such a linguistic decision is beyond the scope of this chapter, but clearly, there are many ways to articulate globalized English in fiction from Asia.

A Final Reflection Then from the Personal Perspective of This Writer

While completing my third book of fiction, *Hong Kong Rose* (1997), a novel set in the seventies of that city, I often said in interviews that I was writing about "courage, cowardice, and compromise." At the time, I had Hong Kong's peculiar political situation in mind; we were arguably "postcolonial" in sensibility, yet still politically a colony, and were poised to transition into a kind of neocolonial state under China, which is where we are now as a Special Administrative Region. I am partial to our peculiar state, where courage and cowardice sometimes seem the same thing, where our very existence has *always* been a compromised one. To articulate that in fiction is, as Appiah suggests, a way of getting at a universalism without sacrificing the values and character of a people from such a nonnation state. You can't help embracing ambivalence knowing that life, and consequently fiction, would have been significantly different if we had had our Gandhi or Lee Kuan Yew, or even pitched tea into our "fragrant" harbor as the Bostonians did. In the late nineteenth century, a rebellious young baker once poisoned the bread sold to Europeans in a little-known historical moment of Hong Kong; he was sent packing back to Guangzhou (where he desperately wanted to return in the first place). The incident did make it into a historical novel, *Hangman's Point* (1999), by Dean Barrett, an American expatriate. The book is a kind of "Asian fiction" in English that is in some ways culturally closer to Asia than say Maxine Hong Kingston's fiction; Barrett is literate in Chinese, while Kingston is not. This *does* make for an ambivalent state of mind, given the debt much Asian fiction in English owes to the likes of Kingston.

In closing, here is the opening and a subsequent excerpt of one of my short stories, "Famine" (*Xu 2004*),[10] which addresses much of what this chapter discusses, in my own offering of globalized English friction-fiction:

> I escape. I board Northwest 18 to New York, via Tokyo. The engine starts, there is no going back. Yesterday, I taught the last English class and left my job of thirty-two years. Five weeks earlier, *A-Ma* died of heartbreak, within days of my father's sudden death. He was ninety-five, she ninety. Unlike *A-Ba*, who saw the world by crewing on tankers, neither my mother nor I have ever left Hong Kong.
>
> Their deaths rid me of responsibility at last, and I could forfeit my pension and that dreary existence. I am fifty-one and an only child, unmarried.
>
> I never expected my parents to take so long to die.
>
> (Xu 2004, 55)

The protagonist arrives in New York, where she checks into the Plaza Hotel and begins indulging in a culinary gluttony. There, she recalls a conversation just prior to departure with a Hong Kong friend, who worried at her strange adventure, and reflects:

> And would she worry, I wonder, if she could see me now, here, in this suite, this enormous space where one night's bill would have taken my parents years, no, *decades,* to earn and even for me, four years' pay, at least when I first started teaching in my rural enclave (though you're thinking, of course, quite correctly, *well, what about inflation,* the thing economists cite to dismiss these longings of an English teacher who has spent her life instructing those who care not a whit for our "official language," the one they never speak, at least not if they can choose, especially not now when there is, increasingly, a choice.)
>
> (Xu 2004, 59)

"Universal" is as universal does in fiction, which arises from the human condition as it is in Asia, and elsewhere, out of this strange and fascinating globalized world, in English or whatever globalized language the current moment in time chooses to articulate. If we, as writers, increasingly also have a choice in the matter, are we better off aligning with the globalized language of commerce and power, as English is today, for our literary expression? Or are we better off staying true to whatever language and culture we come from, *even if English is our more natural medium of expression?* Was Rushdie better off in his exiled state, under a *fatwa,* because at least the literary world in English acknowledges his contribution to contemporary literature?

For myself, the choice is becoming increasingly simple. My language and culture *are* globalized and the world I wish to write about is equally so. The *actual* language happens to be English, but it is the language that allows me to teach creative writing in places as disparate as Guangzhou, Hong Kong, Stockholm, Bali, and Beijing, as well as in Vermont or Iowa. What is also true is that the aspiring fiction writers in my classrooms and workshops use that global English language to write, increasingly, of Asia, regardless of where they were born or grew up, or what their ethnicity might be. Increasingly too, the younger writers especially are conversant in Asian languages and cultures, and write of Asia as it is, without the lens of exotica or Orientalism, and are less constrained by the traditions of English language fiction. Asia is globalized. It should therefore follow that its language for fiction can and will be equally as global, assuming we still believe the Greeks and their logical construct. There is no reason not to do so, until a newer model eventually takes over, as we imagine our world in fiction, and what it could become.

Notes

1. *The Book of Salt* by Monique Truong and *Fake House* by Linh Dinh (Vietnam); *A Thousand Years of Good Prayers* by Yiyun Li (China); *The Foreign Student* by Susan Choi (Korea); and *Sightseeing* by Rattawut Lapcharoensap (Thailand).
2. As of 1997, the three official languages of Hong Kong are Cantonese, English, and Putonghua (or Mandarin Chinese).
3. "FrictionFiction" is also the name of a show that features edgy music; see http://odeo.com/channel/223413/view, but this usage is independently coined.
4. The *Asia Literary Review* (formerly, *dimsum*) is also published in Hong Kong and features Hong Kong writers in English on a regular basis.
5. Conference at Baptist University, Hong Kong, "This is Home, This is Not Home" in 1999.
6. *Asian Voices in English,* ed. Mimi Chan and Roy Harris (Hong Kong: Hong Kong University Press, 1991) and *Asian Voices in English: A Symposium on English Literature by Asian Authors/Organized by the British Council, Hong Kong*

and Department of English, University of Hong Kong, Pokfulam Road, Hong Kong (Hong Kong: British Council, 1990).

7. *Prizewinning Asian Fiction* was an annual anthology, chosen from stories published in the regional news magazine *Asiaweek* from 1981 to 1991; the anthology is not being published now.

8. Publishers in Hong Kong of English language literary work include Chameleon Press, Sixth Finger Press, Haven Books, Blacksmith Press, Proverse Press, and Asia 2000 Ltd.

9. See www.aaww.org.

10. "Famine" subsequently appeared in *Ploughshares*, vol. 30, no. 4 (Winter 2004–05); and in the *2006 O. Henry Prize Stories* (New York: Anchor Books).

References

Appiah, Kwame Anthony. 2005. *The Ethics of Identity.* Princeton, New Jersey: Princeton University Press.

———. 2006. *Cosmopolitanism: Ethics in a World of Strangers.* New York: W.W. Norton.

Ashcroft, Bill, Gareth Griffiths, and Helen Tiffin. 1989. *The Empire Writes Back: Theory and Practice in Post-Colonial Literatures.* London and New York: Routledge.

Baratham, Gopal. *Sayang.* 1991. Singapore: Times Books.

Barrett, Dean. 1999. *Hangman's Point.* New York: Village East Books.

Camens, Jane. 2007. A Case for Literary Contamination with Asia. *The Griffith Review* Edition 18: 67–78.

Ch'ien, Evelyn. 2004. *Weird Englishes.* Cambridge, MA: Harvard University Press.

Cher, Ming. 1995. Spider Mother's Milk [Chapter 7]. *Spider Boys.* Auckland: Penguin Books.

Comber, Leon, ed. 1991. *Prizewinning Asian Fiction.* Singapore: Hong Kong University Press & Times Editions Pte. Ltd.

Compact Edition Oxford English Dictionary, The. 1981. New York: Oxford University Press.

Iyer, Pico. 2000. The Burning House. In *The Global Soul: Jet Lag, Shopping Malls and the Search for Home,* 1–38. New York: Vintage Books, Random House.

Jin, Ha. 1999. *Waiting.* New York: Pantheon.

———. 2000. *The Bridegroom: Stories.* New York: Pantheon

Kuo, Alex. 2001. The Connoisseur of Chaos. In *Lipstick and Other Stories,* 71–74. Hong Kong: Asia 2000 Ltd.

Lim, Shirley Geok-Lin. 2001. *Joss and Gold.* New York: Feminist Press at the City University of New York.

Melvin, Reine Arache. 1999. When I Am Dead. In *A Normal Life and Other Stories.* Manila: Office of Research and Publications, School of Arts & Sciences, Ateneo de Manila University.

Xiaolu, Guo. 2007. *A Concise Chinese-English Dictionary for Lovers*. New York: Nan A. Talese / Doubleday.

Xu Xi. 2004. *Hong Kong Rose: A Novel*. 2nd edition. Hong Kong: Chameleon.

———. 2004. *Overleaf Hong Kong: Stories and Essays of the Chinese, Overseas*. Hong Kong: Chameleon.

———, and Mike Ingham, eds. 2003. *City Voices: Hong Kong Writing in English 1945 to the Present*. Hong Kong: Hong Kong University Press.

Yan, Geling. 2006. *The Banquet Bug*. New York: Hyperion East.

———. 2006. *The Uninvited*. Cheltham: Faber and Faber.

CHAPTER 3

Glocalization through Global Brand Transposition

Shiao-Yun Chiang and Hanfu Mi

Introduction

Chinese economic growth, especially after the country's accession to the World Trade Organization (WTO) in 2001, has opened new markets for global companies in the last decade. With the headline "Globalization Gone Wild" on September 19, 2007, an ABC news report described the opening of a new Beijing branch of Hooters as a "barometer of globalization" in China:

> Regardless of its exotic location, walking in to Hooters Beijing feels exactly like walking into any other Hooters location . . . While this chain may seem routine here in the United States, the Hooters phenomenon for most Chinese is a new and exciting import from the West. Like with any cross-cultural trend, some things get lost in translation, including the name's reference to the female anatomy. In Beijing, "Hooters" simply means "owl," but that doesn't mean the point goes overlooked. The opening of Hooters Beijing follows a long line of American food chains into the Chinese market, such as McDonald's and the Hard Rock Cafe. However, the introduction of this chain brings a relatively new cultural idea—the idea that sex sells.

The global appeal of American products, services, and pop culture for the Chinese is deeply rooted in their marketing strategies. While Americans are certainly familiar with the direct appeal to sex in the consumption culture at home, few would bother to figure out why Hooters is no longer used as a euphemism for "large breasts" but simply as "owls" (猫头鹰 pronounced as "Mao-Tou-Ying") in China. In fact what is lost in the Chinese translation is intentional. China is a high-context culture (cf. Hall 1989) that values an indirect communication style. While the Chinese can understand the idea that sex sells, it still would be highly inappropriate to use "large breasts" in public signs. What is lost in the American euphemism (though Hooters may not be euphemistic any more in American English) is regained in the Chinese translation of "owls" as a metaphor in the sense that owls are nocturnal birds of prey that should remind Chinese consumers of night life, in particular with the original logo. Besides, reports show that the success of Hooters Shanghai, the very first branch in China, does not entirely rely on sex appeal but friendliness and courteousness, and it is common to hear parents in Shanghai saying, "Let's take Grandmom and the kids to Hooters tonight" (Johnston 2005). Hooters is the most recent example of how globalization works.

This study looks at how globalization works through brand transposition across linguistic and sociocultural boundaries in Chinese marketing communication. Globalization is defined here as a "rapidly developing process of complex interconnections between societies, cultures, institutions, and individuals world-wide" (Tomlinson 1991, 170). Our observation is that these interconnections find typical expression in the specific manner in which global brands are transposed from their original language into Chinese. To market a global brand in a society different from its own is not only an economic activity but also a sociolinguistic process that involves the interplay of at least two different languages and cultures (Eckhardt and Houston 2002). Drawing on the linguistic signs of the top 100 global brands marketed in China, this article provides a close analysis of the specific ways in which global brands are presented in the Chinese language.

Global Appeal and Local Appeal

One of the main debates on globalization is whether the global mobilization of business, capital, technologies, and information may bring about cultural homogenization in the world (cf. Guillén 2001). Some studies maintain that globalization may lead to the obliteration of local cultures and the dominance of Western culture (Barker 1999; Friedman 1994; Hall 1991). For example, Hall (1991) argues that globalization creates a global mass culture that consists of images and stories from the West and speaks only English. In contrast, other studies suggest that globalization does not necessarily generate a uniform Western culture across the world, but contributes to the continual development of cultural diversity (Garrett 1998; Hamilton 1994; Tomlinson 1999). For example, Tomlinson (2003) contends that globalization does make imprints on local cultures, but local cultures can revive and even enrich themselves in the process of globalization.

This global/local imperative is one of the key themes in marketing communication. Wherever an international company intends to sell a product or service in a foreign market, the most critical strategy is to communicate with and engage the prospective consumers through attractive brands. Hence, to transpose brands across linguistic and sociocultural boundaries is the most challenging undertaking in marketing communication. Studies suggest that there are two ways to transpose a global brand in a foreign market: a globalized approach and a localized approach (cf. Chan 1990; Chan and Huang 1997, 2001; Farrall and Whitelock 2001; Leclerc et al. 1994; McDonald and Roberts 1990; Pan and Schmitt 1995; Schmitt and Pan 1994; Zhang and Schmitt 2001; Zhou and Belk 2004). The globalized approach maintains that many international corporations tend to keep their brands consistent worldwide so that local customers' consuming values and behaviors can be globalized in the presence of global images. There are successful examples of the globalized approach such as those of McDonald's, which transformed the local fabric of Hong Kong in surprising ways (Watson1997), and Frontier Foods, which actually turned the Chinese people into cheese-eaters (Buckman 2003). In contrast, the localized approach argues that local customers' sociocultural expectations influence their consuming behaviors, and a global product or service should be re-presented in a sign that fits into the local cultural context and meets with local consumers' needs. Most global marketers are found willing to adapt their advertising to the Chinese market (cf. Eckhardt and Houston 2002; Marr and Hatfield 1997; Tai 1997; Yin 1999).

As indicated in marketing communication, globalization is not necessarily a one-way process from the West to the rest (Tomlinson 1996). Empirical studies show that economic developments may bring about pervasive cultural changes, but the cultural heritage of a society as "historically shaped by Protestantism or Confucianism or Islam" exerts "enduring effects" (Inglehart and Baker 2000, 49). It seems more reasonable to say that globalization is a dialectical process (cf. Giddens 1991) that creates convergence and divergence simultaneously. Robertson (1992, 1994) contends that the cultural experience of the contemporary world is under the process of "glocalization" in which globalization and localization interpenetrate each other and are mutually implicative. In Robertson's view, the question of globalization is not about whether globalization promotes or produces homogeneity or heterogeneity. Rather, the question of globalization is an empirical one that requires us to describe, analyze, and explicate the strategies, operations, and mechanisms for global mobilizations within specific sociocultural contexts. Taking Robertson's perspective, this study describes how global brands cross linguistic and sociocultural boundaries in China.

Chinese Transpositions of Global Brands

China has emerged as the largest consumer market in the world since it joined WTO in 2001. Its enormous market has attracted many international companies, and almost all global products and services, from food, cosmetics, fashion, electronics, and automobiles to finance, hospitality, retail, insurance, and recreation, have been marketed in China. While global brands always have been appealing to Chinese customers, they must adapt one way or the other to the local culture in China. Take Coca-Cola for example. While the can still remains red, its logo has been replaced with Chinese characters – 可口可乐 (Ke-Kou-Ke-Le). The Chinese linguistic transposition sounds very similar to the English brand name Coca-Cola, but means "really palatable, really enjoyable" in the Chinese language. 可口可乐 is considered to be the most successful brand transposition in China as it helps to enhance the product image and attract Chinese consumers (cf. Hatfield 1997). Language, in a sense, is the carrier of culture, and the linguistic transpositions of global brands may function as a channel of communication through which the global interacts with the local in China.

The Chinese linguistic system often poses a big challenge for global marketers who want to transpose a brand name. The Chinese language adopts a logographic writing system in the form of characters called 汉字 (Han-Zi). Unlike a phonographic writing system with only a small number of letters, the logographic system consists of many different symbols because the correspondence between speech and writing is largely conventional. A standard Chinese dictionary contains about 50,000 characters, many of which have a similar pronunciation. Unlike a letter in the alphabetic system, each Chinese character stands for a syllable and carries its own meanings (including connotation and denotation). This is problematic as the characters selected for transposing a global brand can convey different kinds of meanings or simply make no sense to Chinese customers. For example, when Coca-Cola was first introduced into China in the 1920s, it was transposed by shopkeepers into four Chinese characters that could mean "Bite the wax tadpole." The company took eleven years to make a profit after it came back to China in 1979 because of its poorly transposed brand name in the past. Coca-Cola now dominates the vast market of soft drinks in China with its new brand transposition 可口可乐.

The traditional Chinese naming practices may also pose a big challenge for global marketers who want to transpose a brand name. Confucius said that "if names be not correct, language is not in accordance with the truth of things; if language be not in accordance with the truth of things, affairs are not carried to success" (Legge 2004, 88). A name, for the Chinese, is not only informative but also formative in terms of its referent's life, career, and future. The meaning of a name must be associated with its verbal form, phonetic structure, family status, social expectations, etc. The basic criteria for naming practices are that a name must express the very essence of the named, the bearer's appreciation for fine arts, and the name-giver's educational level, moral orientation, socioeconomic status, and augury for the future of the named (cf. Schmitt 1995). A brand name is like a person's name as they are both identity markers. Many global brands bear the founders' personal names that are almost sacred to the companies while Chinese cultural traditions require that names should be consistent with their referents. This is problematic as local consumers may not know what the product or service is at the first sight of the brand name. For example, Benz used to be phonetically transposed into 本茨 that bears no practical meaning in Chinese, and now 奔驰 has been used as the official sign that sounds like the original brand, but means "run fast" or "speed on" or "gallop".

Data Analysis

The data under study here consist of the top 100 global brands jointly reported by *Business Week* and Interbrand in 2008. According to the report, these global brands can be grouped by countries, such as the United States (53), Germany (10), France (8), Japan (7), Switzerland (5), Italy (4), Netherlands (3), United Kingdom (2), Canada (2), Korea (2), Sweden (2), Finland (1), and Spain (1). All these top brands have been marketed in China, and their linguistic transpositions have been officially announced as the standard signs for marketing across the nation. A close examination of the linguistic signs shows six types of transposition methods: phonetic, semantic, phonosemantic, transformative, phonetic with a semantic component, and switching.

1. Phonetic Transposition

Phonetic transposition selects those characters that correspond closely to the pronunciation of the original brand names. Chinese characters carry meanings and concepts. In phonetic transposition, the individual characters, once chosen and put together in a sequence as a sign for a global brand, are not supposed to retain any meaning. Theoretically, the characters in that sequence function as purely phonetic symbols that are similar to the meaningless syllable in the alphabetic system. It is notable in Table 3.1 that most phonetic transpositions are proper names.

Table 3.1 Phonetic transposition (34%)

Brand	Character	Pronunciation
Nokia	诺基亚	nuò jī yà
Intel	英特尔	yīng tè ěr
Disney	迪斯尼	dí sī ní
Google	谷歌	gǔ gē
Gillette	吉列	jí liè
Louis Vuitton	路易斯-威登	lù yì sī wēi dēng
Marlboro	万宝路	wàn bǎo lù
Sony	索尼	suǒ ní
Dell	戴尔	dài ěr
JPMorgan	JP摩根	mó gēn
Morgan Stanley	摩根士丹利	mó gēn shì dān lì
Philips	飞利浦	fēi lì pǔ
Thomson Reuters	汤姆森路透社	tāng mǔ sēn lù tòu shè
Accenture	埃森哲	āi sēn zhé
Siemens	西门子	xī mén zi
Ford	福特	fú tè
Harley-Davidson	哈雷戴维森	hā léi dài wéi sēn
Heinz	亨氏	hēng shì
Amazon.com	亚马逊	yà mǎ xùn
Yahoo	雅虎	yǎ hǔ
Audi	奥迪	ào dí
Caterpillar	卡特皮勒	kǎ tè pí lè
Adidas	阿迪达斯	ā dí dá sī
Rolex	劳力士	láo lì shì
Herm's	爱马仕	ài mǎ shì
Gap	盖普	gài pǔ
Cartier	卡地亚	kǎ dì yà
Tiffany & Co	蒂芙尼	dì fú ní
Motorola	摩托罗拉	mó tuō luó lā
Lexus	雷克萨斯	léi kè sà sī
Prada	普拉达	pǔ lā dá
Ferrari	法拉利	fǎ lā lì
Armani	阿玛尼	ā mǎ ní
Hennessy	轩尼诗	xuān ní shī

2. Semantic Transposition

Semantic transposition selects those Chinese words or expressions that correspond closely to the literal meanings of the original brand names regardless of their phonetic structure. Basically, the original brand is translated word for word into a Chinese equivalent. This type of transposition is possible only if the original brand name happens to be a single word or an expression that has a clear meaning or reference (e.g., Nestle and Apple)

Table 3.2 Semantic transposition (22%)

Brand	Character	Pronunciation
Microsoft	微软	wéi ruǎn
GE	通用电气	tōng yòng diàn qì
Toyota	丰田	fēng tián
American Express	美国运通	měi guó yùn tōng
Honda	本田	běn tián
Samsung	三星	sān xīng
Oracle	甲骨文	jiǎ gú wén
Apple	苹果	píng guǒ
UPS	联合包裹	lián hé bāo guǒ
Nintendo	任天堂	rèn tiān táng
UBS	瑞银	ruì yín
Volkswagen	大众	dà zhòng
Nescafe	雀巢咖啡	què cháo kā fēi
AIG	美国国际集团	měi guó guó jì jí tuán
Nestle	雀巢	què cháo
Hyundai	现代	xiàn dài
BlackBerry	黑莓	hēi méi
BP	英国石油	yīng guó shí yóu
Panasonic	松下	sōng xià
ING	国际集团荷兰保险	guó jì jí tuán hé lán bǎo xiǎn
Shell	壳牌	ké pái
FedEx	联邦快递	lián bāng kuài dì

and not a proper name (e.g., Ford and Dell). It should be noted here that some of the global brands on the list with a clear meaning or reference are not semantically transposed (e.g., Caterpillar, Accenture, Audi, and Yahoo).

3. Phonosemantic Transposition

Phonosemantic transposition selects those Chinese linguistic symbols that not only sound like the original brand name, but also carry a meaning related to the service or the product or the product/service category. In contrast to phonetic transposition and semantic transposition, phonosemantic transpositions are mostly phonetic transpositions, but with self-evident semantic associations. It should be noted that these semantic associations are not exactly contained in the original brands, but they appeal to Chinese consumers' sociolinguistic competence. This type of transposition is not exactly a translation, but a transcreation of the original brand name in the Chinese language.

Table 3.3 Phonosemantic transposition (21%)

Brand	Character	Meaning	Pronunciation
Coca-Cola	可口可乐	Really palatable and enjoyable	kě kǒu kě lè
McDonald's	麦当劳	Must labor for wheat	mài dāng láo
Mercedes-Benz	奔驰	Speed on or run fast	bēn chí
Cisco	思科	Think science	sī kē
Pepsi	百事可乐	Everything can be fun	bǎi shì kě lè
Nike	耐克	Hard to be worn (Durable)	nài kè
Ikea	宜家	Good for home	yí jiā
Canon	佳能	Best capability	jiā néng
Kellogg's	家乐氏	Happy family	jiā lè shì
Gucci	古姿	Classic looks	gǔ zī
L'Oreal	欧来雅	European elegance	ōu lái yǎ
Colgate	高露洁	Highly clean as dew	gāo lù jié
Xerox	施乐	Bring you happiness	shī lè
Chanel	香奈尔	Fragrance on you	xiāng nài ěr
Danone	达能	Reaching capability	dá néng
Avon	雅芳	Elegance & fragrance	yǎ fāng
Porsche	保时捷	Get you there on time	bǎo shí jié
Allianz	安联	Safe union	ān lián
Johnson & Johnson	强生	Strong life	qiáng shēng
Nivea	妮维雅	Keep girls elegant	ní wéi yǎ
Visa	威士	Power man	wēi shì

4. Transformative Transposition

Transformative transposition uses some Chinese expressions or combines some characters into a linguistically and culturally acceptable expression that appeals to some characteristics associated with the global brand logo or the product/service. For example, 皇冠 for Smirnoff means "crown" that refers to a part of the brand logo. 惠普 for Hewlett-Packard means "benefit all," which stresses the good quality of the product. 安盛 for AXA means "safe and prosperous," which helps to project a desirable image of the service. Transformative transposition does not tend to keep the original brand names phonetically and semantically consistent in the transposed signs. Rather, this type of transposition highlights the positive characteristics or desirable qualities associated with the product/service category.

5. Phonetic Transposition with a Semantic Component

Phonetic transposition with a semantic component is partly phonetic and partly semantic. Usually, a part of the transposed linguistic sign has a Chinese

Table 3.4 Transformative transposition (15%)

Brand	Character	Meaning	Pronunciation
Hewlett-Packard	惠普	Benefit all	huì pǔ
BMW	宝马	Treasured horse	bǎo mǎ
Citi	花旗	Flower flag (American flag)	huā qí
HSBC	汇丰银行	Funds abundant bank	huì fēng yín háng
Budweiser	百威	Hundred prowess	bǎi wēi
Merrill Lynch	美林	Beautiful forest (literal)	měi lín
Goldman Sachs	高盛	Highly prosperous	gāo shèng
AXA	安盛	Safe & prosperous	ān shèng
Wrigley's	箭牌	Arrow brand	jiàn pái
M & Chandon	酩悦香槟	Fragrant champagne	míng yuè xiāng bīn
Kleenex	舒洁	Comfortable & clean	shū jié
Pizzahut	必胜客	Must win customers (literal)	bì shèng kè
Duracell	金霸王	Golden Great King (literal)	jīn bà wáng
Smirnoff	皇冠	Crown	huáng guān
Marriott	万豪酒店	Wealthy & powerful people hotel	wàn háo jiǔ diàn

Table 3.5 Phonetic transposition with a semantic component (2%)

Brand	Character	Pronunciation
KFC	肯德基 (phonetic) 炸鸡 (semantic)	kěn dé jī zhá jī
Starbucks	星 (semantic) 巴克 (phonetic)	xīng bā kè

equivalent of a component of the original brand while the other part is phonetic. This type of transposition for foreign brands is common in China, but only two examples are found in the list of the top 100 global brands.

6. Switching

Switching is not exactly a transposition as it simply makes a direct use of the original brand logo. Six of the top 100 global brands are directly switched into the Chinese advertising discourse, and five of the switched brand names are abbreviations. They are not transposed because they are all short and convenient (e.g., IBM) or because they are too familiar (e.g., MTV). It should be noted that some of these abbreviations may be semantically transposed in a more formal discourse (e.g., IBM and SAP) while ZARA and eBay have

Table 3.6 Switching (6%)

Brand logo	Switched brand name
IBM	IBM
H&M	H&M
eBay	eBay (电子港湾 or 亿贝)
SAP	SAP
MTV	MTV
ZARA	ZARA (飒拉)

Chinese transpositions that are used in Chinese consumers' everyday discourse but are not officially recognized by the companies.

Discussion

A brand name is designed to produce phonetic, semantic, and visual effects in order to influence customers cognitively and behaviorally. The phonetic, semantic, and visual attributes of a brand are mostly tied to one language and culture and are well understood by native speakers. This means that a global brand transposition must appeal to local consumers' sociolinguistic competence in China while maintaining its global identity. The classification of the transposed linguistic signs above has revealed some explicit or implicit interactions between the global and the local in China.

First, the global/local interaction finds its expression in the phonetic structure of the linguistic signs of the global brands. Traditionally, Chinese people favor short names that are fair-sounding and easy to say. Table 3.7 shows that 72 percent of the transposed linguistic signs consist of two or three syllables. Also, the Chinese language is abundant in homophonic words, which are differentiated by the linguistic system of four tones. This means that a combination of two characters can often sound like many different things. On the one hand, the Chinese phonetic characteristics may pose a big challenge for phonetic transpositions. All the Chinese characters in the transposed linguistic signs must be carefully selected to restrict their semantic associations, and especially to eliminate any negative meaning. This phonetic characteristic may be the primary reason for transformative transpositions. It is notable in Table 3.4 that a transformative transposition is adopted whenever the global brand name is too long or hard to pronounce or liable to create extra meanings if chosen for phonetical transposition—for example, Budweiser (百威), Goldman Sachs (高盛), and Merrill Lynch (美林). On the other hand, the

Table 3.7 Length of transposed linguistic signs

Number of syllables/characters	Number of brands
2	44
3	28
4	15
5 or more (including switched brands)	13

Table 3.8 Referential characteristics of transposed linguistic signs

Reference	Example	Total
Product/Service	GE, UPS, UBS, Toyoto, FedEx, Marriott, HSBC	20
Quality/Function	Benz, Nike, Ikea, Colgate, Kleenex, Duracell	21
Value/Belief/Customs	BMW, Gucci, Xerox, Kellogg's, McDonald's	14
Brand Logo	Wrigley's, Smirnoff, Shell, BlackBerry	15

Chinese phonetic characteristics may provide means and tools for glocalizing a global brand. As shown in Table 3.3, a phonosemantic transposition is made possible only if there is a large set of homophonic words in the language. Chinese consumers particularly like phonosemantic transpositions (as exemplified by Coca-Cola and Benz) because they display a globally stylish sound with a positive Chinese meaning.

Second, the global/local interaction finds its expression in the references of the linguistic signs of the global brands. Traditionally, Chinese people believe that names are supposed to reflect the true nature or marked characteristics of their referents. A name that does not refer to reality (名不副实) may be perceived as a disgraceful thing in China. Table 3.8 shows that 70 percent of the transposed linguistic signs contain an obvious reference to the product/service, its quality/function, or other semantic components. It should be noted here that some brand names (e.g., GE and FedEx) have a reference, but many others (e.g., BMW and Colgate) do not. The referential meaning of a brand name is mostly reformed to facilitate Chinese consumers' understanding. For example, there is a connotation of durability in the name Duracell while the transposed linguistic sign 金霸王 refers to its incomparable power in Chinese.

Third, the global/local interaction finds its expression in the rich semantic associations of the linguistic signs of the global brands. Traditionally, Chinese people believe that a good name may bring about good luck and fulfill social expectations. This symbolic value of global brand names is embedded in their transposed linguistic signs. For example, Kellogg's is transposed into 家乐氏, which literally means "happy family" in the Chinese language. Chinese people purchase products or services not only for their own consumption, but also for relatives and friends as presents on holidays and special occasions. It is a long-standing social custom in China that some presents are more desirable than others for a home visit. Thus, the symbolic meaning of 家乐氏 (Kellogg's) may be the most decisive factor for Chinese consumers before they purchase any product. As shown in tables 3.3 and 3.4, almost all the phonosemantic and transformative transpositions have a positive or desirable semantic association that is not contained in the original brand names. Characters with positive semantic associations, such as 宝 (treasure, preciousness), 吉 (luck), 美 (beauty), 雅 (grace, elegance), 佳 (fine, good), 乐 (joy), 益 (beneficial), 能 (capability), 富 (wealth), 福 (happiness), 盛 (prosperous), 特 (special), 芳 (fragrance), and 利 (profit), are pervasive in the transposed signs of global brands.

Lastly, the global/local interaction finds its expression in the visual appeal of the linguistic signs of the global brands. Traditionally, Chinese people place a great emphasis on the meaning of a name by selecting certain favorable characters that can create certain desirable visual effects. In the logographic writing system, lexical meanings can be mostly identified in the verbal forms. Chinese characters were originally pictures of people, objects, animals, and other things, but over centuries of linguistic evolution, they have become less iconic but more symbolic. Take Benz (奔驰), for example. The visual images of the two characters 奔驰 (especially, 驰 with a horse 马 as radical) produce a vivid mental picture of performance, power, dynamism, and speed—the exact attributes that the company expects all its consumers to remember and think about. The effort made for visual appeal is also a main indicator of social attributes that a global brand wishes to convey. For example, Nivea (妮维雅) and Disney (迪斯尼) contain Chinese characters (妮 and 尼) that have the same pronunciation, but 尼 is more often used as a neutral character while 妮 (with a girl 女 as radical) refers only to a girl. Thus, the transposed linguistic signs for cosmetics help to project a feminine image while the sign for an amusement park is socially expected to look neutral.

Conclusion

The transposition of global brands is strongly conditioned by linguistic and cultural differences. As shown above, to transpose a global brand is not just to give it a Chinese name, but to represent it in a distinctive local image. Take BMW, for example. For Chinese consumers, BMW is not just a driving machine, but a treasured horse (宝马). The horse has a mostly positive image in Chinese arts and literature. There are many idiomatic expressions and legends about the positive characters or qualities of horses in traditional

Chinese culture. This transposition certainly succeeded in tapping into Chinese consumers' cultural consciousness.

While Chinese consumers like global brands that adopt Chinese names, they also prefer brands that sound and look globally stylish. This almost paradoxical feature is reflected in the six types of transpositions above. On the one hand, there is an overt preference for making the transposed linguistic signs meaningful and referential. On the other hand, there is an obvious orientation to keeping the global brands phonetically consistent in the Chinese transpositions to some degree. For example, 耐克 (Nike) has a Chinese semantic association "durable" while it sounds globally stylish.

The key challenge to this global/local interaction is probably to find and keep a fine balance between globalization and localization. A global brand that does not adapt to local cultures may not look sensible as Chinese consumers must find out what the product or service is at the sight of the brand name. The linguistic signs of global brands must match Chinese consumers' sociolinguistic competence. On the other hand, a global brand that has a fully localized image will find it difficult to compete with local brands. The global situation in China is different and more complicated than that in some European and African countries. While Chinese consumers as well as scholars can be just as patriotic in terms of their consumption behaviors as people in any other country, they mostly favor global brands over local brands as the former are usually perceived to have better quality and higher status. The present study shows that there are both advantages and disadvantages in the globalized and the localized approaches, and the risks should be self-evident if a global brand goes to either extreme.

References

Barker, C. 1999. *Television, Globalisation and Cultural Identities*. Buckingham, UK: Open University Press.

Buckman, R. 2003. Let Them Eat Cheese. *Far Eastern Economic Review*, November 12.

Chan, A. K. K. 1990. Localization in International Branding: A Preliminary Investigation on Chinese Names of Foreign Brands in Hong Kong. *International Journal of Advertising* 9: 81–91.

Chan, A. K. K., and Y. Y. Huang. 1997. Chinese Brand Naming: From General Principles to Specific Rules. *International Journal of Advertising* 16(4): 320–335.

———. 2001. Principles of Brand Naming in Chinese: The Case of Drinks. *Marketing Intelligence and Planning* 19(5): 309–318.

Eckhardt, G. M., and M. J. Houston. 2002. Cultural Paradoxes Reflected in Brand Meaning: McDonald's in Shanghai, China. *Journal of International Marketing* 10(2): 68–82.

Farrall, N., and J. Whitelock. 2001. A Comparative Analysis of Advertising Characteristic, Style, Strategies, and Form in Global and National Brand Advertising. *Journal of Marketing Communication* 7: 125–136.

Friedman, J. 1994. *Cultural Identity and Global Process.* London: Sage.

Garrett, G. 1998. *Partisan Politics in the Global Economy.* New York: Cambridge University Press.

Giddens, A. 1991. *Modernity and Self Identity.* Cambridge: Polity.

Guillén, M. F. 2001. Is Globalization Civilizing, Destructive, or Feeble? A Critique of Five Key Debates in the Social Science Literature. *Annual Review of Sociology* 27: 235–260.

Hall, E. T. 1989. *Beyond Culture.* New York: Anchor Books.

Hall, S. 1991. The Local and Global: Globalization and Ethnicity. In *Cultural Globalization and the World-System: Contemporary Conditions for the Representation of Identity,* ed. A. D. King, 41–68. Binghamton: State University of New York.

Hamilton, G. G. 1994. Civilizations and Organization of Economics. In *The Handbook of Economic Sociology,* eds. N. J. Smelser and R. Swedberg, 183–205. Princeton, NJ: Princeton University Press.

Hatfield, A. 1997. Selecting Brand Names that Shanghai Esteems. *AgExporter* 9(7): 3.

Inglehart, R., and W. E. Baker. 2000. Modernization, Cultural Change, and the Persistence of Traditional Values. *American Sociological Review* 65(1): 19–51.

Johnston, N. 2005. East Meets West in Funny Ways. *Christian Science Monitor* 10 (January).

Leclerc, E., B. Schmitt, and L. Dubé. 1994. Foreign Brand Naming and its Effect on Product Perception and Attitudes. *Journal of Marketing Research* 31: 263–270.

Legge, J. 2004. The Confucian Analects. Whitefish, MT: Kessinger.

Marr, J., and A. Hatfield. 1997. Fast-Food Restaurants: Just What Eastern China's Consumers Ordered. *AgExporter* 9(7): 1.

McDonald, G. M., and C. J. Roberts. 1990. The Brand-Naming Enigma in the Asia Pacific Context. *European Journal of Marketing* 24(8): 6–19.

Pan, Y., and B. H. Schmitt. 1995. What's in a Name? An Empirical Comparison of Chinese and Western Brand Names. *Asian Journal of Marketing* 4(1): 7—16.

———. 1996. Language and Brand Attitude: Impact of Script and Sound Matching in Chinese and English. *Journal of Consumer Psychology* 5(3): 263–277.

Robertson, R. 1992. *Globalization: Social Theory and Global Culture.* London: Sage.

———. 1994. Globalization or Glocalization? *Journal of International Communication* 1(1): 33–52.

Schmitt, B. H. 1995. Language and Visual Imagery: Issues of Corporate Identity in East Asia. *Columbia Journal of World Business* 30(4): 28–36.

———, and Y. Pan. 1994. Managing Corporate and Brand Identities in the Asia-Pacific Region. *California Management Review* 38 (Summer): 32–48.

Tai, S. 1997. Advertising in Asia: Localize or Regionize? *International Journal of Advertising* 16(1): 48–61.

Tomlinson, J. 1991. *Cultural Imperialism: A Critical Introduction.* Baltimore, MD: Johns Hopkins University Press.

———. 1996. Cultural Globalization: Placing and Displacing the West. *European Journal of Development Research* 8(2): 22–35.

———. 1999. *Globalization and Culture.* Chicago: University of Chicago Press.

———. 2003. Globalization and Cultural Identity. In *The Global Transformations Reader: An Introduction to the Globalization Debate,* ed. D. Held and A. McGrew, 269–72. Cambridge: Polity.

Watson, J. L. 1997. McDonald's in Hong Kong: Consumerism, Dietary Change, and the Rise of a Children's Culture. In *Golden Arches East: McDonalds in East Asia,* ed. J. L. Watson, 77–110. Stanford, CA: Stanford University Press.

Yin, J. 1999. International Advertising Strategies in China: A Worldwide Survey of Foreign Advertisers. *Journal of Advertising Research* 39(6): 25–35.

Zhang, S., and B. Schmitt. 2001. Creating Local Brands in Multilingual International Markets. *Journal of Marketing Research* 38: 313–325.

Zhou, N., and R. W. Belk. 2004. Chinese Consumer Reading of Global and Local Advertising Appeals. *Journal of Advertising* 33(3): 63–76.

PART II

Identities

CHAPTER 4

Maintenance of Spanish as a Heritage Language in a Global World

María Cristina Montoya

Introduction

This research focuses on the idea that a mixture of human interaction involving diverse cultural, social, and linguistic backgrounds in an era of globalization generates change in two stages. First, previous ideologies supporting assimilation require replacement with those that encourage multilingualism. Second, multilingualism creates an environment for a reconstruction of identity by second-generation bilingual, Spanish/English speakers. The newly constructed identity emphasizes greater cosmopolitanism with adherence to a strong ethnic and linguistic identity base.

This study will examine a generation that transformed the use of Spanish in the United States. This generation included the mixed Spanish-speaking population in New York's urban areas and its surroundings. Data were collected from two groups: immigrants (i.e., first-generation Spanish speakers) and their children born in the United States, who were brought up bilingual and who, as young adults, exhibited proficiency in both languages.

A point of departure in the current study was to differentiate between the two processes lived by the two groups of participants. The first group was made up of parents who came into a new country as immigrants. They needed to pursue cultural and linguistic assimilation in order to help their children integrate into the dominant local society. The second group consisted of the immigrant parents' children who were attending college in New York State. The study found that a reconstruction of identity was occurring where new social networks and technologies were affecting the decisions of bilingual second-generation speakers. Evidence indicates that these college students were in the process of finding out what it is to be a global individual when they started to integrate a private experience into a public one.

The research included seventeen interviews with second-generation speakers that were conducted during the period 2002–2006; all were fluent, bilingual, college students from the five New York City boroughs and Westchester. Interviews with first-generation Spanish-speaking immigrant parents were not conducted until later, after interviews with college students had been completed, and they agreed to extend the invitation to participate to their parents. Fifteen interviews were collected from first-generation participants. The places of origin of the participants were diverse: Colombia, the Dominican Republic, Puerto Rico, Mexico, El Salvador, Honduras, Ecuador, Argentina, and Spain. Thirteen second-generation participants were born in the United States, and four immigrated before they were of school age. All were very fluent in Spanish due to close contact with their parents' culture and countries and the fact that Spanish had a dominant presence in the homes of a majority of them.

The Case of Spanish in the United States

Lipski, in his chronological narrative (2000) about Spanish-speaking people in the United States, presents a brief summary of the main historical events that brought about Spanish-English language contact. Lipski mentions that contact between English and Spanish in the United States has been long known to have roots in the country's history from colonial times and after independence. The two languages have always been active in the social dynamic of the country, with the integration of some southwestern parts of the continent, mostly Spanish-speaking, into U.S. territory. Other examples are the adoption of earlier Spanish colonies such as Florida, and later Puerto Rico. By the 1920s, Spanish was a permanent facet of the U.S. linguistic profile. Around this time, English language use in schools was a main governmental policy for forcing southwesterners to transition to English (Lipski 2000, 5). In the 1950s, scholars and educators became more interested in describing the language of certain Spanish-speaking communities, and research advanced with the target of teaching standard Spanish to those communities. The idea of "Spanish degradation" by its contact with English became a topic, and the variety of Spanish used by young lower social classes was described as an argot used by gangs (Lipski 2000, 8–10).

The influence that the United States has had over its southern neighbors promoted language contact and the development of a particular variation of Spanish in the United States. Continuous immigration of South American populations has generated not only language contact, but also dialect contact.

This language and dialect contact strengthens itself by the diversity of U.S. territories, and it is present among second-generation immigrants for whom the parents' language becomes a heritage language (Fishman 2004, 115–132).

The term "heritage language" in the current study refers to first-generation speakers' native language passed to their children at home. The 1970s brought bilingual education into schools where large Spanish-speaking communities existed. The program did not promote bilingualism, but worked for a transition to the dominant language. Also, by this decade, the study of Spanish in the United States became a major scholarly pursuit (Lipski 2000, 3–28; Torres 1991, 255–270; Zentella 2004, 182–204; Bayley 2004, 268–286).

Academically, the transition in language studies from prescriptive language analysis to an effort to make it more of a "living" entity became of importance, and scholars moved into the barrios to take notes and to observe and record the language in real use. Fishman (1971) is a major example of this kind of work done with the Puerto Rican community. During the 1980s, increasing numbers of Spanish-speaking people escaping from the civil wars in Central America, sought political asylum in the United States.[1] By the 1990s, large numbers of Mexicans arrived in the northeast to work in agriculture. The amnesty provided by the 1986 Immigration Reform Act, IRCA, facilitated family reunification and more open settlement (Zentella 2004).[2]

Table 4.1 presents data extracted from the U.S. Census Bureau on the foreign-born population of the United States from 1850 to 1990 (Gibson and Lennon). This table focuses on the origins of Spanish-speaking

Table 4.1   Region and country or area of birth of the foreign-born population: 1960 to 1990

Region and country or area	1990	1980	1970	1960
Southern and Eastern Europe	2,285,513	2,748,547	3,090,991	3,907,020
Spain	76,415	73,735	57,488	44,999
Latin America	8,407,837	4,372,487	1,803,970	908,309
Cuba	736,971	607,814	439,048	79,150
Dominican Republic	347,858	169,147	61,228	11,883
Central America	5,431,992	2,553,113	873,624	624,851
Mexico	4,298,014	2,199,221	759,711	575,902
El Salvador	465,433	94,447	15,717	6,310
Honduras	108,923	39,154	19,118	6,503
South America	1,037,497	561,011	255,238	89,536
Argentina	92,563	68,887	44,803	16,579
Colombia	286,124	143,508	63,538	12,582
Ecuador	143,314	86,128	36,663	7,670

Source: U.S. Bureau of the Census. Internet release date: March 9, 1999

Table 4.2 Hispanic or Latino population in the State of New York; a three-year estimate 2005–2007

New York	*Estimate*
Total:	19,280,753
Not Hispanic or Latino	16,154,035
Hispanic or Latino:	3,126,718
Mexican	375,617
Puerto Rican	1,079,477
Cuban	69,076
Dominican (Dominican Republic)	630,243
Central American:	290,503
Honduran	58,455
Salvadoran	119,705
South American:	498,103
Argentinean	22,654
Colombian	140,028
Ecuadorian	213,895
Other Hispanic or Latino:	183,699
Spaniard	23,821

Source: U.S. Census Bureau, 2005–2007 American community survey

immigrants from the 1960s to the 1990s. The table was modified to include only the countries pertaining to the participants in the current study.

Table 4.2 presents a three-year population estimate (2005–2007) from the census of 2000. Data include only the state of New York, and it was modified to include only the participants' countries of origin.

These demographic changes of Spanish-speaking Americans, in the chronological perspective discussed above, provide some insights into the existing diversity within the state of New York. Standard Spanish is a common variety for all of them; however, multiple dialects coexist depending on origin, class, education, and other social factors. Some cultural aspects may be common among all due to early Spanish colonization; yet, rituals and beliefs differ in their contact with pre-Columbus and African cultures. This study describes processes of assimilation and identity formation in a group of immigrants who speak different Spanish varieties and share a common space within the urban area of New York City.

The Concept of Globalization

The term "globalization" was formed from the Latin term *globus,* which signifies "ball" *or* "sphere," and refers to the earth. The term became popular in all languages at the end of the twentieth century with the massive internationalization of the economy and new communication technologies. Since then, it has expanded to describe people and processes under this innovative human interaction (www.elcastellano.org/dictionaries). In general terms, there are two approaches to globalization. On the one hand, a global individual is one who understands an integrated diverse society, beyond physical and political boundaries and complex cultural differences. On the other hand, a global individual could be immersed in social practices that lead one to homogenization, and eradication of cultural diversity, or languages; this person seeks to speak the language of the global market and understand the common cultural values that dominate the societies that are interacting (Lee 2006).

According to A. Dal Lago (2002), relations between communities have always been mediated by power. The economic driver of such power in modern societies has been capitalism, which has been global since its birth, through its capacity to promote market expansion and universal cultural frameworks. Along with a neoliberal economic and political agenda, advanced technologies in communication have allowed capitalism to expand virtually (e.g., the Internet), not only exchanging concrete products, but ideologies, values, and representations of people within the world. In this global economic system, time and space are "shrunk and expanded" simultaneously by interconnections, networks, and flows. Kempny observes, "Because the social world cannot be seen any longer as orderly and divided into fixed territorial cultures with clear-cut boundaries, it ultimately brings about the obfuscation of the criteria of exclusion and inclusion, or difference and similarity" (2002, 9). A global person who lives in this system is required to have some degree of assimilation to the promoted common value system and language, and, at the same time, is exposed to a diverse world where he or she can find localities that might reinforce who he or she is culturally and aid in maintaining old identities within new ones. Children of Spanish-speaking immigrants generally place their dual upbringing as a condition to define who they are as U.S. citizens and in the Spanish-speaking world. Their self-image and identity as U.S. Hispanics/Latinos is a process of hybrid identity construction (Eriksen 1993, cited in Kempny 2002, 9).

Mar-Molinero (2006) discusses how the use of Spanish throughout the United States impacted the relationship of immigrants with their host country. That, in turn, redefined their identity. The close proximity of Spanish native speakers to their country of origin provides significantly greater cultural and linguistic continuity than that provided by many other immigrants. Geographical proximity allows them to be in contact with their roots, as well as with high-tech communication networks. The Spanish-speaking world shares media and cultural production beyond the private sphere; therefore, the Spanish language becomes a "commodity" that second-generation immigrants need to maintain and recover along with English, the popular globalized language. Second-generation Spanish-speaking immigrants value their heritage language as a tool for acquisition of goods, services, and interaction between people from the United States and Latin American countries.

The status of Spanish as a major language in the American continent and its use in Europe encourage its maintenance among second-generation speakers. As Rainer Enrique Hamel mentions (2006), Spanish is the lingua franca in most language-contact situations in central Spain and Hispanic America. In the United States, after the mid-nineteenth century, Spanish became the language for daily communication and not, as was previously seen, a transitional language. Because immigration from Spanish-speaking countries has not stopped or diminished, and new generations find numerous opportunities for Spanish interaction, this trend will continue. Furthermore, Spanish is the official language of various international political, social, and economic organizations in Latin America, for example, South America's Common Market (MERCOSUR), Central America System of Integration (SICA), and Area of Free Market of the Americas (ALCA), and plays a leading role in Pan American Health Organization (PAHO) and Organization of the American States (OAS). The secure status of Spanish as a regional language that does not compete with the large socioeconomic space enjoyed by English reinforces the message to bilingual Spanish second-generation speakers that Spanish facilitates their capacity to participate in globalization.

Language as an Identity Marker

Due to globalization and democratization of technology and modes of transportation, the scope of locality has expanded to include environments that were once difficult to reach in daily contact. Interactions surpass the immediate physical space, and access to knowledge is gained not only through the local school, by means of books, or experience with local communities, but through communication media. These technologies advance rapidly and change human access to world awareness. Advances in transportation facilitate human movement, while social and political conflicts and economic opportunities in various parts of the world promote human mobility. Consequently, new technologies and human movements result in diverse communities in which people meet and interchange cultural values. New multimedia human interactions encourage diversification and generate global individuals, those whom Richard Lee describes as citizens that understand an integrated society beyond physical and political boundaries and complex cultural differences (2006, 21–34).

Children in most large metropolitan areas, such as New York, meet peers with different cultural and linguistic backgrounds. Through social tradition, the United States has supported an ideology of assimilation that pretends to erase differences in its aim to create a unified nation (Fishman 1966). Historically, various immigrants coming into the United States gave up their native languages and adopted English as the common language of their new citizenship. Some parents did not deem it worth the effort to pass their languages to their children because English was the path to grasping the "American Dream." At the same time, socioeconomic contexts, class, and education also played a part in immigrants' decisions when they made the effort to pass their native languages on to their children in a society dominated by English.

Globalization and access to new communication technologies modified private and public human interaction. Assimilation processes in U.S. society varied as new generations recognized their particularities within the global space, and their interactions expanded beyond their home and immediate localities to a more open space that was accessible through the Internet. The concept of globalization became a personal quality—people may adopt behaviors to fit into the global society, and such behaviors may involve the addition or retention of other languages and the experiences of other cultures. Assimilation ideologies are challenged by the limitation that monolingualism presents to the individual searching to become "global." In other words, a person prepared to interact beyond his immediate physical and cultural frontiers seeks to learn a second language or to experience more than one locality.

The search for a "global" quality becomes complex when languages and dialects serve as identity markers. A language is not only something that a person uses to communicate globally or locally, privately or publicly, but the variation that exists among vernacular versions of any language and its standards. Spanish speakers in the United States use vernaculars of English and Spanish that are maintained as strong markers of local self-identity, and standards that are learned in school serve as identity markers within a much wider community (Silva-Corvalán 1995). The imposition of globalization's social dynamic is encouraging a reevaluation of those identity markers; second-generation immigrants reconstruct their own images when interacting globally—they need to be of one kind, but also capable of understanding and communicating with many.

J. Edwards (1985) discusses how languages serve two functions: communicative and symbolic. He defines language as a tool of communication and as an emblem of a group. This latter function elaborates precisely into the identity marker mentioned above. People retain certain features of language use in order to belong to and identify with a particular group. These two aspects, the communicative and the symbolic, are separable; a person may experience a shift to the dominant language (global language, in this case) and still hold strong cultural symbolic markers that identify them with a group. Later, as persons assume roles within societies, language attitudes may evolve in two directions: integrative or instrumental. Colin Baker (1995) explains integrative attitudes in terms of cultural association within the group and instrumental attitudes rooted in practical implications for an individual wishing to obtain socioeconomic benefits. Second-generation immigrants may hold onto their parents' languages in order to communicate within the extended family, and celebrate traditions. In this manner, they maintain cultural practices and beliefs; on the other hand, they may also maintain the inherited language for practical socioeconomic reasons, more likely if it is Spanish, considering the overwhelming presence of this language in the United States, its national locality, and its use in a vast area of the world. Knowing Spanish as well as English would represent better opportunities for socioeconomic mobility. These two language attitudes, the integrative and the instrumental, may be present in second-generation Spanish speakers in New York City and the surrounding areas. Depending on their dual upbringing, their public and private interactions, and the attitudes of their parents, the hold of one may be stronger than the other. However, in any situation, children of Spanish-speaking immigrants who are provided with the opportunity to become highly educated and enter the global social dynamic seem to be realizing that the linguistic and cultural capital passed from their immigrant parents is as useful as their knowledge of the English language. Both languages become part of their identity as global American individuals.

A global individual, in earlier times of historical modernization, might have been considered to be a person with the means for traveling and accessing other cultures. As transportation and communication advanced, more and more people had the opportunity to become global. People migrate for various reasons; the reason behind any decision to move voluntarily is to find better living conditions. First-generation immigrants often referred to their children's education and well-being as the purpose of their immigrant experience, which has not always been pleasant or easy. Therefore, beyond escaping from poverty or violence in their homelands, the move into the United States guarantees access to standard English for the second generation, and the possibility of connecting to the rest of the world in a country that may provide better living conditions. Furthermore, the second generation may count on one more factor that, if perceived positively, enhances its global experience.

This is the immigrant experience lived by the parents, which results in their bicultural/bilingual upbringing and frequent contact with a world outside the United States. Their social networks expand early in life, beginning in a private domain that later becomes an advantage in the public domain. The dual experience may initially be assumed unconsciously and may generate some conflict among immigrant children who are encouraged to assimilate into dominant and linguistic practices; however, they become more conscious as they access higher education and perceive support by a wider community with which they can identify and interact.

Children of immigrants can have better opportunities to become global individuals because of their exposure to different localities. Their parents' physical mobility provides linguistic and cultural assets for children. At school, they learn the dominant language and experience other cultures brought into the classroom. Later, communication media and technology allow them to connect virtually to the world at their fingertips. Mass media bombard them with cultures as products to be consumed, including those cultural practices experienced at home and transformed by contact with the wider national and international communities. An example of a merged cultural practice in the United States is Latin pop music. This product is the result of a cultural and linguistic hybridization process; what is consumed is not a Latin American or Spanish product, but a commodity created by the second generation of Spanish heritage speakers and the wider locality, meaning media and cultural practices in the United States and the rest of the world. Cepeda (2003) describes how the music business has generated great capital by utilizing Latino cultural markers, language among those, in a profitable market. Latinos are not the only ones responsible for its consumption; an entire youth culture has been created by the media and fed by contact with Spanish-speaking immigrants and their offspring. Geographical proximity to Latin America, historical events, and economic relationships with the Latin world have secured the presence of Spanish in the United States.

Social Network

Second-generation immigrants enter a dynamic of reidentification, away from previous assimilation processes of integration into one nation, to a process of globalization seeking to integrate into a broader world community, and within the process, social networks established by Latinos become complex as Del Valle (2006, 28) states:

> Latinos are active participants of multiple and complex networks of interaction: the neighborhood, the local community, the nation-state, the heritage country,

the Spanish-speaking world, and the global markets. Their linguistic practices, therefore, influence and are influenced by diverse environments; and similarly, their linguistic beliefs are produced, reproduced, and transformed in multiple ideological settings.

As noted, social networks become part of this emerging identity experienced by second-generation Spanish speakers. The issues of private language versus public become blurred in a context where transnational interaction is a requirement for new generations. The private environments are invaded by the public language, English, which becomes the "native" language among siblings from the second generation. Their parents insist on its use due to their own perceptions regarding the need to assimilate.

The mass media and technology available to the Spanish-speaking world affects the public language of immigrants. Second-generation Spanish speakers, who have been encouraged to speak their parents' language and for whom higher education is an option, seek to transform the vernacular and private Spanish they use into a more public and standard Spanish that allows them to interact globally. Consequently, the reconstruction of their identity requires various tasks that ultimately must be woven together. Chronologically, it may occur as follows, varying according to specific locations and opportunities for complex networking to take place: early childhood is experienced predominantly under Hispanic/Latino (both terms are used as synonyms to mean people of Latin American or Spanish origin) customs and language; late childhood provides the input from the dominant society's language, customs, and values when children attend school; preadolescence may favor practices and values from the dominant society and reject minority practices, language, and values from private domains as the group establishes a secure self as U.S. citizens; late adolescence may provide an opportunity to study the Spanish language in formal settings, away from private practices, and it is observed how it gains value as a second language for English-speaking classmates; finally, at college, second-generation Spanish speakers experience analysis of the issues of their dual upbringing, and through formal education, modify their Spanish vernaculars into a standard Spanish language variety with more instrumental attitudes that allow them to be part of a global economy, while maintaining an integrative attitude toward the heritage language. By maintaining Spanish, these groups are seeking to reconstruct their identity as bicultural individuals in a multicultural context. Retaining their biculturalism and bilingualism provides them with a more holistic understanding of the cultural differences in the global community to which they belong.

The Lived Experience of College Students and their Immigrant Parents

The discussion above on the concept of an individual who lives in a globalized system in relation to immigrant experience and the dual cultural and linguistic upbringing of children provides a good opportunity to examine the construction of identity in the context of the multicultural and lingual networks in New York State, particularly those of the cohorts of the second generation.

First of all, it is necessary to define the types of networks that are present in the current research. Definitions are based on Milroy's study of language and social networks (1987). Figure 4.1 represents the high-density networks in urban areas of mostly Spanish-speaking populations, where the participants in this study lived. This signifies that many of the people interacting know each other. A large number of the persons to whom "ego," the self, is linked are also linked to each other. The areas of high-density networking identified by the participants are the Bronx and Brooklyn. In high-density networks, it is common to find a multiplex functional network; this is when each individual is likely to be linked to others in more than one capacity.

The participants also identified low-density networks presented in Figure 4.2. These networks consist of people interacting who do not know each other. Interviewed participants who moved to the areas of Westchester or Long Island find themselves participating in a low-density network, where Spanish is rarely used in public domains and most public transactions are separated from private ones. In low-density networks, it is common to find

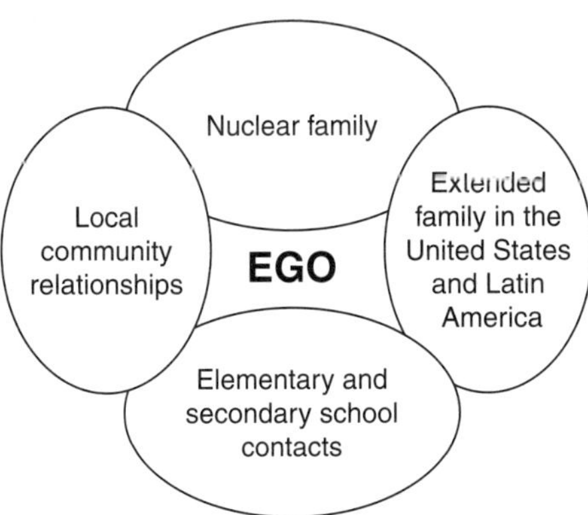

Figure 4.1   High-density, multiplex networks while growing up.

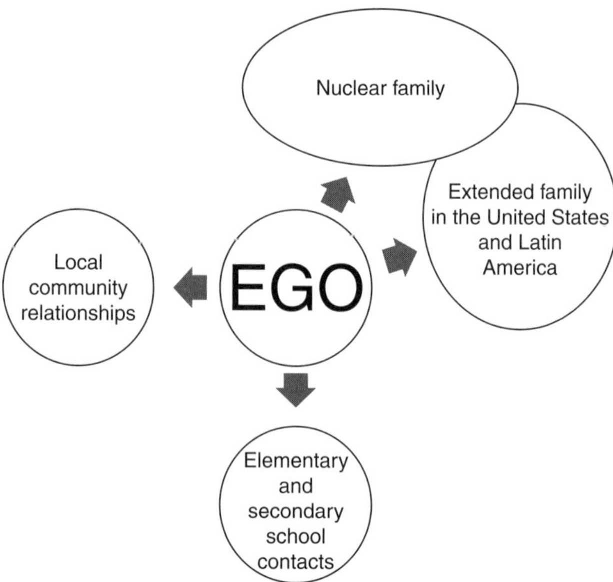

Figure 4.2 Low-density, uniplex networks while growing up.

a uniplex functional network; this is when individuals relate to each other in only one capacity.

The importance of social networks lies in their acting as a mechanism for exchanging goods and services and for imposing obligations while constructing self-identity through the means of belonging. Such networks extend to the practices of a broader society, which imposes behaviors as well. A more open construction of identity that is developed to nurture a sense of belonging to a society is no longer a private or public endeavor, but diffused and global.

Data collected among first-generation Spanish speakers contributed to an understanding of the social networks among their children, who are the focus of the study. It was found in the data that the role of kin relationships within the established network was a mechanism for survival among immigrant parents. Family members helped each other to find jobs, save money, adapt to their new immigrant status, and take care of children. Family celebrations, one home for extended and nuclear families, and frequent trips to a Spanish-speaking country, if possible, were a strategy for heritage language retention and a construction of bilingual/bicultural identity for the second generation. The following is a fragment from an interview highlighting the importance of extended family networking for heritage language maintenance.

> Ella pasa más tiempo con mi mama, porque es la primera nieta de ella, entonces ella entiende más el español, que siempre están juntas, entonces ella ve las novelas y todo eso y ella también se pone a ver las novelas.
>
> [She spends more time with my mom, because she is her first granddaughter , so she understands more Spanish, they are always together, so she watches the soap operas and all that, and she also watches the soap operas.]
>
> Anonymous

Moreover, the language attitude developed by the first generation was identified as being more of an integrative type, rather than instrumental. Although parents would like to see their children in better jobs and integrated in the global society, they believe that Spanish language retention is important for their children's self-identification as Hispanics in a multicultural setting and for maintaining communication with family networks. The attitude mainly held by parents provided a foundation for the second generation in their reidentification process. Holding onto their roots and cultural practices provided them with an understanding of being part of a diverse world.

Moreover, in regard to the linguistic aspect, a key element present among members of the first generation that affected heritage language maintenance among their children was the education and skill level of parents and their command of the English language. All parents interviewed had been in the United States for at least eighteen years. This length of time does not relate directly to their English fluency or the jobs they hold. Some families that have resided in New York for a long time still rely on their family and friends' connections to find unskilled jobs, and they do most of their networking transactions in Spanish. The second generation of this kind of family tends to identify strongly with its Spanish values, customs, and language. Its language attitude remains integrative and its social network is of the high-density multiplex type, where family, friends, and community as a whole interact in both private and public domains.

On the other hand, there were those parents with advanced levels of education and better proficiency in English; they moved away from high-density networks to low-density ones in order to expose their children to the dominant society and, consequently, to social mobility. However, they still believed that Spanish language retention was important for integrative and instrumental reasons, and made the home environment the space for Spanish interaction and development of Hispanic/Latino identity. Family networking was important for this group of parents as well, and celebrations, along with frequent trips to the home country, were strategies for heritage language maintenance. A participant reports on their appreciation of their cultural heritage:

> Me encanta, me encanta la cultura, me encanta hablar con mi gente, comer comida típica, comer, andar con mis amigos, este … y a observar la cultura como es, me encanta ir a Colombia.
>
> [I love it, I love the culture, I love to talk with my people, eat traditional food, eat, walk with my friends, ummm … and observe the culture just like it is, I love to go to Colombia.]
>
> Anonymous

Religious practices were present in two types of networking described above: (1) for some families, who lived in Hispanic communities, the church was part of a neighborhood network and Spanish was adopted as the language of religion; (2) for others, who were not part of the community network, the religious practices were part of the extended family network with the Spanish-speaking country, and often, children were sent to their parents' home countries to comply with the required practices, and their children had religious education in Spanish; (3) some parents preferred to send their children to religious schools, all Catholic, and religious practices became part of the school network where English was the language of religious instruction.

Primary and secondary school environments served as places for networking as well; parents were often welcome to participate in their children's education, mostly during elementary schooling and particularly if their children were part of English as a Second Language (ESL) or bilingual education programs. Connecting to the school was difficult for some parents due to lack of English proficiency, lack of confidence in interacting with the dominant society, or extended work hours that limited family time for involvement in children's education. Moreover, children placed in ESL or bilingual programs reported conflict as well. Their assimilation to school practices and development of friendships were affected by their own perception of being "different."

> Me sentía osea que no llegaba a entender todo como ellos. Osea entendía todo pero yo vi como si ellos me vieran como si yo fuera menos que ellos, pues no sé, pues estudié en una clase apartada de ellos y cuando me llegué ya a incluir en la clase que fue un año nada más, que me llegué a integrar con ellos fue raro. Fue como no sé como nunca se acostumbraron a verme en la clase.
>
> [I felt like that I couldn't understand everything like them. Like I understood everything, but I saw like if they saw me like if I were less than them,

so I don't know, so I studied in a separate class from them and when finally
I joined their class, that was only one year, that I finally mixed with them,
it was strange. It was like they were never used to see me in class.]

Anonymous

Furthermore, parents who were not necessarily highly educated moved to low-density Hispanic networking neighborhoods. These parents were not fluent in English. However, they saw English proficiency and interaction with the dominant society as key elements for the success of their children. Within this type of home environment, the private space acted as reinforcement for Hispanic/Latino cultural values and heritage language retention. Some immigrant parents experienced difficulties in the process of raising children, related to the lack of understanding of the sociocultural practices of the public sphere and the pressure that parents experienced to adapt and change moral values and cultural practices according to the public life of their children.

The college students in the current study had a life course that was different from that of their parents. Their experiences showed how children within Spanish-speaking immigrant families become aware of their dual upbringing very early. First, American mass media present a different language and family structure based on a more concrete representation of the nuclear family. Television rarely portrays the larger extended family network with contacts in other countries, which is found only in those few television shows that highlight ethnicity or immigrant status. Second, during elementary schooling, immigrant children begin to notice the difference in moral values often associated with religious practices and beliefs. They find their parents to be stricter than those of their classmates; they also find difficulties if their parents lack interaction with the dominant English-speaking society. Usually, parents do not understand peer practices that occur in schools.

Like mi mama no me dejaba pintar las uñas temprano y la gente Americana sí deja a sus hijas que se pinten las uñas temprano, que se saquen las cejas temprano o que salgan al cine.

[Like my mom didn't let me polish my nails young and the American people allow their daughters to polish their nails young, and get their eyebrows out young, and let them go out to the movies.]

Anonymous

Proficiency in Spanish varied regardless of their parents' effort to maintain it. Bilingual children who are more fluent in Spanish are found within those households where English is not spoken (known) by parents who hold a strong integrative attitude toward Spanish retention; in addition, there are other households with very educated parents, who are fluent in English and hold strong instrumental attitudes toward Spanish retention. These kinds of parents recognize the advantage of bilingualism in global networking. It is important to clarify that having more education may be class-related within their countries of origin. More education is generally obtained by the middle or upper classes. However, when they immigrated to the United States, the concept of class became less clear as they were classified as immigrants looking for opportunities to advance up the social ladder. Their legal status also plays a role in opportunities available in the new country regardless of their previous social class.

Spanish fluency is affected as well by the local communities where children live. In dense, multiplex networks (figure 4.1) within immigrant populations, children are most likely to learn values such as respect for elders and the presence of an extended family. The Spanish language is a medium in these relationships. On the other hand, less fluent bilinguals are found within households that do not relate often to the extended family or to Spanish-speaking countries, and who live in English-dominated communities. These two factors break, drastically, the contact between the private and the public space. Parents from these types of households are often less educated, but fluent in English and allow the dominant language to enter the home. Parents in this kind of home environment may still hold the idea of assimilation as a key element for their children's future success and may show a lack of an instrumental or integrative attitude toward the maintenance of Spanish by the second generation. The following speech fragments reveal student participants' perceptions about Spanish retention and use.

Si puedo cambiar algo en mi vida, yo quiero cambiar que no sé español porque es importante que alguien, I mean, que las personas saben más de un idioma y hay más trabajos si saben dos idiomas. Estoy un poco mad, furiosa que mis padres no me enseñó español, pero por eso es porque estoy estudiándolo ahora porque quiero cambiar eso.

[If I could change something in my life, I want to change that I don't know Spanish because it is important that one, I mean, that people know more than one language, and there are more jobs if they know two languages. I'm a little mad, furious that my parents did not teach me Spanish, but that is why I'm studying it now because I want to change that.]

Con el español me siento que puedo ir a cualquier país y siento como que es algo que la gente admira, ser bilingüe, y entre más lenguas sepas mejor.

[With Spanish, I feel that I can go to any country and I feel like it is something that people admires, being bilingual, the more languages you know, the better.]

No lo practico mucho solo lo hablo con la gente con la que me siento cómoda puedo hablar mejor y hay veces que esa misma gente sabe un poco de inglés entonces no hablo el español completamente, siempre es spanglish.

[I don't practice it much, only when I talk to people that I feel comfortable, I could talk better and there are some times that the same people know some English so I don't talk in Spanish completely, it is always Spanglish.]

Anonymous

The college students interviewed were immersed within a new social network (figure 4.3 illustrates participants' college experiences); they left the local communities where they grew up and were not in physical contact with their immediate and extended family. Their choices for networking changed due to the mix found at college. Exposure to world dynamics was practiced in classes and through constant analysis. They studied the socioeconomic aspects of their parents' immigrant status, became conscious of their dual upbringing, and identity reconstruction became a concrete weaving of private and public selves into globalized individuals. Spanish becomes a valued form of capital in their particular experience and is reinforced by knowledge acquired about the world within their college setting. Before arriving at college, some of the students held a strong conscious desire, linked to an integrative language attitude, to maintain Spanish; for others, it was simply there due to family practices and community environments. However, Spanish recovery and maintenance through academic engagement developed into a conscious instrumental language attitude at college. Mass

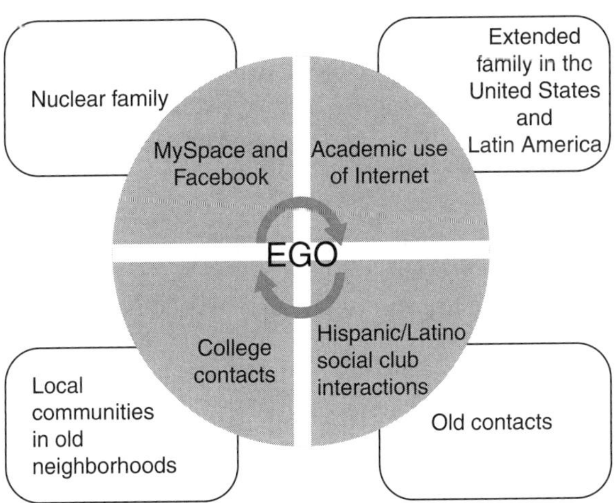

Figure 4.3 New college network.

media at college not only represented the local or national community, but Internet search engines and multimedia communication exposed the second generation to a broader locality of interaction—the world. Spanish became useful in this new space. The difference from their educational experience before college is that while attending primary and secondary school, they were part of social networks granted by the family and the local communities, which provided them with a set of language use and cultural practices. In the higher education setting, they had the opportunity to generate their own social network, making it more global and less local.

Observing the three types of networks above, while growing up and at college, the students reported that the main difference at the college level was the social domain outside—the nuclear family, the disengagement from the local community where they grew up, and the incorporation of world communication through a more interactive/multitasking use of the Internet. The Internet served the educational requirement of increasing world knowledge, while mediating local communication among college friends and immediate communities in their college town. The Internet is also a medium of communication with their localities back in New York City and with their parents' countries of origin. Networks at college also combine low- and high-density levels; regardless of the shared space, not everyone interacts or knows each other though one common characteristic is that everyone relates to the local world and the wider world outside through Internet communication. In this new social network (see figure 4.3), second-generation Spanish speakers become aware of the globalization processes that mediate their daily interactions. Localities become virtual spaces where they interact regardless of distance or physical contact. Languages play a part in this virtual communication and holding on to their heritage language provides a channel for global interaction. Within this new social network, students make use of their language varieties: standard and vernacular English and Spanish, as well as the tech-language variant used in cyber communication.

In contrast, while students were attending high school, their use of the Internet was mediated by constant local interaction. They all reported that they had shared common spaces at a school facility and neighborhood services; the Internet was mainly a peer communication and search engine tool mediated by their local school experience. At college, it became more than a tool. It was the door to extend their knowledge and feed the analysis provided in classes, as it also became the main communication medium with the family and community, locally and globally. By this amplified use of the tool, students realized that their Spanish cultural and linguistic capital became available for integration into a more global society, and they recognized the hybrid identity within them as an asset imperative to maintain.

Moreover, at college, some Hispanic social contacts are sought and maintained. Membership in a Hispanic club acts as a replacement for the weakened network with extended family members and with local Hispanic communities. At club meetings, an opportunity to communicate in Spanish and reinforce their integrative attitude is accomplished in a college environment that is not generally supportive of public Spanish interactions. Classes become determinant settings for strengthening instrumental attitudes toward maintaining Spanish. In previous networks, the second generation may have perceived, unconsciously, the importance of being bilingual; however, in classes where Spanish is the content or the topic relates to cultural, social, and economic issues of the global dynamic, the importance of retaining linguistic and cultural capital becomes a priority. The new network generated by college experience reconstructs the immediate locality as a more diverse environment where space becomes virtual through Internet communication, and where the choices for human contact mesh students' Hispanic upbringing with an academic understanding of identity roles in a global society.

One last concept of great importance for the maintenance of heritage languages, those passed on by parents and not a requirement of the dominant society, is the existence of "linguistic bands" as presented by Hurtado and Vega (2004). The concept refers not only to the possibility of two or more people speaking the same language in particular contexts, but also to the exposure to different language media, such as television, radio, recorded music, and the Internet. It is observable in the participants of the current study that they were part of those different linguistic bands while growing up in a metropolis like New York City and, consequently, upon arriving in college. They tended naturally to seek and create bands of the same type through the Hispanic club's activities, Hispanic roommates, and recorded music accessed through the Internet. Language and aspects of culture, such as music and food, were retrieved as strong symbolic markers in a diverse environment during the establishment of their own identity. These bilingual/bicultural students implemented the use of "Spanglish," a mixture of their two linguistic systems, as a marker of identity in informal conversations within their "Facebook" or "MySpace" accounts. It is clear that they wanted to be identified as having a different linguistic and cultural upbringing. Music such as regeton, salsa, and merengue was uploaded onto their iPods and MP3s and proudly played at student social gatherings. The second generation of Spanish-speaking immigrants reveals an antiassimilation behavior; they do not want to appear like everyone else and they want to show openly their parents' cultural input while becoming competent citizens immersed in an English-dominated environment.

Conclusion

This exploratory study examines how a small group of college students perceives the importance of maintaining Spanish as a way to participate in "the global," and how their living environment in their home cities and college impacts this perception. At college, families and small localities are not the main sources of transmission. Internet-mediated communication, the academic face-to-face interaction with professors, and the social meetings with diverse student populations as well as with Spanish-speaking peers are the new sources of interaction. Support for their "new" image as global citizens is sought in this diverse environment that is neither private nor public, but virtual. The college represents a "spatial station" from where they access the globe. At the station, they recreate the image of themselves being transmitted. The result becomes a hybrid individual that is made of a reconstruction of public versus private domains experienced at first while growing up bilingual/bicultural, and later modified as they enter a new locality, the college. At college, they are not members of public or private domains with particular language interactions, but representations of bilingual/bicultural individuals who are in constant search for their place in the global society. Identity is transformed as the second generation integrates its upbringing with academic and professional understanding of its own identities. Being a citizen in the era of globalization does not necessarily grant the condition of global citizenship. Bilingual/bicultural participants in the current study recognize the importance of their linguistic capital, bicultural upbringing, and college experience in their understanding of and relationship to the rest of the world.

These research observations could help develop guides for future studies needed to determine what is happening to the maintenance of Spanish as a heritage language in the United States. However, it is clear that Spanish is not following the same path of transition into English monolingualism, as was suffered by other heritage languages. The presence of the Spanish language is being benefited by the momentum experienced in the country: the change in national ideologies for global understanding and conformation to a culturally and ethnically diverse global society.

Notes

1. This is revealed in the government's census data between the years of 1981 and 1990. The total number of immigrants by country of birth was 7,338,100. There were 214,600 Salvadorians, 87,900 Guatemalans, 49,500 Hondurans, and 44,100 Nicaraguans in that group.

2. The Immigration Reform and Control Act of 1986 (IRCA) allowed two groups of illegal aliens to become temporary and, then, permanent residents of the United States: aliens who have been in the United States unlawfully since January 1, 1982 (legalization applicants) and aliens who were employed in seasonal agricultural work for a minimum period of time (Special Agricultural Worker, or SAW, applicants). The application period for temporary residency for legalization applicants began on May 5, 1987, and ended on May 4, 1988, while the application period for SAW applicants began on June 1, 1987, and ended on November 30, 1988. Legalization applicants became eligible for permanent residence beginning in the fiscal year 1989. Beginning in 1989, immigrant data included temporary residents who were granted permanent residence under the legalization program of IRCA. (Source: www.census.gov.)

References

Baker, Colin. 1995. *Attitudes and Language*. Philadelphia: Multilingual Matters.

Bayley, Robert. 2004. Linguistic Diversity and English Language Acquisition. In *Language in the USA: Themes for the Twenty-First Century*, ed. E. Finegan and J. Rickford, 268–86. Cambridge: Cambridge University Press.

Cepeda, María Elena. 2003. Mucho Loco for Ricky Martin: Or the Politics of Chronology. Crossover, and Language within the Latin(o) Music Boom. In *Global Pop, Local Language,* ed. Berger and Thomas Carroll, 113–29. Mississippi: University Press of Mississippi.

Dal Lago, Alessandro. 2002. The Uneasiness of Globalization: Notes on the Role of Migrations in the World Society. In *Which "Global Village"?* ed. Valeria Gennaro Lerda, 23–39. Westport, Connecticut: Praeger.

Del Valle, José. 2006. *US Latinos, La Hispanofonía, and the Language ideologies of High Modernity.* In *Globalization and Language in the Spanish-Speaking World. Macro and Micro Perspectives*, ed. Molinero and Stewart, 27–46. New York: Palgrave Macmillan.

Edwards, John. 1985. *Language, Society and Identity.* New York: Blackwell.

El castellano dictionaries. http://www.elcastellano.org (accessed in November 2008).

Fishman, Joshua. 1966. *Language Loyalty in the United States.* The Hague: Mouton.

———. 2004. *Multilingualism and Non-English Mother Tongues.* In *Language in the USA: Themes for the Twenty-First Century*, ed. E. Finegan and J. Rickford, 115–32. Cambridge: Cambridge University Press.

———. Robert Cooper, and Ma Roxanne. 1971. *Bilingualism in the Barrio.* Bloomington: Indiana University Press.

Gibson, Campbell J., and E. Lennon. Historical Census Statistics on the Foreign-Born Population of the United States: 1850–1990. In *Population Division: U.S. Bureau of the Census, 20233–8800.* Washington, D. C.

Hamel, Rainer Enrique. 2006. *Language Conflict and the Micro-Macro Link in the Spanish-Speaking World.* In *Globalization and Language in the Spanish-Speaking*

World. Macro and Micro Perspectives, ed. Molinero and Stewart, 47–75. New York: Palgrave Macmillan.

Hurtado, Aída, and Luis A. Vega. 2004. *Shift Happens: Spanish and English Transmisión between Parents and Their Children. Journal of Social Issues* 60: 137–155.

Kempny, Marian. 2002. Introduction: On "Identity," Fixity, and Change in Social Theory and Social Life under Globalized Conditions. In *Identity in Transformation: Postmodernity, Postcommunisim, and Globalization,* ed. Marian Kempny and Aldona Jawlowska, 1–18. Westport: Praeger.

Lee, Richard. 2006. *Globalization, Language, and Culture.* Philadelphia: Chelsea House.

Lipski, John. 2000. Back to Zero or Ahead to 2001? In *Issues and Challenges in U.S. Spanish Research*, ed. A. Roca, 1–41. Sommerville, MA: Cascadilla.

Mar-Molinero, Clare. 2006. Forces of Globalization in the Spanish-Speaking World: Linguistic Imperialism or Grassroots Adaptation. In *Globalization and Language in the Spanish-Speaking World. Macro and Micro Perspectives,* ed. Molinero and Stewart, 9–26. New York: Palgrave Macmillan.

Milroy, Lesley. 1987. *Language and Social Networks.* New York: Basil Blackwell.

Silva-Corvalán, Carmen, ed. 1995. *Spanish in Four Continents Studies in Language Contact and Bilingualism.* Washington, D.C: Georgetown University Press.

Torres, Lourdes. 1991. The Study of US Spanish varieties: Some Theoretical and Methodological Issues. In *Sociolinguistics of the Spanish-Speaking World: Iberia, Latin America, United States,* ed. C. Klee and L. Ramos-García, 255–70. Tempe, Arizona: Bilingual Press.

The U.S. Census Bureau. 2005–2007. American Community Survey 3-Year Estimates Survey: American Community Survey. *Table B03001. Hispanic or Latino Origin by Specific Origin Universe: Total Population.* http://factfinder. census.gov/servlet/DTTable?_bm=y&-context=dt&-ds_name=ACS_2007_3YR_ G00_&-mt_name=ACS_2007_3YR_G2000_B03001&-tree_id=3307&-redo Log=true&-_caller=geoselect&-geo_id=01000US&-geo_id=04000US36&- search_results=01000US&-format=&-_lang=en (accessed on December 13, 2009).

Zentella, Ana Celia. 2004. Spanish in the Northeast. In *Language in the USA: Themes for the Twenty-First Century,* ed. E. Finegan and J. Rickford, 182–204. Cambridge: Cambridge University Press.

CHAPTER 5

Language Choice among Mayan Handicraft Vendors in an International Tourism Marketplace

Walter E. Little

Introduction

Ethnographic research on the effects of globalization has demonstrated a wide range of impacts, negative and positive, on indigenous peoples throughout the world (Appadurai 2002; Friedman 2003; Gregory 1998; Little 2004; Zorn 2004). Sometimes, globalization has radically altered their economic and political lives, transforming their cultural identities. Related linguistic or language-oriented research has looked at the impact of globalization from the position that most indigenous languages are threatened and may become extinct without some sort of intervention; language standardization is often part of this (Garzon et al. 1998; La Ponce 2004; Mandal 2000; McCarty 2003; Whaley 2003). Although there are counterarguments that attempt to explain the perpetuity of some languages (Mühlhäusler 2003), most (i.e., cited above) either look at the intrinsic nature of the language, its structure, or the agency or volition of the speakers—the language can survive if the speakers want it to persist.

A more productive approach is to look at the material conditions in which languages are used, not just language structure or the agency of speakers. Approaches based on structure or agency tend to divorce languages from the lived realities of the people who actually speak them, ignoring why they continue to speak their languages, give them up, or in the case presented here, increase the number of languages that they speak. This argument will be presented through ethnographic examples that are contextualized within the political economy of Antigua, Guatemala, an internationally known tourism destination and the location of a large handicraft marketplace, populated primarily by Mayan vendors. Examples of handicraft vendors' sociolinguistic interactions will help illustrate how linguistic practices relate to the economic and political contexts in which they live and work. In particular, language interactions between and among Mayan vendors, between Mayan vendors and customers, and Mayan vendors and Ladinos[1] will highlight the productive use of Mayan languages and the use of language as a form of resistance to politically and, most often, economically dominant Ladinos.

The structural characteristics of Mayan languages and the vendors' "will" to keep their language alive are not under analysis, but the contexts in which Mayan vendors use multiple languages are analyzed to point out that economy and politics play an important role in maintaining one's native language, as well as in adding additional languages to one's linguistic repertoire. The ethnographic and linguistic data discussed in this essay was collected at the time of and after the Peace Accords, which officially ended the civil war between the Guatemalan government and leftist guerrillas, were signed in 1996 (Warren 1998). The postwar period has ushered in positive (increased economic mobility and opened the country to more tourist consumers) and negative (increased crime: theft and international gangs) changes for Mayan handicraft vendors (Little 2005; Little and Smith 2009). It is within the postwar context that Mayan vendors' language choices and strategies are shaped by internal Mayan vendor interactions, touristic forms of cultural consumption, and political hierarchies that still privilege Ladinos.

An Ethnographic Example

In the course of any given day, Ixajpub',[2] a Kaqchikel Mayan woman from Santa Catarina Barahona, codeshifts between Kaqchikel Maya, Spanish, English, and an Esperanto-like language that is midway between Kaqchikel Maya and K'iche' Maya. While selling in what is locally called the New Artisan Marketplace, the language she uses is highly contextual. On one June morning, she sits in her marketplace locale talking with her female cousin about business classes at the national university. Her dialect of Kaqchikel is specific to her community, especially her neighborhood. As vendors from neighboring locales pass by greeting and asking questions about her inventory, when the next marketplace association meeting will be, or how members of her family are, she and her cousin change their dialect or language, code switching to a more generic Kaqchikel or Spanish.

Such linguistic encounters among vendors, which commonly occur in the course of daily life in the marketplace, are interrupted by visits from middlepersons and customers. With regard to the former, a linguistic middle ground is often forged between Ix'ey and the middleperson, both merchants trying to accommodate the other to facilitate conversation. Neither vendor strictly speaks Kaqchikel, K'iche', Ixil, or one of the other official Mayan languages; rather they create a hybrid of a couple of these, especially if they are Kaqchikel and K'iche' speakers. During encounters between vendors and new middlepersons, enterprising middlepersons will try to speak Kaqchikel, as a way of building rapport and showing respect. If this is not possible, then Spanish will be used.

Interruptions of these Maya-language exchanges by vendors trying to attract customers introduce additional language-use strategies. Most commonly, Spanish is the bridge language between the Mayan vendors and their foreign, tourist customers. But Ix'ey, like many other vendors, tries to predict what the native language of the customer is, using this technique to make the person feel comfortable and draw them into conversation and eventual purchase. These conversations then transform into curious mixtures of Spanish, the native language of the customer (English, German, Italian, French, or Japanese), and even Kaqchikel. Individual words and phrases are exchanged like gifts with each party increasing their respective linguistic repertoire. Ideally, such exchanges, especially those that go beyond simple greetings, end in the sale of merchandise. For Ix'ey, this friendly banter with customers helps improve her English skills, allows her to promote her own language, Kaqchikel, and sell.

Depending on the person with whom she is engaged in conversation and the context—social or economic—Ix'ey will use the language that is most appropriate. Rather than yield to Spanish, the dominant and official language of Guatemala, or facilitate foreigners by speaking English, the most common language spoken by tourists, she uses her language in pragmatic and playful ways. For example, she employs Kaqchikel words for textiles (*uq* rather than skirt or the Spanish word *corte*) or adjective descriptors to flatter the customer who tries on a *po't* (blouse, or *huipil* in Spanish), by saying "*jeb'el ok*" (very pretty).[3] When such words are introduced into the sale transaction, conversation invariably turns toward language, and Ix'ey will explain to the customer what her language is and may even suggest that the customer learn to speak it.

Kaqchikel Maya language use can also keep conversations private, but, as Ix'ey knows, introducing Kaqchikel Maya words into conversations with customers who speak English or Spanish can make the sales interaction seem more authentic and fun. Besides, the customer comes away from the encounter having learned a few words in Kaqchikel Maya, not just acquiring a handloomed textile. Rather than acquiesce to political pressure from local Ladino business and community leaders to not speak Mayan languages or allow market exchanges with customers to drift exclusively to Spanish, Ix'ey and other Mayan vendors resist by using the Mayan languages among themselves and introducing customers to them in a fashion that makes the marketplace exotic and authentic. It should be emphasized that Mayan vendor language interactions are not simply a matter of acquiescence versus resistance, but rather a more complex phenomenon in which language use relates to the consumption of Mayan ethnicity by international tourists. Hence, choosing to use a Mayan language over Spanish can serve multiple aims: political (overt resistance to Ladinos), pragmatic (it is their first language), and economic (capitalizing on tourists' desire to experience authentic Mayan culture).

The above, albeit general, example, calls attention to the fluidity of language use by handicraft vendors. No two vendors use the same complex combination of languages. In fact, family members and coworkers often try to develop complementary and different languages, just to outpace their competition. In the context of the New Artisan Marketplace and in general with respect to the handicrafts market in Antigua, vendors regard learning new languages and using multiple languages as a matter of good business practice. Aside from establishing rapport and respect with middlepersons and customers, knowing the others' respective languages contributes to more efficient use of time, since language is less of a barrier. Maintaining one's hometown— even household—dialect can also allow vendors to discuss personal matters or price adjustments among themselves before making or countering the offers of middlepersons and customers. In short, using their indigenous language can have immediate benefits.

In addition, language use takes on playful characteristics, where joking involves fusing words within linguistic interstices where no specific language exists. In arriving in such conversational spaces, vendors mark linguistic boundaries, only to take them apart and manipulate them. For example, vendors will say to English-speaking customers, "*Takwaj jun jacket*" ("you take one jacket") and "*Chula ok' ri a koton my friend*" ("very pretty, that sweater, my friend," where *chula* is Spanish). A casual observer would mistake the encounter by thinking that the Kaqchikel Maya used here was riddled with loan words from English and Spanish, but that would miss the context and point of using such words, which operate more like bait to draw in the customer who may not even realize at first that the vendors speak Kaqchikel Maya.

The material conditions outlined here will be taken up later in two short "language negotiation" examples to show how language use plays out within the particular economic, social, and political context of the marketplace.

Language Loss/Endangerment Politics and Globalization

Unlike linguists, Mayan handicrafts vendors are not generally concerned about language loss, language endangerment, or language rights. Nor do they worry much about the ways that their native language indicates historical continuity. Such concerns are part of contemporary linguists' anxieties about the life, vitality, and perpetuation of indigenous languages (see Mufwene 2004). Mayan linguists (Batz and Roquel 1999; Esquit 1997), however, share the concerns of foreign linguists (England 2003), and both are actively working together to strengthen Mayan language use, especially in public education (Maxwell 2009).

In recent years, linguists have been preoccupied by the loss of languages throughout the world due to globalization. The United Nations Educational, Scientific, and Cultural Organization (UNESCO's) Web page on Endangered Languages presents startling statistics about disappearing languages and languages with dramatically shrinking numbers of surviving native speakers.[4] It reports, for instance, that "over 50% of the world's 6000 languages are endangered" and that "one language disappears on average every two weeks." The National Science Foundation (NSF)[5] funds scholars to study endangered languages to protect, promote, and understand the conditions in which the languages of the world are disappearing. The language-loss alarm has sounded and is inspiring linguists to an almost Boasian quest, hoping—ideally—to save languages, or, failing that, at least to document them before they are gone. In this context, languages become living things that can be saved, which, ironically unlike actual living things, are not allowed to change. The work of saving languages, in essence, freezes them and, I emphasize, can strip them of their vitality.

Most linguists treat globalization as a force, which threatens the lesser-spoken languages of the world and can even lead to language death (Errington 2003; Mufwene 2002). The treatment of language almost as a biological organism has resulted in a rhetoric of lifesaving and human rights. Language, specifically the use of one's native language in contrast to colonial languages, has become a fundamental right and important identity marker. According to England (2003, 735), Mayan languages "are widely considered the single most important symbol of Mayan identity, both because they are still spoken by the majority of the population and because they are unequivocally 'authentic.'" For some linguists and speakers of threatened languages, language is used to indicate primordial roots, connections with specific territories, and ties to historical social, political, and economic relationships. Scholarship on Mayan languages is replete with this perspective (Brown 1996; Cojtí Cuxil 1996; England 1996, 2003;

Maxwell 1996; Richards and Richards 1996). These scholars have commonly emphasized these continuities and connections with the past. In other words, academic reconstructions and collective memories of Mayas have the tendency to fix Mayan languages and essentialized Mayan identity, making them easier to grasp, defend, and empower Mayas acting in political spheres (England 2003; Fischer and Brown 1996). Members of Mayan linguistic communities, like other linguistic communities throughout the world, have used this rights rhetoric to secure funding—some of which is language-oriented—for themselves, to renegotiate education policies and systems, and to promote multiculturalism though language diversity. Because Mayas have been relegated to the bottommost rungs of society since Spanish colonization in 1526, they have had the least access to basic services, education, political offices, and economic opportunities (see Carmack et al. 2007). As England (2003) and Cojtí et al. (2007) argue, language and cultural activism are beneficial to the economic, political, and social lives of these speakers of lesser-spoken languages.

This political maneuver has not resulted in a negative turn of events. In fact, as the above-cited authors effectively demonstrate, linguists and Mayan language activists have done much to raise language awareness among Mayas in Guatemala in ways that bridge native language use with identity politics and lead to greater political participation. Saving languages, however, has resulted in academics and native speakers themselves separating language into ideal and idealized forms that are inextricably linked to political ideologies, but ignore the material conditions of productive language development and change that occurs in everyday life among people who do speak their native languages. For example, in highland Guatemala where Kaqchikel Mayas live, debates have emerged among Kaqchikel Mayas themselves about what is the "standard" or "correct" form of Kaqchikel.[6] This has resulted in some youths alternately worrying about how they speak and giving up entirely on their birth language because it does not conform to the standard. Fortunately, in some cases, how linguists and organizations like UNESCO and the NSF and a myriad of human rights organizations regard language is not exactly the same as how people speaking or not speaking those languages use them.

The concerns of linguists, rights activists, governments, and members of linguistic communities themselves are embedded in material conditions and related power relations. To varying degrees, all of these parties are involved in missions to reverse language loss resulting from globalization. In Guatemala, this has taken multiple dimensions from local- to national-level interventions and help from foreign and national linguists. For decades now, Mayan languages have been studied and analyzed, but profound political changes, including those related to language policies, have occurred only over the last twenty years (see Cojtí et al. 2007). School programs from primary to university levels have been implemented to teach Mayan languages (Batz and Roquel 1999; Maxwell 2009; Richards and Richards 1996). Local community and national politicians celebrate Guatemala's linguistic diversity, hailing it as a distinctive, proud feature of the nation (Chacach 1997; Esquit 1997). Such ideologies, however, do not always reflect the material conditions in which Mayas use and continue to use their native languages. Moreover, they do not permit space for Mayas to play with their language, to keep it vital—link it to real-life concerns—and open new spaces where they can adopt and use additional languages.

Language Use in an International Tourism Market

Blommaert et al. (2005) offer an example of the material conditions of language use—particularly multilingualism in an urban setting—that contradicts the language-loss literature. According to Bloommaert et al., rather than having a homogenizing effect and causing distinct speakers of different languages to use one dominant language, globalization becomes a force that encourages diversity and, like the Mayan examples above, contributes to conceptions of space and identity. The tourism marketplace in Antigua offers a comparable ethnographic situation.

There are thirty-odd Mayan languages in use in Mexico, Guatemala, and Belize. Of these, twenty-four Mayan languages are spoken in Guatemala, but only Kaqchikel Maya, K'iche' Maya, Tzutijil Maya, Mam Maya, Ixil Maya, and occasionally Q'eqchi' Maya are regularly used in the handicraft marketplace in Antigua. Tourism, the primary reason this market exists, further contributes to linguistic diversity, adding Spanish, English, German, French, Italian, and other languages. Antigua is one of the main hubs of the Guatemalan tourism circuit. It indirectly links highland Mayan life to globalization and provides an urban context for multilingualism and encourages participants, especially the vendors, to use multiple languages, as mentioned earlier, to keep conversations private, to bridge cultural differences, and in general, to help conduct business.

Linguistic diversity is not a recent development. Since it was founded in 1543, Antigua has been a place where business and social life are conducted in multiple languages: European, Mesoamerican, even African to some degree (Lutz 1994). Despite the prevalence of Mayan and other Mesoamerican languages, Nahuatl, for instance, Spanish is the dominant language orientation. This language hierarchy was first cultivated by the original Spanish and Creole political administrators and has been continued into the present by the non-Maya Ladino administrators, who conceive of the city as a Ladino place in which the local official language is Spanish. It is conceived as the language of commerce and politics. This language ideology stands in direct contradiction to actual practice, since most vendors and laborers who serve the city come from Maya-speaking communities. Furthermore, as my research on the Mayan handicraft vendors and tourists reveals (Little 2004), irrespective of Ladino administrators' conceptualizations and preferences of Spanish use, international tourists look forward to experiencing Antigua as a place populated with Mayas who speak their respective languages and dress in their distinctive traditional clothing. Vendors are more than willing to accommodate them. The following examples highlight the two principle domains, one economic and one political, in which handicraft vendors use Mayan languages in Antigua.

Language Negotiation I: Vendors and Tourists

Aside from the obvious economic negotiations, each encounter between Mayan handicraft vendors and tourists involves a linguistic interaction that can best be framed as language negotiation. Vendors assess potential customers to decide which language to use. Through trial and error they have learned that yelling out, "Hey mister" or "Hello lady" or "Hello, my friend," tends to prejudice tourists against making purchases. At the same time, as curious as some tourists find it, listening to the vendors speak only Mayan languages presents a barrier that most tourists find insurmountable. Mayan languages are so different from European languages on phonological, morphological, and grammatical levels that tourists, coming upon a couple of vendors speaking to each other in Kaqchikel or K'iche' Maya, will pause a few moments, watch and listen with curiosity, then move on to another vendor's locale.

Just as Mayan languages can be a barrier between tourists and vendors (Little 2004), they can also be used as a way to build rapport and gain the confidence of the customer. Savvy vendors know that speaking a Mayan language, like wearing handwoven clothing, can verify a vendor's indigeneity and, even, authenticity to their international tourist customers (see Little 2004). However, experienced vendors also know that they need to drop their conversation in the Mayan language and address the customer in a language that she understands.

Finding the best language to establish rapport with a customer involves guessing which language the customer would prefer. Since these tourist-customers do not wear signs indicating this, vendors make guesses based on prior experience and the assumption that most tourist-customers will also be foreign students in one of Antigua's many Spanish-language schools. Aside from obvious formal greetings (*Buenos días, señorita*, Good morning, young lady) or direct sales pitches (*Compréme algo señor*, Buy something from me, sir), some overtures to customers are playful. Young female vendors will say to an older man, "*Joven, compré una tapete bonita para su novia*" (Young man, buy a beautiful textile for your girlfriend).[7] Or they will say with sincerity to a younger woman, "*Este huipil se vería más bonito que la blusa que se pone*" (This *huipil*[8] would look prettier than the blouse you are wearing). If Spanish does not work, they will generally resort to English, which is a risky strategy if the person is European.

Figure 5.1 A Kaqchikel Mayan vendor discusses prices with tourists.

When a potential customer responds positively, vendors continue to use that language to construct a sense of intimacy. Conversation is about topics, which are seemingly unrelated to sales: where the person is from, if that person is married and has close kin, what kind of job the person holds, what they like best about Guatemala, and when the person left on her trip. Conversations frequently turn to language issues, especially since vendors interrupt each other and are interrupted by middlepersons. These side conversations are often in Mayan languages. Less sophisticated vendors maintain parallel conversations, clearly keeping the two conversations and languages separate. Some, however, use these moments to create a feeling of inclusion for their tourist customers. The vendor will introduce the other person as family (even when this is not the case) and include Mayan words in the conversation. If the interruption comes after the vendor and customer have talked for a few minutes, the customer may have already been taught some Mayan words and be asked to practice them with the other vendor. At the same time, armed with some knowledge of the customer's interests, family, and itinerary, the two vendors will conspire about what they will try to sell and how best to go about it. Because the language divide is great and Mayan and European languages are completely incomprehensible to each other, there is little chance the customer will understand what is happening. Letting the customer participate by teaching her words and allowing her to ask questions about the language tends to reduce customer suspicions that the vendors are merely trying to make sales. The best scenario is that after this bilingual and cross-cultural banter has occurred for some minutes, the vendors will ask the customer to buy something. Although the use of Mayan languages helps highlight the vendors' cultural distinctiveness and is inclusive when they teach customers some words and phrases, this use also helps hide price-fixing and masks marketplace disharmony, which occurs because of competition and can dissuade tourists from buying.

Language Negotiation II: Vendors and City Officials

Politics in Antigua are a Spanish-language domain. Business in City Hall, as well as within the social and economic spaces that city officials occupy for official business and in which they have a presence, is done in Spanish. At beauty pageants, commemoration and dedication ceremonies, Chamber of Commerce meetings, and any other event they may attend, city officials speak Spanish and expect that the language will be spoken by the other attendees. There are pockets of resistance where Mayan languages are used, such as research and language institutes like the Centro de Investigaciones de Mesoamérica and the Fundación Proyecto Lingüístico Francisco Marroquín. In most businesses where Mayas work, Mayan language use is discouraged. The handicrafts marketplace, however, is one place in which Mayan languages are spoken freely in everyday life, be it for commerce, personal matters, and other reasons. This has been problematic and a source of annoyance for city officials, especially when they have to contend with vendors in the marketplace or in City Hall.

The legacy of Spanish-language use in Antigua, which is the historical legacy of how that language dominates everyday life and political and economic spheres, was established with Spanish colonization and the founding of the city. Although Spaniards made Spanish the official language of commerce and government, this was certainly not uncontroversial. Given that the city was constructed and serviced by legions of Mayas and Nahuas and other Mexican indigenous language speakers (Lutz 1994), prohibiting indigenous languages was simply not pragmatic. Although language politics have not been the focus of historical research on Antigua (Few 2002; Herrera 2003; Lutz 1994), one can easily interpret that Antigua was effectively a multilingual place, where, especially in court cases and in commerce, Guatemalan and Mexican indigenous languages were commonly used.

The official language then and now may be Spanish, established through a long historical legacy of domination, but it has been countered by indigenous language use. Speaking indigenous languages in Antigua, however, should not be construed only as a form of resistance. In fact, given the inefficiency of the Guatemalan education system (Batz and Roquel 1999; Richards and Richards 1996), the slowness of state institutions, in general, in instigating educational change in the countryside (Taracena Arriola 2002), and internal Mayan cultural practices and concepts (Carmack et al. 2007), Mayan language use persisted throughout the colonial and early national periods (1500s until the 1940s). The Mayas spoke their languages over Spanish because they were the most pragmatic, serving them best in their everyday lives. This opposed the official language, Spanish, and highlighted the weakness of the state. This tension between the official language and unofficial Mayan languages, from the colonial period to the present, meant that individuals commonly negotiated which language or languages would be used whenever political officials and Mayas interacted.

The contemporary period of globalization—manifested in the intensification of international tourism, new international, Evangelical, religious missionization strategies, and the transnational migration of Mayas, among other political, social, and economic forces—has impacted the Mayas in more profound ways than the previous 500 years.[9] The language endangerment literature related to Guatemala and discussed earlier in this chapter applies most to this contemporary period in which language loss is most severe. In many instances, younger generations are not maintaining the same language traditions as their parents and grandparents (Garzon, et al. 1998). At the same time, language negotiations between government officials and Mayas today, in contrast with past situations, can be categorized as a form of resistance. In fact, Mayas actively conceive of speaking Mayan languages in public and in official state domains as an act of resistance. The reasons for this shift in attitude are complex, but partially relate to the increased social, economic, and political spheres that place Mayas and Ladinos together (England 2003; Hale 2006; Little 2004). Prior to the 1970s, Mayas and Ladinos (but also Spaniards and Creoles in the more distant colonial past) lived largely separate, but highly unequal lives (see Carmack et al. 2007).

The following example is limited to a local case, a visit to a handicraft marketplace by the mayor and other city officials in 1996, which I have discussed elsewhere (Little 2004, 132–133). I did not discuss the sociolinguistic dimensions, especially the language use and language negotiations that occurred that day, in that analysis, which focused on the organizational abilities of the vendors. Here, the emphasis will be on the strategic uses of Mayan languages and the language negotiations that occur in public space under official political contexts.

The occasion for the Mayor's visit that day was a ceremony to recognize the physical reorganization of the marketplace. City officials mandated that the vendors in the Compañía de Jesús Artisan Marketplace deconstruct their marketplace and rebuild it so that all individual locales and aisles conformed to the same dimensions. Vendors suspected that the city's call for major reorganization of marketplace space was aimed at removing them from the Compañía de Jesús, a city-block-sized structure that was originally a Jesuit monastery and church. For the last one hundred years, it had been the site of, first, a utilitarian market and, then, a handicrafts market. City officials believed that the vendors would not succeed; hence, justifying the removal of the vendors. Because the vendors succeeded in reorganizing and rebuilding the marketplace, that day in 1996 was cause for celebration for the vendors.

Vendors decorated the marketplace with banners and balloons. A temporary stage was constructed for speeches and the presentation of awards and gifts. A marimba band was hired to play *sones*, a traditional form of music. The marketplace was closed for the day, but the gay decorations and music attracted onlookers, some of whom were invited to participate, giving the event an international flair, as many were foreign tourists and expatriate businesspersons and retirees. Linguistically, it was a typical globalized Antiguan social space with discussions occurring in various languages and most people speaking and code switching between two or more languages.

With the arrival of the mayor and other city officials, who did not speak Mayan languages and only had rudimentary speaking skills in other languages, Spanish became the "official" language of the event. Unlike meetings at City Hall and in Antigua's business associations, the speeches and discussions in Spanish were frequently interrupted by Kaqchikel Maya, K'iche' Maya, and even English. At that time, the president of the vendor association was a Ladino who only spoke Spanish. Introducing himself, he opened the ceremony, greeting the city officials and members of the audience. He showered the mayor with compliments and thanked him for his "vision to improve the marketplace," where they and "tourists will benefit from a much more enjoyable place." He presented a plaque to him, so that he "would recall this momentous event in which the vendors of the Compañía de Jesús Artisan Marketplace and the municipality worked together."

From the onset, it was clear that the market association president was merely a figurehead. Mayas comprised the vast majority of the 200-plus stalls of the marketplace and Mayas, in the course of their monthly association meetings, were in charge. Having a Ladino president seemed to be ironic, in that it conformed to the stereotypical neocolonial situation of indigenous people needing continued management by those believed to be more Europeanized. However, the Mayan vendors realized that city officials tended to refuse to negotiate with them. By placing a Ladino in the role of president, but by giving him no power, the vendors were able to speak indirectly to the mayor. In fact, the negotiations that took place between city officials and a small subcommittee of vendors in the months prior to the day's ceremony were conducted in Spanish, but with the market association president acting according to the vendors' collective decisions.

Unlike the previous meetings when the vendors were in City Hall, on that day in 1996, they were in their marketplace, where they spoke their own languages when they felt like it or when it was beneficial to them. The vendors around me expressed their anger at the mayor for having wasted their time. The official speeches by the vendors themselves, the mayor, and other city officials were interrupted with pauses permitting interpretation for "the indigenous women who could not speak Spanish well enough to understand." What the officials and the president of the vendor association did not understand was that these pauses were not about making these speeches comprehensible; rather they were interjections of social critique and humor in which they made fun of the mayor and even the president of the market association for acting important. For instance, one Mayan woman from San Antonio Palopó called out in Kaqchikel, "Ask the mayor how he will steal money from the city when there are no tourists coming and spending money on us." The mayor, however, was asked to "consider the important economic role Mayan handicraft vendors play in the city."

In contrast to the previous examples, vendors did not try to find a common language for the participants, which they all knew was Spanish. They, likewise, did not play with their languages to draw the city officials into conversations that would introduce Mayan words to them. Instead, they used Kaqchikel and K'iche' to construct a linguistic barrier between themselves and the officials. They also created a very confusing linguistic social space. Not only were official speeches interrupted by the critical and, sometimes, humorous interpretations, they were sometimes drowned out by the side conversations and commentaries by members of the audience.

Aside from speaking with the vendor association president, a few other Ladino vendors, and other city officials, I was the only person the mayor voluntarily approached. He had spent the whole ceremony avoiding the Mayan vendors, not speaking more than a greeting and that only in reply. At the end of the ceremony, he crossed a group of Mayan vendor women who were intent on asking him what the city was doing with the rents they had paid over the years, since they had not seen improved services. Ignoring them and probably denying that I was engaged in a conversation in Kaqchikel with a friend about how the new physical arrangement of the marketplace would affect business, the mayor held out one hand for a shake and patted my shoulder with the other. "Thank you for coming to this event," he said. "It is important for foreigners to see how we *Chapines*, Ladinos and *indígenas* can work together." One of the women shouted to me in Kaqchikel, "Ask him when he's going to help us fight the thieves." At about the same time, another vendor approached and asked me in English how my family was and if they were coming to visit soon. To which another commented in Kaqchikel, "Yes, you've been very sad without them." Flustered and annoyed at being in a linguistic situation that he could not control or understand, the mayor excused himself.

Globalization, Language Use, Power, and Difference

At the time of the ceremony, the linguistic complexity—in terms of which languages were used, the interruptions of one language by another, the code switching among several languages, and the dual, often contradictory, Mayan and Spanish languages that existed within the same social space—was lost on me. I was too disappointed about losing a chance to talk with the mayor to really understand what had happened. It is important to locate the previous examples of language negotiation within a contemporary economic and political context that places Mayan language use and interruptions with forms of resistance.

Given the long history of designating Spanish as the official language (as described earlier) in contrast with the equally long continued use of Mayan languages due to everyday practicalities, it is not surprising that language use in the handicraft marketplace tended toward Mayan languages in intra-vendor communication, be it for commerce or personal family matters. They were easier and ensured more privacy in the presence of Ladinos and tourists. Even communication between vendors of different Mayan languages—especially Kaqchikel and K'iche'—drifted toward Mayan language use, especially in cases where Ladinos and tourists were present. By contrast, in dealing economically with tourists and politically with Ladinos, conversations ultimately drifted toward Spanish, usually the lingua franca. Injection of Mayan words and phrases by vendors into conversations with tourists can be construed both as minor resistances to the political domination of Spanish and as a strategic ploy. This latter use plays into tourists' desires to experience difference through clearly marked signs of language and distinctive costumes. The marketplace, hence, is the physical space where global forces act out in distinctive ways that contradict national and local Ladino notions of order, especially with respect to language use. In the tourism market, intravendor communication, vendor-middle person communication, and vendor-customer communication, each demand different sets of languages that are often determined by economic goals.

Mayas and Ladinos engage the local-in-the-global and global-in-the-local social situation that typifies everyday interaction in Antigua in quite different ways. The attempted enforcement of Spanish in economic, political, and social domains by Ladinos tends to deny the place as a site of multiple languages—something that has now gone on for 500 years. Ladinos—at least many of those talking to me—conceptualize Antigua as an intrinsically Spanish-speaking place. Certainly, they hear other languages being spoken, but few tend to actively embrace other languages, and when they do, it is in favor of English over the local Mayan language, Kaqchikel. The preponderance of Spanish language schools contributes to this attitude, since they serve, among various functions, to reinforce Spanish, facilitating communication between the language learners and their hosts. Only one school, operated by the Fundación Proyecto Lingüístico Francisco Marroquín, offers regular language instruction in Mayan languages—something that few students realize.

Globalization, in this case the conflation of diverse and mobile groups (international tourists, foreign businesspersons, retirees from the United States, and Mayan vendors themselves) and local Ladino residents, acts to unsettle Ladino identity, much as Hale (2006) describes in his analysis of multicultural neoliberalism. This state agenda "holds out the promise of both equality and cultural recognition, but grants only the latter, and then promotes intercultural exchange anyway" (Hale 2006, 38). According to Hale, the gains—really cultural concessions by the national government—made by Mayas in recent years have contributed to Ladinos'—especially middle-class and poor Ladinos'—feelings of losing political and economic power. Hale very effectively shows how these sentiments do not correlate with any significant gains by Mayas in economic and political contexts, except in relatively rare cases. Basically, Ladinos are not yet threatened by Mayan economic and political ascendancy. However, the context of globalization in Antigua—international tourism—dovetails with the national, multicultural, neoliberal agenda in that it creates similar effects in Ladino attitudes.

The tourism market opens Antigua's economic, political, and social spaces to the use of multiple languages that undermine attempts by local Ladino politicians and businesspersons to effectively enforce Spanish as the only language of politics and commerce. There is little chance that some other language will displace Spanish as the lingua franca in Antigua, but Mayan vendors have seized upon Ladino insecurities to expand the domains in which they speak their respective languages. It would be an overstatement to claim that globalization was acting to reverse the general trend toward language loss occurring throughout the Guatemalan highlands, just as it would be to claim, as many scholars have done, that globalization may "account for the loss or endangerment of several non-European languages" (Mufwene 2004, 206).

From the perspective of Mayan vendors, international tourism (or processes of globalization) opens more spaces for them to use their own languages. Those same processes also allow them to use Mayan languages in local political spaces—this was not possible in earlier periods of Antigua's history. What was just beginning to happen in the marketplace ceremony described previously—the public use of Mayan languages to critique Ladinos—has now expanded into City Hall and other public places. Mayas, especially vendors, increasingly try to use their languages to gain an advantage over monolingual Ladino businesspersons who are in most direct competition with them. Language, costume, and specific products allow them to highlight how different they are from their Ladino competitors, who often call foul and demand that the city council mete out penalties to the vendors. In essence, Mayan handicraft vendors use their ethnicity, as expressed through costume and language, to gain economic advantage, which is then converted into political power against Ladinos.

International tourism, alone, is not responsible for this turn of events, nor can credit be given just to the Pan-Mayan movement (Fischer and Brown 1996; Hale 2006; Warren 1998). Instead, these events, in combination with the influx of nongovernmental developmental organizations and human rights groups in the postwar period following the 1996 signing of the Peace Accords between the national government and guerrillas, have opened a political space in which vendors (not to ignore other Mayas) have been emboldened to stand up for cultural, political, and economic rights. They have been quick to seek out the legal assistance of these aid organizations, framing Ladino acts to restrict their commerce as distinctly racist and culturally anti-Mayan. For example, male vendors, who rarely dress in the traditional costume of their home community, will say in Spanish to human rights lawyers, "Ladinos discriminate against us because we were speaking our language. Because they cannot compete with us, they use force to remove us." Hence, struggles for power, at least in economic domains, become associated with the politics of ethnicity and language use. Specific languages, Mayan languages in this case, become tools for economic and political leverage, as well as intentional manifestations of Mayan resistance to Ladino authority. Mayan handicraft vendors, in contrast to Mayan linguists and cultural activists described earlier, do not apply specific grammatical and lexiconical standards to the Mayan languages they use in everyday economic or political spheres.

Conclusions: Mayan Languages and Pragmatic Concerns within the Global Economy

In this chapter, I have endeavored to present this sociolinguistic case of language negotiations between Mayan vendors and others as an example of how globalization does not necessarily hasten language death. That this example is situated within an economic context—a handicraft marketplace aimed primarily at foreign tourists—shows how Mayan languages continue to have utility in pragmatic, contemporary, everyday work contexts. As Mufwene (2004, 206) puts it, "The vitality of languages cannot be dissociated from the socioeconomic interests and activities of their speakers."

On the surface, economic, political, and cultural forms of globalization appear to homogenize. In Antigua and elsewhere, one does not have to go far to find a McDonald's restaurant, Coca-Cola, or Mickey Mouse, but such global cultural and economic expressions do not necessarily replace or displace more historically and locally situated cultural and economic expressions. Mufwene (2004, 208) explains, "The correlation of language death with globalization as an economic network of production and consumption interdependencies is partly correct." The problem with assuming the inevitability of language death, according to Mufwene, is that the local, material, and historical contexts of globalization are highly variable in terms of how indigenous languages are impacted. The case, here, attempts to provide an example that contests commonly held popular and scholarly beliefs that globalization necessarily leads to language death. Furthermore, given the specific local history of Mayan language use in Guatemala in relation to Spanish, the language of Ladino political and economic dominance, globalization appears to open new spaces from which Mayas can more securely challenge Ladino forms of power. This gets played out linguistically in the daily business of the handicraft marketplace, as well as in many other public and private economic and political spaces in Antigua.

To borrow from Blommaert et al. (2005, 229), Antigua is one of those urban global places that "allows semiotic orientations to different centers active at different scales: the strictly local scale of the street or the neighborhood, the scale of [the city], the scale of [the nation], the scale of [the country] and its neighboring countries, and so on. The different orders of indexicality that emanate from orientations to such centers allow for a generous, multiple register of interactional patterns." Both Spanish and Kaqchikel are local and global at the same time. Antigua itself and these languages are interconnected through the circulations of what Antigua and Mayas and indigenously produced handicrafts mean as they circulate in the global economy and in local politics.

The tension between language endangerment policies and the actual use of indigenous languages, however, has not been resolved. Mayas, including these relatively self-confident vendors, still question how well they actually speak their own languages when confronted by language standardization efforts that appear critical of nonstandard speech and would make language use more rigid. In this context, globalization creates social and political spaces that mutually support Mayan language use and resistance to Ladino power manifested through Spanish language use. The ability to use multiple languages, not just a Mayan language or Spanish, is pragmatic in the context of Antigua. This makes life easier and leads to economic or political successes for Mayas and Ladinos alike. A language may serve as an identity marker, but its continued use relates less to sentimental attachments than to pragmatic realities.

Notes

1. In Guatemala, Ladino is a complex socioracial concept, based in part on phenotypic characteristics but more on cultural practices, including language use. A Ladino is, simply, non-Maya. However, such clear delineations between Ladino and Maya are not always part of daily life or self-conceptualizations (see Hale 2006; Little 2004).
2. Names of people are pseudonyms, to protect their anonymity. Ixajpub' and Ix'ey are names based on the 260-day ritual calendar. "Ix" denotes that the person is a female.

3. In Kaqchikel Maya, *jeb'el* is pretty. The second word, *ok'*, is commonly used as a affectionate diminutive ("little pretty") and as an adjective to add emphasis ("very pretty").
4. Web site last accessed on September 23, 2007; http://portal.unesco.org/culture/.
5. A report by the National Science Foundation presents similar startling statistics; accessed on September 25, 2007; http://www.nsf.gov/news/special_reports/linguistics/endangered.jsp.
6. This is an example of the development of ethnic nationalism as discussed by Benedict Anderson (1983).
7. Brian Haley called to my attention, in his review of my essay, the fact that such linguistic exchanges are indicative of flirtations, which can be used as a sales mechanism.
8. A *huipil* is a handwoven blouse worn by Maya women in Guatemala and Mexico.
9. See Walter E. Little, ed. (guest), "Maya Livelihoods in Guatemala's Global Economy," special issue of *Latin American Perspectives* 32, no. 5 (2005): 3–127.

References

Anderson, Benedict. 1983. *Imagined Communities: Reflections on the Origin and Spread of Nationalism*. London: Verso.

Appadurai, Arjun, ed. 2002. *Globalization*. Durham, NC: Duke University Press.

Batz, Juan, and Jamie Roquel. 1999. Escuelas mayas y bilingües interculturales. In *Valores de la cultura maya y desarrollo con identidad: Compilación de documentos y experiencias*, 275–95. Iximulew-Guatemala: Fundación CEDIM.

Blommaert, Jan, James Collins, and Stef Slembrouck. 2005. Polycentricity and Interactional Regimes in 'Global Neighborhoods.' *Ethnography* 6(2): 205–235.

Brown, R. McKenna. 1996. The Maya Language Loyalty Movement in Guatemala. In *Maya Cultural Activism in Guatemala*, ed. Edward F. Fischer and R. McKenna Brown, 165–77. Austin: University of Texas Press.

Bulag, Uradyn E. 2003. Mongolian Ethnicity and Linguistic Anxiety in China. *American Anthropologist* 105(4): 753–63.

Carmack, Robert, Janine Gasco, and Gary Gossen, eds. 2007. *The Legacy of Mesoamerica*. Upper Saddle River, NJ: Prentice Hall.

Chacach, Martín. 1997. El arte de la lengua en los últimos 20 años. *Cultural de Guatemala* 18(2):13–34.

Cojtí, Waqi' Q'anil Demetrio, Ixtz'ulu' Elsa Son Chonay, and Raxche' Rodriquez Guaján. 2007. *Ri k'ak'a runuk'ik ri Saqamaq': Nuevas Perspectivas para la Construcción del Estado Multinacional*. Guatemala City: Cholsamaj.

Cojtí Cuxil, Demetrio. 1996. The Politics of Maya Revindication. In *Maya Cultural Activism in Guatemala*, ed. Edward F. Fischer and R. McKenna Brown, 19–50. Austin: University of Texas Press.

England, Nora. 1996. The Role of Language Standardization in Revitalization. In *Maya Cultural Activism in Guatemala*, ed. Edward F. Fischer and R. McKenna Brown, 178–94. Austin: University of Texas Press.

————. 2003. Maya Language Revival and Revitalization Politics: Linguists and Linguistic Ideologies. *American Anthropologist* 105(4): 733–743.

Errington, Joseph. 2003. Getting Language Rights: The Rhetorics of Language Endangerment and Loss. *American Anthropologist* 105(4): 723–32.

Esquit, Alberto Choy. 1997. La oficialización de idiomas: el caso de Guatemala. *Cultura de Guatemala* 18(2): 219–31.

Few, Martha. 2002. *Women Who Live Evil Lives: Gender, Religion, and the Politics of Power in Colonial Guatemala.* Austin: University of Texas Press.

Fischer, Edward F., and R. McKenna Brown, eds. 1996. *Maya Cultural Activism in Guatemala.* Austin: University of Texas Press.

Friedman, Jonathan. 2003. Globalizing Languages: Ideologies and Realities of the Contemporary Global System. *American Anthropologist* 105(4): 744–52.

Garzon, Susan, R. McKenna Brown, Julia Becker Richards, and Wuqu' Ajpub' (Arnulfo Simón). 1998. *The Life of Our Language: Kaqchikel Maya Maintenance, Shift, and Revitalization.* Austin: University of Texas Press.

Gregory, Steven. 1998. Globalization and the 'Place' of Politics in Contemporary Theory: A Commentary. *City & Society* 10(1): 47–64.

Hale, Charles. 2006. *Mas que un Indio: Racial Ambivalence and Neoliberal Multiculturalism in Guatemala.* Santa Fe, NM: School of American Research Press.

Herrera, Robinson A. 2003. *Natives, Europeans, and Africans in Sixteenth-Century Santiago de Guatemala.* Austin: University of Texas Press.

La Ponce, J. A. 2004. Minority Language and Globalization. *Nationalism and Ethnic Politics* 10: 15–24.

Little, Walter E. 2004. *Mayas in the Marketplace: Globalization, Tourism, and Cultural Identity.* Austin: University of Texas Press.

————, ed. (guest). 2005. Maya Livelihoods in Guatemala's Global Economy. Special issue of *Latin American Perspectives* 32(5): 3–127.

————, and Timothy J. Smith, eds. 2009. *Mayas in Post-War Guatemala: Harvest of Violence Revisited.* Tuscaloosa: University of Alabama Press.

Lutz, Christopher H. 1994. *Santiago de Guatemala, 1541–1773: City, Caste, and the Colonial Experience.* Norman: University of Oklahoma Press.

Mandal, Sumit K. 2000. Reconsidering Cultural Globalization: The English Language in Malaysia. *Third World Quarterly* 21(6): 1001–12.

Maxwell, Judith M. 1996. Prescriptive Grammar and Kaqchikel Revitalization. In *Maya Cultural Activism in Guatemala,* ed. Edward F. Fischer and R. McKenna Brown, 195–207. Austin: University of Texas Press.

————. 2009. Bilingual Bicultural Education: Best Intentions across a Cultural Divide. In *Mayas in Post-War Guatemala: Harvest of Violence Revisited,* ed. Walter E. Little and Timothy J. Smith, 84–95. Tuscaloosa: University of Alabama Press.

McCarty, Teresa L. 2003. Revitalising Indigenous Languages in Homogenising Times. *Comparative Education* 39(2): 147–63.

Mufwene, Salikok. 2002. Colonialization, Globalization and the Plight of 'Weak' Languages. *Journal of Linguistics* 38: 375–95.

———. 2004. Language Birth and Death. *Annual Review of Anthropology* 33: 201–22.

Mühlhäusler, Peter. 2003. Language Endangerment and Language Revival. *Journal of Sociolinguistics* 7(2): 232–45.

Richards, Julia Becker, and Michael Richards. 1996. Maya Education: A Historical and Contemporary Analysis of Mayan Language Education Policy. In *Maya Cultural Activism in Guatemala,* ed. Edward F. Fischer and R. McKenna Brown, 208–21. Austin: University of Texas Press.

Taracena Arriola, Arturo. 2002. *Etnicidad, estado y nación en Guatemala, 1808–1944.* Guatemala: Nawal Wuj.

Warren, Kay M. 1998. *Indigenous Movements and Their Critics: Pan-Maya Activism in Guatemala.* Princeton, NJ: Princeton University Press.

Whaley, L. 2003. The Future of Native Languages. *Futures* 35: 961–73.

Zorn, Elayne. 2004. *Weaving a Future: Tourism, Cloth, and Culture on an Andean Island.* Iowa City: University of Iowa Press.

CHAPTER 6

Making of the Pacific Mall: Chinese Identity and Architecture in Toronto

Ho Hon Leung and Raymond Lau

An ethnic icon in the Toronto Chinese communities, the Pacific Mall is a shopping mall, and probably the best-known "Chinese shopping mall" in Canada, possibly in North America. When the Chinese in Toronto say "Go to 'Tong Yin' mall [referring to the Chinese shopping mall in Cantonese]," they very likely have the Pacific Mall in mind. When Chinese-American tourists visit Toronto, they demand a visit to two places: Niagara Falls and the Pacific Mall. Every day, someone passing by the mall can see tourist buses loaded with visitors. They are busy dropping off and picking up their clients. The popularity of the mall has expanded beyond the Chinese communities, and non-Chinese visitors can be seen anywhere and at anytime in the mall, which has also attracted attention from different media. The Pacific Mall was introduced in a short film by the Canadian Broadcasting Corporation (CBC) in 2002. It also appeared in several mainstream magazines in Toronto. It made its appearance in the *New York Times* in March 2002. The intriguing question is under what circumstances the mall became an ethnic icon that signifies the "Chinese mall." Why is the mall important to the Chinese community? The purpose of this chapter is to use the Pacific Mall to illustrate a theoretical framework that conceptualizes an intertwining relationship between ethnic identity and architecture. This particular relationship was established in a Chinese immigrant community in Toronto; the development of the mall reflects a phenomenon of globalization, which is a neoliberal capitalist system that facilitates the flow of people, images, ideas, and commodities across national boundaries.

Studies of ethnic identity / cultural identity[1] have made important contributions to the discipline of architecture, and students of ethnic identity can learn much about the life of an ethnic group by studying architecture. On the surface, ethnic/cultural identity and architecture are seemingly different disciplines, but they share at least one essential common component—land. Many theories of ethnic identity formation, by using various cultural venues and resources, stress the importance of territory and homeland to a group, while architecture is built and is to be built on a piece of land. What an ethnic group builds signifies the dynamics of its essentiality at different (developmental/historical) phases. Yet, both what has been built and what is going to be built also shape the ways that an ethnic group perceives and identifies who they are. Such theoretical observation is constructed upon a literature review and several case studies by the authors in Canada, the United States, Greece, China, Hong Kong, and Macau. The following sections will briefly introduce the theories of ethnic identity and architecture that inform our framework; then, the application of the framework, a synthesis of these two disciplines, will be used to examine how "Chineseness" is constructed at the Pacific Mall, Markham, Ontario, Canada. The narrative on the Pacific Mall presented in this chapter is derived from in-depth interviews with mall shoppers, retailers, shop owners, and some members of the management board. Their views are interpreted in the theoretical framework of ethnic identity and architecture that takes into consideration Canadian immigration policies, architectural space, demographics of the users, and a business model in the context of globalization. Before we present our case study, we will examine the concepts of ethnic identity and architecture that inform the theoretical framework.

Studies of Ethnic Identity

There is much debate about what ethnic identity is and how it is formed. The debate usually considers two theoretical perspectives: primordial and instrumental/constructivist. The primordial approach argues that ethnic identity, a sense of belonging to the group, comes rather naturally because it is innate. It is blood-like (see Geertz 1973; Isaacs 1989); it is in the DNA of a person, metaphorically speaking. However, the recent debate has been dominated by the instrumental/constructivist approach (see Prazniak and Dirlik 2001), because scholars are more convinced that the sense of belonging to the group expressed in ethnicity is a social and cultural construct. It is always in the process of being formed. Ethnicity emphasizes the cultural traits of a group through which it expresses a sense of belonging and solidarity. Culture can be seen as the shared practices, the know-how of a group, and a learning process that deals with everyday challenges. Everyday challenges emerge out of the social, economic, and political changes in a given system within a given time frame. The conditions change, the culture changes; therefore, the cultural practices of an ethnic identity can change accordingly. In short, the behaviors of an ethnic group can change across time and space. The study of an ethnic group inevitably involves an examination of the cultural components a group uses to mobilize its identity. De Vos (2006, 11) sums up the definition of ethnic identity from this perspective: "The ethnic identity of a group consists of its *subjective, symbolic,* or *emblematic* [italic in original] use of any aspect of a culture, or a perceived separate origin and continuity, in order to differentiate themselves from other ethnic groups. In time, these emblems can be imposed from outside or embraced from within." The concept of "we" versus 'them" is formed.

Hutchinson and Smith (1996, 6–7) articulate the six elements that contribute to the formation of an ethnic identity: a common proper name, a myth of common ancestry, shared historical memories, common culture such as language, customs or religion, a link with a homeland, and a sense of solidarity. On the one hand, the complexity of ethnic identity lies in how a group constructs their sense of belonging, by using some or all the six elements. It varies from group to group. On the other hand, some groups might use their identities to form a nation, but some groups do not follow this pattern. The construction of ethnic identities can take place in four scenarios: (1) a majority group as a nation within their homeland (Germany, France, Japan, and China), (2) a majority group outside their homeland (Jews), (3) a minority group as a nation in their homeland (Afrikaners in South Africa), and (4) a minority group outside their homeland (any immigrant groups such as Fijians in Australia). But, in many cases, all these four scenarios can exist at the same time and in the same space, such as multiethnic nations, and the political and economic power of the state can fall into the hands of either an ethnic majority group or a minority group. Place-bound ethnic dynamics vary tremendously.

Many studies have already explored how different cultural components, such as media use, language, religious practices, marriage patterns, ethnic friends, residential patterns, use of ethnic food, and so on, contribute to ethnic identity. But they often neglect the contribution of architecture. Architecture is definitely a cultural practice. Before we theorize the intertwining relationship between ethnic identity and architecture, we must first explore what architecture is in the following section.

Architecture

Architecture can be conceptualized as a way in which humans build to meet their need for shelter, climatic control of their living environment and its accessibility, monumentalization of activities, creation of physical boundaries and segregation, and also for the expression of the desire to identify themselves. The execution of such desire, the material culture, and the formal expression in relation to function can result in different constructions as technology advances. In short, architecture amplifies the generality of the human desire to shape the land to suit itself (Shepheard 1994).

To build something to represent oneself is part of the generality of human desire. Graves and others argue, "In making a case for figurative architecture, we assume that the thematic character of the work is grounded in nature and is simultaneously read in a totemic or anthropomorphic manner" (1982, 13). Barthes' observation on the symbolic meaning of the Eiffel Tower (1997, 172) is a case in point. The reader can easily find numerous pieces of totemic architecture around the world that stand for an ethnic group, its ethnic pride, or the nation of the ethnic group.

However, the meaning of architecture can change across time and space. The Eiffel Tower was once considered to be an eyesore, but now it is an icon of Paris and France. The pyramids of Egypt were once tombs of some pharaohs; now they are the national icons of Egypt. In contemporary Taiwan, the previous government under Chen Shui-bian (Democratic Progressive Party), who advocated a sovereign state as a nation independent of mainland China, passed a law to rename any building associated with the Nationalist Party. This political move was meant to "erase" the influence of the Nationalist Party, which is still hoping to reunite Taiwan with mainland China one day. Chiang Kai-shek Memorial Hall in Taipei has been renamed Taiwan Democracy Memorial Hall, for example. Architectural structuralism conceptualizes the dynamics of the (re)interpretation of the meanings of a piece of architecture. Leach (1997, 164) states, "Structuralism has obvious applications to the world of architecture through the discipline of semiology—the science of signs. Semiology offers a mechanism by which the built environment can be 'read' and 'decoded'" (also see R. King 1996). The (symbolic) meaning of architecture can change across time, varying along with the social, cultural, political, and economic conditions of a given society.

Ethnic/Cultural Identity and Architecture: An Intertwining Relationship

The discourse concerning architecture and ethnic identity reveals some interesting intersecting and intertwining relationships. Ethnic identity and architecture share an important common component—land. An occupied land or territory, be it a nation, a province (Catalonia, Quebec), or an ethnic community (Chinatown, Greektown, Little Italy), is the heart of an ethnic group. Land is the foundation of architecture. In most instances, that land is a driving force in both ethnic identity and architecture and in separating the inside and outside, the in-group and out-group. Koolhaas and Mau state that architecture seduces, separates, limits, defines, and excludes from the rest by setting boundaries and accessibilities (1995, 961). These spatial relations manifest attributes very similar to ethnic relations. At the same time, architecture and ethnic groups connect and communicate, since most human activities, ethnic activities included, take place in buildings (Beaman 2002), particularly in modern times. It is the continuum of the flows of messages, ideologies, people, and materials between the inside and outside (referring to architecture)—the in-group and out-group (referring to ethnic groups) that is manifested in space and in social/ethnic relations.

Further, similar to the (symbolic) meaning of architecture, the (re)interpretation of an ethnic identity, such as Chinese or German, changes. What is the "Chineseness" (the cultural practice of Chinese people) then? It is a very fluid concept. For example, "Chineseness" in mainland China, Taiwan, Hong Kong, Macau, and overseas and "Chineseness" in ancient and contemporary Chinese civilizations vary a great deal culturally. What we can observe is that the meanings of architecture and ethnicity always undergo de/re/construction and (re)interpretation that are subjected to the social, economic, and political conditions where a group lives.

The analysis of the intertwining relation between ethnic identity and architecture leads to a theoretical framework that guides future research in this field. This framework demands a vigorous investigation of the complex and fluid relation between these two variables that reinforce each other. The dynamics between the conceptual levels and the actual practice of the people in the process of de/re/construction and (re)interpretation of identity and architecture can only be realized by empirical investigation. The analysis requires sensitive consideration of the social, economic, and political conditions under which this process takes place.

The Pacific Mall, as a case study, shows the application of this theoretical framework that analyzes and understands the (re)construction and (re)interpretation of "Chineseness" in the Pacific Mall located in Markham, a major city next to Toronto. This case study takes place in one of the four majority-minority ethnic relation scenarios: a minority group, Chinese as immigrants, outside their homeland.

The Development of Chinese Communities and "Chinese" Shopping Malls

The conceptualization of the Pacific Mall took place in the midst of the flourishing establishment of ethnic malls and plazas in the late 1980s in

Scarborough, Ontario, Canada. These commercial developments consisted of Chinese shopping centers, Cuban strip plazas, or Japanese malls. Qadeer categorizes this phenomenon as "a new genre of suburban commercial development" (1998). According to Lai (2003, 332), there were fifty-eight Asian-themed malls in December 1999 in Scarborough, which is part of the Toronto metropolitan area, and two other neighboring regions, Markham and Richmond Hill, which are smaller cities just north of the Toronto metropolitan area. Such economic development in these areas is a result of the most recent Canadian open-door immigration policy that recruits immigrants based on merit, rather than country of origin. The following section outlines the history of Chinese immigration in Canada.

Chinese Immigrant History in Canada

The Chinese have a long history in Canada. This history can be categorized into three distinctive waves. Instead of coming directly from China, the first small wave of Chinese migrants came to Canada from the west coast of the United States around 1858 for the Gold Rush in the Fraser Valley of British Columbia. The Canadian Census of 1880–81 reported that there were about 5,000 Chinese present in Canada and 22 in Ontario (Lai 2003, 313).

The second wave of Chinese migration was recruited for the mega-project of building an intercontinental railroad. The challenge and cost of building the railway, particularly the most dangerous part along the Rocky Mountains in the west coast, were the reasons for importing Chinese workers. Chinese workers could do very dangerous work for much less pay than other workers due to racist and discriminatory pay scales (Li 1998, 16). Upon completion of construction of the railway, the Chinese workers were dismissed because they were no longer needed. Because of the unusually poor remuneration, many of the Chinese workers could not save enough money for the return trip to China (Chan 1983, 67). In fact, despite getting help from the newly established Chinese Benevolent Association, no more than 3,000 out of 17,000 were able to return to China (Chan 1991, 17). The rest were forced to seek work elsewhere, within Canada or outside Canada; some stayed in Victoria and Vancouver, while others followed the Canadian Pacific Railway route and moved eastward. Facing strong racial discrimination and prejudice, including an exclusion act and head-tax system, they could only take unwanted jobs in the Prairies and eastern Canada. Along the way, some established themselves as peddlers, grocers, and cooks, while others worked as laundrymen and servants for white families. Chinatowns were then formed in cities and towns along the route (Chan 1991, 28). Between 1881 and 1884, there were about 15,000 Chinese in Canada (Lai 2003, 314). The demographic characteristics of these waves of Chinese immigrants were those of poorly educated laborers.

The third wave of Chinese immigration, the largest of all, was a result of the implementation of the new Immigrant Act in 1967, which recruited newcomers based on a point system, instead of their country of origin. The point system selected immigrants based on their level of education, occupational skills, knowledge of English and French, and other merits. Along with many immigrants who came from a nontraditional European background, many Chinese from Hong Kong, Taiwan, China, and other overseas countries entered Canada under the "independent category," which required a total of merit points exceeding seventy out of a possible one hundred points under this new system. As a result, the ethnic diversity of Canada became even more prominent. Unlike the previous two waves of Chinese immigration, family reunions were permitted. This new policy profoundly changed Chinese demographic characteristics in Canada as newcomers could establish their roots in Canada with their family members.

This wave of Chinese immigration is also called the Hong Kong Tide. Between 1967 and early 1990, China exercised a closed-door policy, whereby out-migration was tightly controlled and restricted. The Chinese in Hong Kong have been the main source of immigrants in the Chinese population. Other than the fact that Chinese from Hong Kong have greater freedom to migrate to other countries than their counterparts in China, the return of the sovereignty of Hong Kong to China in 1997 created a huge push factor that induced this third wave of Chinese immigration. Their favorite destination was Canada, followed by the United States and Australia. Not only were the Chinese from Hong Kong highly educated, skilled immigrants, but many of them who entered Canada as entrepreneurs or investors were relatively wealthy. This development is a response to the Investment Canada Act of 1986. The purpose of the Immigrant Investor Program was to promote economic growth in Canada. There are three types of business migrants under this program: investors, entrepreneurs, and self-employed persons (Lai 2003, 325). The business migrant must fulfill the following conditions: "(1) a migrant investor must maintain a residence in Canada and make a three-year investment of not less than Can$250,000, which would create jobs; (2) a migrant entrepreneur must have bona fide financial and managerial ability, and buy or start a business where he or she would have an active managerial role, and create jobs for Canadians; and (3) a self-employed migrant must maintain employment and contribute to the economy or enrich Canada's cultural-artistic life" (325–6). These opportunities created a powerful pull factor that attracted many Chinese and money from Hong Kong to Canada. Many of these immigrants sought haven in Canada because of the 1997 sovereignty factor.

For almost a decade, Hong Kong led the list of birthplaces for newcomers, with 96,500 of the 1.24 million recent immigrants (Statistics Canada 1994, 13). However, the tide has ebbed because Hong Kong's future is becoming less uncertain. In addition to this Hong Kong tide, the number of Chinese immigrants from other places such as China and Taiwan has increased at the same time. Among the immigrants who came to Canada between 1981and 1991, Chinese was the most frequently reported ethnic origin at 236,810. Among all immigrants, the Chinese have become the second largest ethnic group in Canada at 425,800, just after those from Britain (Statistics Canada 1994, 22).

While Hong Kong Chinese constituted the leading immigrant group within the Chinese community, China has assumed the lead recently. This is a result of two factors. One is that China has implemented a more open-door policy that allows more freedom of migration. The second factor is that more Chinese from China are more highly educated and affluent than before; therefore, they are qualified to apply for immigration to Canada. This current development in the Chinese immigrant population has not only changed the demographic characteristics of the Chinese community in Canada again, but has also induced a rapid growth of the Chinese population in Canada. In 2001, there were 1,029,400 Chinese (or 3.5 percent of Canada's total population), up from about 300,000 in 1981 (Chui et al. 2005, 27). From 1986 to 1990, there were 74,905 Chinese from Hong Kong, and 42,320 from China. From 1991 to 1996, these two groups were almost equal in number—130,790 and 107,420, respectively. From 1996 to 2001, 184,780 Chinese came from China, while only 54,655 came from Hong Kong. Although the number of Chinese immigrants from Taiwan is also increasing, their share of the Chinese community has always been small (Chui et al. 2005, 26). In Canada, 40 percent of the Chinese population lives in Toronto and 33 percent lives in Vancouver. In 2001, the size of the Chinese community in the Toronto metropolitan area increased 50 percent, and the percentage of the Chinese population as a proportion of Toronto's total population increased from 6 percent to 9 percent (27). In the same year, 409,535 Chinese lived in the Toronto metropolitan area (Statistics Canada 2001a), up from 335,185 in 1996 (Statistics Canada 2002a). Markham also experienced a rapid rise in its Chinese population. In 2001, 62,355 Chinese lived in Markham (Statistics Canada 2001b), up from 43,285 in 1996 (Statistics Canada 2002b). The Chinese population has added a huge piece of ethnic fabric to the already ethnically diverse Canada.

Development of "Chinese" Shopping Malls

These changes in the Chinese population impacted the formation of Chinese communities in suburban areas such as Scarborough, Markham, and

Richmond Hill, and the development of these shopping malls. According to Lai (2003), several Chinese investors started to construct some of these indoor malls and open plazas in the early 1980s, and many non-Asian developers also took this opportunity to develop shopping malls and sell the individual units to Hong Kong and Taiwan investors. Unlike mainstream shopping malls, this type of mall is operated like a condominium corporation, or categorized as a commercial-condominium. The term commercial-condominum means that the shop units are sold to different owners in the manner of tenants buying units in a residential building. Unlike mainstream malls, the owners can decide the types of merchandise sold, the business hours, and the resale of units for profit. Like a residential condominium, the shop owners elect representatives to form a management board, which oversees the overall operation of the mall. The developer of the Pacific Mall claimed that it was the pioneer in this operation in all of North America.

Our study interviewed the developer of the Pacific Mall, who, interestingly, is not Chinese. He said that the units were mainly sold in Hong Kong within two weeks. Very few of them were sold in Toronto. These businesses indicate two points. The size of the Chinese community has reached a critical mass. The flourishing "Chinese" shopping malls are intended to meet the everyday needs of the rapidly increasing number of Chinese residents in those areas. Another point is that some Chinese immigrants gained their entry visas through these business opportunities under the Immigrant Investor Program. One of the veteran retailers in the Pacific Mall said that a sizeable number of investors started their businesses here to fulfill the requirements of the Immigrant Investor Program. Some resold their units to other immigrant applicants after fulfilling their requirements. The same unit might have changed hands many times under this circumstance.

In short, the development of these new Chinese communities in suburban areas is due to a set of internal social, economic, and political factors in the immigrant-receiving country (Canada) and the same set of external factors in immigrant-sending countries (mainly Hong Kong and China). On the one hand, the current Canadian immigration policies are a response to its low birth rate, market and economic needs, and the continuing nondiscriminatory and non-race-based multicultural politics. On the other hand, immigrants from Hong Kong and China seek greater political freedom, a better living environment, and economic opportunities.

The Exterior and Interior and Its Operation: (Re)construction

The architectural design of the mall is a mix of red bricks, steel beams, and glass. The impression that Wallman Clews Bergman, the architect of the mall, wanted to create was that of "a 'fabulous transparent building as different as possible from its surrounding' (Wallman email interview). Rather than a typically internalized shopping mall, the architects had modeled a contemporary and innovative market building with extensive glazing at the exterior walls" (Chen 2005, 95–6). However, the developer of the mall stated, "Yet here is Canada, a mixed [ethnically diverse] country, not China, not Hong Kong. The architectural style should not resemble Chinese [styles] at all. I don't want it to stand out too much. It blends into the neighborhood." Both views are a correct description of the mall. Anyone driving by the intersection of Steeles and Kennedy immediately notices the mall. The glazed structure and its size give a sense of fabulous transparency and distinguish the mall from its surroundings. The lot is huge with nearly a thousand outdoor parking spaces. Yet, aesthetically, it harmonizes with its surroundings, in the same way that the red bricks and the large pieces of glass panels are typical construction materials in Toronto. If the huge sign of "Pacific Mall" were replaced with "Willow Mall," for example, and the vertical signs of "Heritage Town" and "Golden Regency Restaurant" in traditional Chinese with English translations below were also removed, passersby might think that it is a mainstream suburban mall. In other words, it is a typical North American construction with Chinese signs.

The interior design of the mall is a different story. Shoppers can see the exposed roof truss, pipe work, and roof decks that reveal no ethnic characteristics, and its construction is a good representation of shed typology that is characterized by mass production, cost efficiency, and fast construction. When they look at the mall, shoppers, particularly those from Hong Kong, are reminded of some typical Hong Kong malls in Wan Chai or Mongkok, in which shops have very limited floor areas, except for the fact that the Pacific Mall has high ceilings and wider corridors. The mall has about 400 shops with an area under 270,000 square feet and store units with areas varying from 300 to 800 square feet. A Toronto mainstream mall, Yorkdale Mall, on the other hand, has an area of about one million square feet with just over 200 stores (Chen 2005, 95). Yet the grid-like corridors in the Pacific Mall have a North American street layout. Each corridor is given a street name. Those running from north to south are named after some famous streets in Hong Kong like Hollywood Avenue, Queen's Avenue, and Nathan Avenue, for example. Those running from east to west are named in numerical fashion, North American style, such as 218th Street, 188th Street, and so on. These numbers are chosen in order to carefully align with the connotation of "affluence" in Cantonese pronunciation. Most of the shops are located on the first floor. But the center of the mall is not different from that of mainstream malls. A huge space, with a cathedral-like high dome ceiling, is allocated for elevators and a stage that can host different cultural programs and trade fairs.

The north side of the second floor consists of a food court, entertainment centers, shops, a Chinese teahouse, and a medical office. Heritage Town was added to the south side on the second floor in 1999. The developer commissioned artists and clay architects in China to custom-make the decorations that include huge bas-reliefs (dragon pictures). On top of the bas-reliefs, there are elaborate roof tiles showing two dragons vying for a pearl. Other artifacts include 300 very elaborate lanterns, an emperor's chair, dragon panels, a woodwork bridge set at the entrance of the village across a fish pond with rocks and plants, and similar features. The atmosphere resembles a market where people can eat, shop, rest, and wander. Later on, several terracotta soldiers were added to the Town as a permanent display. The mall shows a "Hong Kong flavor with stereotyped Chinese artifacts and images," as a retailer observed.

The Pacific Mall opened in 1996. It has been in business for more than a decade. But the business did not have a good start. According to a man who has been working there since day one, "after the mall opened, the business did not look good. Not all the shops were occupied. The retailers even had time to chat in the hallways; their kids played outside the shops. The management board tried different strategies to boost the business, ranging from sidewalk sales, to rent out booths located in the common area in the middle of the mall. But these did not work all the time."

One of the best strategies was to convert the empty space on the second floor into a Heritage Town in 1999. Heritage Town attracted new mall visitors. Provided with an all-season shopping environment, indoor parking, and popular commodities that kindle nostalgic feelings among many Hong Kong immigrants, the mall has been improving its business. Other strategies that were developed later have also boosted its popularity and business.

After the Pacific Mall added Heritage Town, the board wanted to make it a tourist attraction. It applied for an exemption under which it could keep it open to customers during statutory holidays such as Christmas and New Year. This became an additional "bonus" for many Chinese in Toronto. In the late 1990s, Pacific Mall was still the only mall of that sort and scale in Scarborough and Markham. Many Chinese could mainly shop at the Pacific Mall during statutory holidays. It was common that they said to each other during those holidays, "Go to 'Tong Yin' mall." The literal meaning of "Tong Yin" mall is "the Chinese shopping mall." But in this context, most of the Chinese would associate the Chinese shopping mall with the Pacific Mall.

In addition, the Pacific Mall also promotes its attractions to other Chinese communities, not only in Canada, but also in the United States. It places promotion pamphlets at airports and tourist information centers in major

North American cities. The manager said, "Many Chinese tourists in the United States visit Toronto for two things, the Niagara Falls and the Pacific Mall, as they told me." Visitors to the Pacific Mall can see buses loaded with tourists parked outside the mall. A woman who sold traditional Chinese artifacts in Heritage Town overheard a conversation between her Chinese-American customer and her young son, "If you want to see China, come here." Frequent visitors to the Pacific Mall also find that more and more non-Chinese visit the mall. Anywhere they turn, and at any time, non-Chinese visitors can be seen. Another shop owner who operated a shop on the first floor explained, "In order to keep up the business, we need more than Chinese customers. We should reach out to the non-Chinese customers who are the majority in Toronto." It is fair to conclude that the Pacific Mall has become a shopping icon in both the Chinese community and the larger Toronto community. It has also become one of the tourist hot spots of Toronto.

(Re)interpretation of the Pacific Mall

If architecture is a sign, how do people read this "shed"-like structure? Pacific Mall has been working hard to achieve the current status. Before it succeeded, even before it was constructed, the Mall was an unwelcome sign for many people. Preston and Lo's study (2000) documents well the controversy caused by mall development in the suburban Richmond Hill area. The controversy was sparked by the proposal for an indoor Chinese mall in the Milliken area of Markham, which is the current Pacific Mall (*Toronto Star* 1993). The opposition to the proposal did not just come from the Markham general public, but also from the Chinese community in the area. The opposition was based on the following key points: parking, traffic volume, the architectural style of the proposed replacement to Cullen Country Barns, which had a long history in Markham, and the challenge to deal with many different owners in the condominium-style mall. Later, in 1995, Markham Deputy Mayor Carole Bell stirred up the controversy by saying that the growth of theme malls catering to the Chinese community was driving some Markham residents away (*Toronto Star* 1995a). Her remark was not just aimed at the development of the Pacific Mall, but also toward a total of fifteen retail condominium developments covering 1.7 million square feet that had been either proposed or were in place (*Toronto Star* 1995b). Bell continued to argue, "If everything built right now is catering to the Chinese community, the greater community—the 85 percent—are [*sic*] really not being served." Some called Bell's opposition "racist and discriminatory" (*Toronto Star* 1995a). However, Bell's concern was echoed by both Chinese and non-Chinese people. Some of the opposition from both groups was based on the concern whether Asian-theme malls inhibited the integration of Chinese into the neighborhood (*Toronto Star* 1995c; Preston and Lo 2000). In short, whether the reasons were the cause of traffic issues, a barrier for integration, the cause of conflict on spatial distribution, land use, or conflict between different ethnic groups, the Pacific Mall was not welcome or truly embraced. However, the following paragraphs document the positive development of the mall. The meaning of the mall has changed. Some of these changes can be realized from the mall shoppers' views.

A seventy-five-year-old woman, who immigrated to Toronto from Hong Kong in 1978, avoided the mall due to the traffic, the noise, the crowds, and so on. She said the mall belonged to the young. But she visited it occasionally with her fellow churchgoers if they went to a Chinese supermarket next to the mall to shop for groceries. Once in a while, she enjoyed shopping for jade and crystal at the Pacific Mall. In her opinion, the expansion of the residential areas of Chinese immigrants to the suburbs is a sign of the improvement of their social class. She said with pride, "When I came to Canada years ago, discrimination against the Chinese was very strong. But now, the development of the malls [the Pacific Mall and other Chinese malls in the areas] reflects the successful development of the Chinese-Canadians in the last thirty years, in addition to the recent rapid economic strides in China. We can walk with our head up now." The mall is not her favorite place to visit. It is not "her" mall, but the youngsters'. Yet, it has a symbolic meaning for her ethnic pride. The success of the Pacific Mall and the establishment of other Chinese malls in the area signify a rise in social class for the Chinese. She is proud of the achievement of the Chinese-Canadians.

A conversation with a university student reveals another positive experience of mallgoers. Her experience also raised a very intriguing question on what Chineseness is. This student, who had immigrated to Canada from mainland China, settled in Nova Scotia at the age of four. When she arrived as a young child, the Chinese community in Nova Scotia was very small. The great majority of the people with whom she socialized were white English-speaking Canadians, even though her upbringing had stressed Chinese values. She described herself as very "white-washed." She had moved to Toronto at the age of six with her parents, and she had not had much contact with other Chinese. She had never visited Chinatown until recently. She mainly visited the mainstream malls for everyday shopping. After she had enrolled in high school, she had discovered that her values were quite different from those of other white schoolmates due to her upbringing. Her Asian friends at school had introduced the Pacific Mall to her. Her experience in the mall changed her in many ways. She started to learn how to speak and write Chinese by listening to Chinese pop songs and reading the lyrics. Many of these songs came from Hong Kong. She also fell in love with Japanese animation because it is popular among the Hong Kong Chinese now. She took up martial art lessons until her schoolwork became too demanding. Her new discovery about her ethnic roots was reinforced by more frequent visits to mainland China. The Pacific Mall is her place to discover her "Chineseness," but which type of Chineseness is it? She originally came from mainland China, but the material culture in the Pacific Mall is more like the Hong Kong Chinese culture. Because of the colonial experience, the Hong Kong Chinese culture can be very different from that in mainland China. In a way, this example is related to the concept of ethnic revival. Smith (1981) described "ethnic revival" as an ethnic phenomenon where people rediscover and celebrate their ethnic roots because of the long cycle of the emergence and decline of ethnic feeling. Other scholars also apply this term to describe the phenomenon where immigrants and the well-assimilated descendants of immigrants rediscover and celebrate their ethnic roots (see Jacobson 2006). Yet, this example also reveals the multiple dimensions of Chinese culture.

Other than ethnic pride and ethnic revival, the Pacific Mall can also be seen as a hub for some young Chinese adults who live a transnational life. Basch et al. (1994, 6) defines transnationalism "as the processes by which immigrants forge and sustain multi-stranded social relations that link together their societies of origin and settlement … many immigrants today build social fields that cross geographic, cultural, and political borders." As indicated above, the Pacific Mall adopts a commercial-condominium management style where the individual shop owners can decide which commodities are the hottest to sell at the time. Since the fame of this mall is built upon the theme of "Hong Kong flavors," besides typical Chinese commodities such as tea, jewelries, herbs, Chinese ornaments, and so on, many retailers continue to sell the most recent fads in Hong Kong and Asia. For example, many shops carry the newest models of mobile phones (with Chinese displays and instructions), miniprinters, and cameras that are not yet available in North America. The electricity plugs of some of these devices are of European or British standard. People who buy them need to buy an adapter if they are used in Canada. Many people, especially teenagers or young adults, look for the hottest comics in Hong Kong or Japan.[2] Children are interested in many garments printed with their favorite animation characters, toy versions of animation characters, games, and movies that are not popular or less popular in North America, such as Pokemon and Hello Kitty, but extremely popular in Hong Kong. In other words, shoppers can keep themselves "up-to-date" when shopping at Pacific Mall. That is a shop owner's exact description of some young shoppers at the mall. He further explained, "Many young Chinese adults find the availability of these transnational commodities beneficial."

Since the Canadian economy has not grown as rapidly as that of China, and many Hong Kong firms that do business with China need well-educated fresh graduates with fluency in both English and Chinese (or at least fluency in speaking Chinese), many fresh young graduates want to "take a chance" in their parents' homeland. By staying in contact with the (fad) culture of Hong Kong through the Pacific Mall, they demonstrate that they are not "too foreign" or "too out," when they are in Hong Kong. In short, the Pacific Mall serves as a continuity of an ethnocultural practice.

However, other Chinese interviewed viewed the Pacific Mall differently and less positively. In the opinion of some more recent immigrants from mainland China, it is not a place of their own, and they do not come from the same cultural, social, and dialect backgrounds as many of those who came from Hong Kong and operated the mall. These immigrants did not find enough Mandarin-speaking staff and retailers in the mall, although this has been changing gradually, according to one of the managers of the mall. Due to the lack of language skills and a social network, and credential devaluation, some less financially secure recent immigrants from China found the prices at the Pacific Mall too high. They preferred more affordable shops in mainstream society. Some recent Hong Kong immigrants might not be attracted to the mall as well, although the reasons are different from the above. The Pacific Mall resembles the "A-commodities malls" (A as in the alphabet A), as Hong Kong people called them, in Shenzhen, which is one of the cities in the Special Economic Zone in southern China near the Hong Kong border. The commodities sold in these malls are usually very cheap: counterfeit brand-name garments, handbags, and pirated music and movies labeled as "A-commodities." The construction of the malls there is usually of fast-assembled and factory-like typology. A Hong Kong teenage girl who had arrived in Toronto less than two years back said, "This is, to me, a lower class mall like those located in Shenzhen. This mall [Pacific Mall] is for those who travel back and forth between Hong Kong and Canada."

Pacific Mall: Architecture of Transnationalism and Globalization

Pacific Mall is a "Globurb," using A. King's term (2004, 103–105), and also an "ethnoburg," using Li's term (cited in King 2004). Although the emphasis on these two terms can refer to two different geographical-social spatial concepts, they can overlap each other. "Globurb" is an expansion of the concept of suburban. Contemporary suburban areas have added a new ethnic layer. A. King states, "The new migrations which have largely helped to form them, mostly, but not all, Asian (and later, Asian-American) were, and are, on different degrees, tied to American foreign policy as well as patterns of colonialism and nationalism" (2004, 104). This concept can also be applied to Toronto's situation with ties to British colonialism in Asian regions and North America.

The development of "globurb" is an evidence of globalization, which can be understood as a global capitalist system that facilitates the flow of people, commodities, information, message, images, and ideologies through more liberal trade practices (see Johnston et al. 2002). The Pacific Mall and other Chinese shopping malls in the area and the influx of Chinese immigrants into the area are a result of a series of seemingly unrelated political, economic, and demographic events in the globe (the return of Hong Kong to China, China's economic open-door policies, the decline of the birthrate in Canada, the struggling Canadian economy at the time that needed to attract investments from overseas, non-race-based immigration policies in the 1960s, and so on) that have taken place under a global capitalist system.

Yet, of all the other Chinese mall constructions in the area, the Pacific Mall stands out in terms of the interactive effect of the interior elements (the Heritage Town, the interior layout of the corridors, the naming of the corridors, the innovative commercial-condominium concept, and unique commodities) housed in the shed-like structures that blend in with the surrounding buildings and the community, creating an expected surprise when one enters. All these have created different interpretations depending on the social, cultural, ethnic, political, and economic background of the spectators and users. The (symbolic) meaning of the mall can range from a "barrier," the "integration of the local Chinese community into Canadian society," "nostalgic emotion toward Hong Kong," "ethnic pride and revival," and the "continuity of a transnational living style," to socioeconomic class differences within the Chinese community. If architecture in a city carries multiple voices (R. King 1996), we can also argue that through selling "Chineseness" in a piece of architecture, the Pacific Mall manifests and signifies the multiple voices of the residents and the visitors. The conceptualization of the mall by a non-Chinese developer, the development of Heritage Town, and the cultural practices in the mall reveal the process of (re)construction and (re)interpretation of "Chineseness," be it an essentialist sentiment to many Hong Kong immigrants or stereotypical images to many non-Chinese and Chinese alike, or a Chinese fad culture to some younger consumers. The mall is ethnic; the mall is a Chinese mall.

In conclusion, this is an exercise in theorizing the intertwining relationship between ethnic identity and architecture. In empirical research, this theoretical framework is a powerful tool to explore the meaning of architecture through

the lens of ethnicity; in turn, one can explore the contribution of architecture to the formation and mobilization of ethnic identity. It is a particularly useful research tool for shedding light on ethnic relations in human-built forms, be they in the metropolis, globurbs, ethnoburbs, or even more rural loci, since globalization is a powerful social, cultural, political, and economic force that will further complicate ethnic landscapes all over the world.

Notes

1. Although ethnic identity and cultural identity can be two different topics, in this paper ethnic identity and cultural identity overlap in many ways. Furthermore, this chapter focuses on ethnicity, instead of race, in the theoretical framework. Although scholars (e.g., Woldemikale 2005) recognize that both race and ethnicity are not naturally given, but socially constructed, there are differences. Unlike race, which stresses on biological differences, ethnicity emphasizes the cultural traits of a group through which it expresses a sense of belonging and solidarity. Furthermore, unlike race, which assumes that the behaviors and intelligence of a racial group are closely associated with their genetic inheritance such as physical traits, the behaviors of an ethnic group can be nurtured through cultural practices and therefore can change across time and space. The study of an ethnic group inevitably involves an examination of the cultural components used by a group to mobilize and nurture its identity. That is why ethnic identity and cultural identity are sometimes used together or are interchangeable in order to highlight the cultural uniqueness of a group applied to our theoretical framework.

2. Hong Kong culture has been strongly influenced by the Japanese culture, and even Korean culture. Many Hong Kong Chinese are attracted by Japanese and Korean TV series, soup operas, comics, and fads in these two countries.

References

Barthes, Roland. 1997. The Eiffel Tower. In *Rethinking Architecture: A Reader in Cultural Theory*, ed. Neil Leach, 172–81. New York: Routledge.

Basch, Linda G., Nina Glick Schiller, and Cristina Szanton Blanc. 1994. *Nations Unbound: Transnational Projects, Postcolonial Predicaments, and Deterritorialized Nation-states*. New York: Gordon and Breach.

Beaman, Jean. *Footnotes, American Sociological Association*. December 2002. http://www.asanet.org/footnote/dec02/fn17.html (accessed on May 11, 2006).

Chan, Anthony B. 1983. *Gold Mountain: The Chinese in the New World*. Vancouver: New Star Books.

Chan, Kwok Bun. 1991. *Smoke and Fire: The Chinese in Montreal*. Hong Kong: Chinese University Press.

Chen, Cecillia. 2005. Constructing Pacific Mall. *Journal for the Arts, Sciences, and Technology* 3(1): 89–100.

Chui, Tina, Kelly Tran, and John Flanders. 2005. Canadian Social Trends. *Statistics Canada* Spring, Catalog No. 11–008. Ottawa: Government of Canada.

De Vos, George A. 2006. Introduction: Ethnic Pluralism: Conflict and Accommodation, The Role of Ethnicity in Social History. In *Ethnic Identity: Problems and Prospects for the Twenty-First Century*, ed. Lola Romanucci-Ross, George A. De Vos, and Takeyuki Tsuda, 1–36. 4th edition. New York: Altamira Press.

Geertz, Clifford. 1973. *The Interpretation of Cultures*. New York: Basic Books.

Graves, Michael, Vincent Joseph Scully, Karen Vogel Nichols, Peter Arnell, and Ted Bickford. 1982. *Michael Graves, Buildings and Projects, 1966–1981*. New York: Rizzoli.

Hutchinson, John, and Anthony D. Smith. 1996. Introduction. In *Ethnicity*, ed. John Hutchinson and Anthony D. Smith, 3–14. Oxford: Oxford University Press.

Isaacs, Harold R. 1989. *Idols of the Tribe: Group Identity and Political Change*. London: Harvard University Press.

Jacobson, Matthew Frye. 2006. *Roots Too: White Ethnic Revival in Post-Civil Rights America*. Cambridge, MA: Harvard University Press.

Johnston R. J. et al., eds. 2002. *Geographies of Global Change: Remapping the World*. Oxford, United Kingdom: Blackwell.

King, Anthony D. 2004. *Spaces of Global Cultures: Architecture, Urbanism, Identity*. New York: Routledge.

King, Ross. 1996. *Emancipating Space: Geography, Architecture, and Urban Design*. New York: Guildford.

Koolhaas, Rem, and Bruce Mau. 1995. *S. M. L. XL*. New York: Monacelli.

Lai, David Chuenyan. 2003. From Downtown Slums to Suburban Malls: Chinese Migration and Settlement in Canada. In *The Chinese Diaspora: Space, Place, Mobility, and Identity*, ed. Laurence J. C. Ma and Carolyn Cartier, 311–36. New York: Rowman and Littlefield.

Leach, Neil. 1997. Structuralism. In *Rethinking Architecture: A Reader in Cultural Theory*, ed. Neil Leach, 164–65. New York: Routledge.

Li, Peter. 1998. *Chinese in Canada*. 2nd edition. Toronto: Oxford University Press.

Prazniak, Roxann, and Arif Dirlik. 2001. *Places and Politics in an Age of Globalization*. New York: Rowman and Littlefield.

Preston, Valerie, and Lucia Lo. 2000. "Asian Theme" Malls in Suburban Toronto: Land Use Conflict in Richmond Hill. *Canadian Geographer* 44(2): 182–90.

Qadeer, Mohammad. 1998. Ethnic Malls and Plazas: Chinese Commercial Developments in Scarborough, Ontario. <ceris.metropolis.net/Virtual%20Library/economic/Qadeer1/qadeer1.html> 38k –(accessed on May 21, 2004).

Shepheard, Paul. 1994. *What is Architecture? An Essay on Landscapes, Buildings, and Machines*. London: MIT Press.

Statistics Canada. 1994. *Canada's Changing Immigrant Population*, Catalogue 96–311E. Ottawa: Statistics Canada.

———. 2001a. *2001 Community Profile—Toronto*. Ottawa: Government of Canada.

———. 2001b. *2001 Community Profile—Markham*. Ottawa: Government of Canada.

———. 2002a. *1996 Community Profiles—Toronto*. Ottawa: Government of Canada.

———. 2002b. *1996 Community Profiles—Markham*. Ottawa: Government of Canada.

Smith, A. D. 1981. *The Ethnic Revival in the Modern World*. New York: Cambridge University Press.

Toronto Star. 1993. Mall Project May Have Zoning But Mayor Still Has Concerns. October 21, NY3.

———. 1995a. Bell's Latest Remarks Attacked. November 15, A7.

———. 1995b. Will Bylaws or Market Determine Growth of Chinese Theme Malls? November 9, NY1.

———. 1995c. Bell's Remarks Still Prompt Debate within Community. October 5, NY1.

Woldemikael, Tekle M. 2005. Eritrea's Identity as Cultural Crossroads. In *Race and Nation: Ethnic Systems in the Modern World*, ed. Paul Spickard, 337–55. New York: Routledge.

CHAPTER 7

Citizens or Consumers? British Conservative Political Propaganda toward Women in the Two World Wars*

Matthew Hendley

The question of identity plays a key role in politics. How modern political parties identify their political supporters and foes reveals much about their core beliefs. During times of significant international upheaval, such as the era of globalization in the twentieth century, the sense of identity portrayed by political parties could be especially fluid. An investigation into the construction of identities in political propaganda by the British Conservative Party will illustrate this point and prove to be particularly valuable to this book.

A study of identity could also prove useful in bridging the traditional divide between the political history of the Conservative Party and the history of British women. Women's historians have traditionally shied away from investigating right-wing women. Political historians have dismissed right-wing women as political ciphers. Recent work has begun to survey the interaction of Conservatism and British women (Maguire 1998; Jarvis 2001, 1996). Historians have shown both the flexibility of the Conservatives' approach to female voters and the Conservatives' fluctuating level of political success. One way of understanding these phenomena is to think about how party propaganda conceptualized the identity of the typical female voter. During periods of great political change and political flux, such conceptualizations are of particular importance. As this chapter will show, the Conservative Party conceptualized the British female voter as a citizen at the first general election after the First World War in 1918 and reconceptualized the British female voter as a consumer at the first general election after Germany's defeat in the Second World War in 1945.

The process of globalization and its impact on the place of Britain in the world may well have exacerbated these changes. Britain was a pioneer in the economic globalization process that occurred during the industrial age. The loss of the Thirteen Colonies after the American Revolution coincided with the growth of industrialization in Britain and moved the British economy away from trading solely within the British Empire. After 1815, tariffs were reduced or removed, so that after the 1840s, Britain had the most open economy of any Western country and was succeeding at embracing global trade. As P. J. Cain has written, the British Empire remained a factor in British trade from 1790 to 1914, but "British international economic policy … became infected by the spirit of free trade cosmopolitanism"(Cain 1999, 31). By the 1840s, Britain had embraced free trade to the extent that 60 per cent of its imports came from Europe, the United States, and Latin America, all areas with few or no British colonies (Cain 1999, 32). Free trade was seen as an untouchable dogma that would ensure world peace through greater trade and prosperity for British manufacturers and low food prices for the poor (Howe 1997). In fact, Frank Trentmann has argued that before 1914 free trade was "uniquely central to democratic culture and identity in Britain" (Trentmann 2008, 3).

The British Conservative Party had initially resisted the move toward free trade. As Andrew Gamble has written, "In matters of economic policy, the Conservative party was traditionally the party of the national economy and the party of protection, opposed to the doctrines of free trade and economic liberalism" (Gamble 1980, 29). In the late nineteenth century, the Conservatives officially accepted free trade policy but without much enthusiasm. Britain's open embrace of free trade came into question by 1914. Economists and politicians argued that free trade might have been to Britain's advantage only during the early phase of industrialization when Britain held considerable trade advantages over its rivals. Though officially still a key part of Liberal Party policy, a variety of "progressive" thinkers were beginning to have problems reconciling the individualism inherent in free trade with emerging ideas of collectivist action by the state (Trentmann 1996, 219). Furthermore, by 1914 some industrialists (especially in the metal and engineering trades) believed that free trade no longer made sense because of the threat of competition from mature industrial economies like the United States and Germany (Ramsden 1978, 7). In addition, German and American tariffs blocked full access by British exports to these vital foreign markets. The British Conservative Party continued to question free trade after 1900. In 1903, the Conservative cabinet minister Joseph

Chamberlain argued for tariff reform that would restrict foreign imports into Britain through tariffs and encourage greater trade throughout the Empire. Chamberlain founded the Tariff Reform League, which attempted to convert both the Conservative Party and the British public to his cause. Though unsuccessful, the tariff reform movement represented an entirely new conceptualization of the political economy of Britain and the British Empire (Green 1994). Tariff reform began the process of redefining ideas of identity held by the Conservative Party. It would take moments of major political change to transform the identity-making process even further.

Two key moments of political flux are the First and Second World Wars. The general elections of 1918 and 1945, which followed the end of these conflicts, form key cornerstones for the fortunes of the twentieth-century Conservative Party. The general election of 1918 began a period of interwar Conservative dominance. The election of 1945 marked one of the three worst twentieth-century defeats suffered by the Conservative Party (rivaling poor performances in 1906 and 1997). A fundamentally different notion of the core identity of women voters existed in Conservative propaganda in 1918 and 1945. In the lead-up to the general election of 1918, Conservative propagandists portrayed prospective female voters as newly minted citizens in need of political instruction. In the lead-up to the general election of 1945, Conservative propagandists portrayed prospective female voters as consumers. This transformation of female voters in the Conservative political imagination from citizen to consumer shows both the flexibility of the Conservatives' approach and also helps account for their varying success. This transformation is also a reflection of Britain's changed global position after 1918. Paradoxically, Britain's economic weakness after the First World War meant that Conservative political propagandists felt more confident showing women as consumers. By 1945, British Conservatives could openly express concerns about Britain's economic strength and do so using political images of women. During and after the Second World War, Conservatives no longer feared that their economic arguments would be automatically linked to the unpopular cause of tariff reform. As will be shown in greater detail later, free trade had been undermined by intra-Empire trade after 1918 as Britain's main international economic model. This macroeconomic change would filter down into the way in which the Conservatives constructed the identities of female voters.

The Female Voter as Citizen

The notion of female citizenship poses several theoretical problems. Traditional political theorists like T. H. Marshall argued that citizenship in the British context had three key elements: civil, political, and social (Marshall 1965, 78). To Marshall, the elements of citizenship advanced in progressive stages. The full political rights of citizenship were only conceded to men in 1918 with the concession of universal male suffrage (Marshall 1965, 81, 85–86, 93, 121–22, 188). Feminist critics of Marshall's "model of progressive stages" have pointed to the false assumptions of universality made by such constructions. Citizenship and the assumptions of the "civil body politic" were often modeled after "the image of the male individual" (Canning and Rose 2002, 2–3). As Anne Phillips has noted in her criticism of liberal democracy, "there is no gender-neutral individual, and when liberals try to deal with us only in our capacity as abstract citizens, they are wishing away not only differences of class but what may be even more intransigent differences of sex"(Phillips 1991, 149). The conceptual awareness of gendered understandings of citizenship held by modern political theorists is starting to enter the work of historians.

Gendered constructions of citizenship were a pressing concern for Conservative propagandists in the First World War. Before 1914, many Conservative leaders, including Arthur Balfour and Andrew Bonar Law, had supported limited female enfranchisement, believing that it would benefit their party. The Conservative rank and file tended to be more negative (Phillips 1991, 78; McCrillis 1998, 12–13). Many Conservatives, including Lord Curzon and Lady Bathurst, strongly opposed the entire concept of giving the franchise to women.[1] A final group of Conservatives accepted female enfranchisement grudgingly as a necessary consequence of the electoral reforms brought about by the war.[2] Having conceded the inevitability of enfranchisement, Conservative political propaganda attempted to instruct the newly enfranchised female voters in the "correct" use of their vote. In this way, the Party wished to construct voters in its own image. Both pamphlets issued by the Conservative Party itself as well as the publications of the Primrose League, the largest extraparliamentary political organization allied to the Party, reflected this trend.

Instruction on citizenship took several forms. Some Conservative propagandists assumed that women knew nothing about politics and had to be shown the basics of citizenship. Other propaganda portrayed women voters as having special responsibilities. A closer study of internal memoranda from Conservative organizations at this time reveals plans for wide-ranging instruction in citizenship. Taken as a whole, these Conservative efforts in the First World War reveal a conceptualization of the female voter as an embryonic citizen in need of specific guidance.

One of the first things that become evident when looking at Conservative political propaganda leading up to the general election of 1918 was that it assumed many women knew very little about politics. Conservative estimates calculated that up to six million female voters would be added to the franchise due to electoral reform. In fact, the actual number was closer to nine million (McCrillis 1998, 18). An editorial from the *Primrose League Gazette* in December 1917 noted that "there is likely to be a lamentable ignorance of facts among many of these new voters with regard to their rights, duties and privileges as British citizens" (Editor, *Primrose League Gazette*, hereafter referred to as *PLG,* December 1917, 5). A more charitable interpretation of women conceptualized them as having great potential as future active political citizens. On the eve of the general election of 1918, the Dowager Countess of Jersey (a former president of the Primrose League's Ladies Grand Council) wrote that "many voters, though perfectly capable of forming a just judgment on … [political issues] have not had time or opportunity to study them" (Dowager Countess of Jersey, *PLG,* December 1918, 9). In all of these examples, female voters were conceptualized as lacking skills necessary for citizenship.

Other conceptualizations of female citizens saw them as having special responsibilities. An often repeated idea was that women held the vote as a trust to help others. In March 1918, the *Primrose League Gazette* noted that "the vote means a great trust, a great responsibility" (Editor, *PLG* March 1918, 6). A 1918 Conservative Party pamphlet entitled "To Women Voters" also told women to remember that "the Vote is a great trust given to them. If they fail to use it they fail in their trust" (National Union of Conservative and Unionist Associations, hereafter referred to as NU, no. 1878, Harvester Microfilm collection of the Conservative Party Archives, hereafter referred to as CPA, 1918/53). The ultimate manifestation of this idea came in the pre-Armistice 1918 Conservative Party pamphlet entitled "Trustees for the Silent—A Word to Women." This pamphlet played on Victorian middle class stereotypes of female selflessness and devotion to others. The newly won vote was not to be used "for merely selfish purposes, or even for a class purpose," but as "a great trust … to secure what is best for all the British people." In fact, women were said to be the specific trustees to a large group of people, including those killed in the war (both soldiers and civilians), the women and children of captured lands, those still fighting, and those who were prisoners of war (NU no. 1827, CPA 1918/4). Oddly, all of these people were portrayed as "silent" and in need of the trusteeship of women. It is doubtful that most serving soldiers on the Western Front saw things in quite the same light as they themselves were able to vote through the postal ballot (Turner 1992, 330–32).[3] Regardless of whether the political rhetoric of serving as proxy voters was accurate in reality, this pamphlet introduced a novel idea of female citizenship. The idea of female self-effacement and self-sacrifice on behalf of family was an intrinsic part of the ideology of motherhood and feminine identity in the Victorian and Edwardian periods (Gorham 1982; Ross 1986, 78–80). The novelty of this idea was its application to voting. Women, having gained their own political voice as citizens, were supposed to exercise it only on behalf of others. It is also possible that this conceptualization of selfless female citizenship was fueled by the wartime rise of the Women's Party. This short-lived political creation of the Pankhursts was launched in November 1917. Its platform combined corporatist rhetoric over labor-capital collaboration with a direct appeal to female voters to support their own interests (Pugh 2001, 340–42). Although it failed to make a breakthrough in the 1918 election, the Women's Party seriously unnerved existing organizations of Conservative women such as the Primrose League (*PLG* December 1917, 5; *PLG* February 1918, 4).

Either to combat the ill-proven fears of the Women's Party or to combat supposed ignorance, Conservative organizations during the First World War wanted to take an active role in instructing women voters. In June 1917, while the Representation of the People Bill was still under debate, two local branches of the Primrose League made an unsuccessful attempt to convince the League's Grand Council to begin a campaign to teach "political science" along Conservative lines (General Purposes Committee 1917, 218–220). In March 1918, the Primrose League put forth proposals for speaker's classes for League members and special lectures to help enlighten the new citizenry. The League's past record of large numbers of female members made it well suited for responding to this call. Particularly relevant lectures for women were entitled "The Call to Citizenship and How We Must Answer It," "Women's Part in the New Reform Act," and "Women's Responsibilities for Local Government" (*PLG* March 1918, 5). The Conservative Party followed suit with a number of its own publications. These pamphlets took a similar format. They laid out the specific terms of enfranchisement, delineated the responsibilities of each level of government, and tried to point out the leading issues of the day from a Conservative perspective (CPA 1918/54; CPA 1918/55). Such "political instruction" was clearly intended to do more than provide basic information on citizenship. Women were told that issues like imperial trade and targeted tariffs (known as "safeguarding") were "questions on which most women feel very strongly, and in which woman's influence can do much" (CPA 1918/55). It is doubtful that such concerns loomed large in the calculations of the prewar suffragettes and suffragists, many of whom were Liberal or Labour in their politics. Overall, the tariff issue was not heavily stressed as voters believed tariffs increased the cost of food. Any politician advocating policies to increase food prices faced political suicide in British politics from the mid-nineteenth century onwards. In this way, Britain's free trade economy embraced globalization before many other Western industrial economies as the best way to maintain low consumer prices. Even when free trade was being actively questioned by politicians and economists after 1900, the electoral impact of opposing free trade was overwhelmingly negative. Joseph Chamberlain's efforts toward tariff reform in 1903 had split the Conservative Party and helped contribute to three successive Conservative electoral defeats in 1906, January 1910, and December 1910. One of the most effective Liberal critiques of tariff reform was about its impact on the price of food. The focus on citizenship in Conservative Party propaganda in the lead-up to the 1918 election may well have expressed the understanding among Conservative propagandists not to challenge the free trade status quo. Furthermore, the emphasis on the rhetoric of citizenship (instead of trade) revealed the Conservative feeling that regulating political actions during a time of political upheaval was being seen as more important than regulating economic actions. In this and all First World War publications, Conservative propagandists aimed at the active construction of female voters as political citizens with a definite Conservative point of view.

The Female Voter as Consumer

The Second World War brought with it new ideas of the duties and responsibilities of female citizenship. The construction of the female political identity by the Conservative Party had evolved along with Britain's changed status as a global power. By 1939, women were fully recognized participants in elections, and a small but growing number had been elected to parliament as MPs (Brookes 1967, Parts One and Two). For wartime Conservatives, the challenge of women as citizens was not the presumed lack of basic instruction in politics or fears of mass ignorance. Good citizenship for women in the Second World War was not seen as primarily political. Instead, it revolved around full participation in the war effort while maintaining sexual virtuousness and status as good mothers (Rose 2003, 287).

Perhaps because citizenship was no longer seen in exclusively political terms, the conceptualization of women in Conservative wartime propaganda changed. Equally important, Britain was no longer the global economic power it had been. Furthermore, by 1939, free trade had been undermined. After the First World War, former free traders began to consider "a more active role for the state in protecting consumer interests and towards ideas of trade regulation and coordination" (Trentmann 2008, 4–5). This meant that the Conservatives were no longer fearful of the negative electoral impact of raising economic issues. Thus, it only made sense that as Britain's external position evolved, the construction of political identities would also undergo an important transition. Rather than being presented primarily as citizens, Conservative Party propaganda in the Second World War began to present women as consumers.

The change in political imagery from citizen to consumer is closely linked to the external economic changes Britain had experienced. It is significant that by 1945, Britain's global trading position had eroded considerably. In 1913, "37.2 percent of total British exports were to the Empire and 24.9 percent of British imports came from the Empire" (Fieldhouse 1999, 98). After 1918, these figures increased considerably. Free trade was now seen as threatening, and Britain became more dependent on the Empire for trade. In 1932, at the height of the Great Depression, Britain was forced to abandon free trade with the imposition of wide-ranging tariffs on imports from outside the British Empire, and preferential trade agreements were signed with imperial trading partners. This helped stabilize the British economy although "the proportionate increase in Empire imports to Britain, about 14 percent between 1914 and 1938, was far greater than the increase in British exports to the Empire, about 6 percent" (Fieldhouse 1999, 101). Overall, 1932 was a date of great significance because it ended the confidence the British public and British politicians had previously had in the globalized world of free trade. The Second World War had an even harsher impact as British trade patterns were once again disrupted. All economists and politicians from the major political parties realized by 1945 that Britain faced a very difficult period of postwar economic adjustment. The famous British economist John Maynard Keynes stated in a famous memorandum to the British Cabinet after the 1945 election that Britain faced a "financial Dunkirk" due to the huge net deficit between British exports and imports (Barnett 1995, 41). To help weather this storm, Britain turned to the Empire even further. By 1948 the Empire was providing 45 percent of British imports and receiving 46.1 percent of British exports. All of these transactions could be paid for in pounds sterling, which saved the government precious hard currency (Fieldhouse 1999, 103). In a sense the post-1932 British economy tilted away from the fully global economy and toward its own imperial semiprivate globalized network until the mid-1950s. Worse still, the postwar Labour governments would adopt harsh austerity measures for consumers. Food and clothing would continue to be rationed from 1945 until the mid-1950s (Zweiniger-Bargielowska 2000, 80–102). Even bread, which had never been rationed in the worst moments of the Second World War, was controlled for two years after 1945 (Zweiniger-Bargielowska 1993).

Constructions of female voters as consumers in Conservative propaganda had always existed. If anything, these images often had a defensive tone because Conservatives' dedication to tariff reform put them at a disadvantage. Conservatives had to rebut Liberal and Labour claims that Conservative economic policy would lead to increased food costs, which would hit housewives especially hard (Hendley 2004, 20–21; NU no. 1349, CPA 1910/127; NU no. 1296, CPA 1910/76; NU no. 1261, CPA 1910–44). During the First World War, consumer issues were not generally friendly to the Conservatives. Consumer anger over inflation, profiteering, food quality, and food shortages was intense. Perhaps due to these concerns, Conservative references to women as consumers in First World War political propaganda were quite limited. Only one Conservative pamphlet entitled "Cards and Coupons" issued in 1918 took up opposition to rationing as a potential issue. It argued that wartime regulation was excessive but necessary for victory (CPA 1918/15). The interests of females as consumers also surfaced in a Conservative pamphlet issued shortly after the Bolshevik Revolution, which portrayed Russia as a consumer hell with extremely high inflation that was accompanied by anarchy, godlessness, and moral decay (CPA 1918/21). Overall, such references were relatively rare.

Just as Conservatives in the First World War occasionally conceptualized women voters as consumers, Conservatives in the Second World War expressed fears that women had still not been sufficiently educated as citizens. As victory in the war became ever more certain, political concerns among Conservatives increased. There were fears expressed over both the political clout women voters might hold and their lack of political knowledge. In July 1944, an article by an unnamed male Conservative political organizer noted that women were usually so consumed by practical daily tasks that they did not make enough time for politics. He urged that women make time for politics and become informed. Issues such as national defense and industrial policy would affect women's lives and those of their children (CPA 1944/15). The fear that women were politically unsound and "sentimental" in their attitude to politics had been an issue in the 1920s (Jarvis 1996, 172–93). The interwar Conservative Party had undertaken a large-scale propaganda effort to educate women on the superiority of Conservative ideology (Jarvis 1994; Hendley 1996). Despite Conservative success in interwar elections and despite efforts to keep female Conservatives active in wartime, these doubts became increasingly evident as the election of 1945 approached. A number of election pamphlets aimed directly at women sometimes took a patronizing approach to explaining the political process in simplified terms for a female audience (CPA 1945/4). The tone of these later publications indicates the lack of confidence some Conservatives had in the female vote and the feeling that the efforts to keep the party organization alive in wartime had been insufficient. Nevertheless, for the most part, such fears did not become the centerpiece of Conservative political propaganda. There was no serious effort to revive the campaigns of 1918 to teach the arts of citizenship.

During the Second World War, Conservative political propaganda openly embraced the concept of the female voter as a consumer. This new focus took two main formats. First, the role of women as housewives in dealing with consumer issues was highlighted. Second, as the election approached, Conservative propaganda hammered away at the question of controls and rationing. As previously mentioned, the British economy had been in decline since 1914, was unable to retain an allegiance to free trade, and turned instead to easier markets in the Empire. Consumers also became increasingly subject to controls. With these trends in mind, it made sound political sense for the Conservatives to define women in this way.

Wartime Conservative political propaganda defined British women as consumers first and foremost. One of the most obvious ways in which this was done was through advice for housewives. Women were the main purchasers of the family food and clothing and had to deal with the wartime system of ration cards and wartime controls. Conservative publications like *The Onlooker* gave frequent advice on how to shop effectively in times of shortage. The purchase of nonrationed goods such as potatoes was encouraged, and women were advised not to skimp on children's shoes while increasing the mending of other clothes (*Onlooker* April 1941, 7; May 1941, 7; July 1941, 7; CPA 1941/4, 5, 8). Similar advice showing women's roles as consumers and homemakers included recipe and hospitality advice during a period of wartime shortages (*Onlooker*, January 1942, 7; June 1942, 7; CPA 1941/1, 1942/7). A happier postwar future for housewives' efforts at food preparation was hinted at in discussions of model kitchens of the future (Egerton 1944, 7, CPA 1944/6). The freedom of women to choose as consumers and the need to be aware of left-wing efforts to interfere with the free market through controls and cooperatives were also highlighted (*Onlooker*, January 1944, 7, CPA 1944/5). By the election of 1945, women's role as consumers first and foremost was solidified in Conservative Party propaganda. The main Conservative election pamphlet aimed at women was entitled "Women and the Peace." It was filled with images of women as consumers above all else. A pastiche of images subtitled "What Women Want" was essentially an idealized vision of British middle class existence with a modern house complete with running water, a garden, and a kitchen at the top of the list. The freedom to buy "cheap and varied goods" also featured high (CPA 1945/4). This last reference is interesting. It harkened back to an era of freer trade when the British consumer arguably had the best prices and best choices of goods of any consumer in the Western world. Similarly, a pamphlet entitled "This Controls Question" made a firm distinction between controls necessary for wartime victory and the need for free enterprise to satisfy consumer needs in peacetime. As the pamphlet noted, "As soon as variety begins to matter—as it does in a free country and free world—controls slow down action. They foster lack of enterprise"(CPA 1945/36). Nella Last, a middle-aged housewife who lived in the shipbuilding town of Barrow-in-Furness in Lancashire, kept a diary whose pages reveal the impact of such arguments. Despite her reform-minded sentiments in areas like education, she felt her identity strongly as an autonomous consumer. She wrote in her diary on June 10, 1945:

> Well, I'm voting for Churchill ... I think his policy is the only solid one put forward. I don't like co-ops and combines, I hate controls and if ... they are necessary from the economic point of view, I don't want them so obvious and throat-cramming—and heaven save any Nosey Parkers who intruded into my domestic life with any 'Gestapo' methods.
>
> (Broad and Fleming 1981, 287)

The importance of the presentation of women as consumers in Conservative propaganda in the Second World War cannot be emphasized enough. First, this conceptualization created a "female space" in Conservative propaganda. The presentation of consumption as a particularly female concern and its importance to the war effort helped to highlight female contributions in wartime. The mundane everyday functions of shopping and consuming became actions of utmost national importance. In a war in which ordinary housewives may have felt overlooked compared to wartime heroes, this emphasis was important.

The Conservatives seemed especially eager to end the reliance on wartime controls. This reflected an awareness of the future international challenges that Britain would have. Globalization after 1945 would not initially be to Britain's advantage as it had been during the nineteenth century. In fact, the total amount of British imports from and exports to the British Empire/Commonwealth increased substantially between 1910 and 1950. Faced with increasing global competition, Britain turned away from it and toward the so-called sterling area with which it could trade more easily.[4] In addition, the presentation of female Second World War voters as consumers helped create a precedent for the future. After the Labour victory of 1945 and the intensification of existing controls as well as the imposition of new ones, "the Conservatives favoured a return to individualism and championed the consumer." Consequently, "Conservative propaganda was extremely well placed to exploit the low morale among women and especially housewives during the late 1940s" (Ina Zweiniger-Bargielowska 2000, 207). The politics of consumption would become fertile Conservative territory after 1945, and Conservative propaganda during the war assisted in its creation. The Conservatives would win general election victories in 1951, 1955, and 1959, trumpeting the freedom of British consumers (especially women) to consume as well as the attractions of affluence (Ramsden 1998, 365–67). Ironically, it would take much longer for the British economy to turn back to the global economy, away from the newfound interest in trade with its former imperial possessions. However, it is possible to consider that the Conservative Party, in the long term, was helping to mentally mobilize the British population for leaving the security blanket of intraimperial trade and attempted to reenter an even more globalized marketplace that would lead to even more economic choice and competitive prices.

The meaning of the shift from the Conservative conceptualization of the female voter from embryonic citizen in 1918 to consumer in 1945 is of great significance. It is definite proof that the Conservatives were never static in their political approaches to women. The results of both elections also show that Conservative fortunes varied as much as the types of their appeals. Overall, Conservative conceptualizations of women voters never did full justice to the true reality of British women. However, women were represented in political propaganda in ways that revealed the Conservatives' shrewd political calculations as well as their responses to Britain's changing position in the world. As Britain's seemingly effortless domination of the global economy through free trade waned, new intraimperial trading patterns emerged. With the evolution of Britain's trading arrangements, political identities were also forced to change, and the Conservative Party was adept at making such changes.

Notes

* The author would like to thank the following for their assistance in the writing of this chapter and the preparation of this book: for research and conference funding, I wish to thank SUNY Oneonta's Faculty Research Grant program; the Redfield Fund of SUNY Oneonta's History Department; the Individual Development Awards program of the Joint Labor-Management Committee of the State of New York and the United University Professions and the Social Sciences and Humanities Research Council of Canada. For scholarly advice, I wish to thank my fellow coeditors, Dr. Ho Hon Leung, Dr. Robert Compton, and Dr. Brian Haley; Dr. Ina Zweiniger-Bargielowska for her comments on a conference paper that formed an early effort to think through these issues; Dr. Trevor Lloyd for his sage advice and the Siena College Multidisciplinary Symposium on World War Two.

In addition, I wish to thank librarians at the following libraries—Milne Library, SUNY College at Oneonta; Robarts Library, the University of Toronto; Mills Library, McMaster University; and the Modern Political Papers Room at Oxford University. Finally, I wish to thank my wife Michelle for her continued support and love.

1. Curzon long opposed female suffrage but decided to abstain on the last crucial vote on electoral reform in the House of Lords. He wished to avoid a constitutional crisis with the Commons. On Curzon, see David Gilmour, *Curzon* (London: Macmillan, 1995), 498–99. Lady Bathurst, the proprietress of the right-wing *Morning Post,* was particularly scathing. In particular, see Lady Bathurst's letter to the editor of the *Morning Post,* August 19, 1916, on the inadequacy of women as potential voters and her letter in the *Morning Post,* January 14, 1918, on the unfairness of women becoming voters during the war. See *The Rasp of War: The Letters of H. A. Gwynne to the Countess Bathurst 1914–1918,* ed. Keith Wilson (London: Sidgwick and Jackson, 1988), 5–6.

2. Due to strict residency requirements and the vast numbers of men serving overseas or having moved for munitions work, the existing parliamentary register would have effectively disenfranchised up to 40 percent of existing male voters. However, once reforms were contemplated to correct this problem, it was difficult to deny the long-standing demand for female enfranchisement. See Neal R. McCrillis, *The British Conservative Party in the Age of Universal Suffrage* (Columbus: Ohio University Press, 1998), 10–19.

3. All voters who were on active service in the United Kingdom and the Western Front were entitled to postal votes. During the 1918 general election, 2.7 million postal ballots were issued but only 641,632 postal ballots were cast before the count was closed. Real proxy voting was allowed only to assist the much smaller number of British soldiers serving outside the main theater of war. Many soldiers were in possession of their own political voice but did not bother to vote at all. See John Turner, *British Politics and the Great War: Coalition and Conflict, 1915–1918* (New Haven, CT, and London: Yale University Press, 1992), 330–32.

4. For British imports from the Empire/Commonwealth considered within the pound sterling area (excluding Canada), the overall percentages were 21.3 percent in 1910 and 36 percent in 1950. For British exports and reexports to the Empire/Commonwealth considered within the pound sterling area (excluding Canada), the overall percentages were 26.2 percent in 1910 and 41.5 percent in 1950. See T. O. Lloyd, *Empire, Welfare State, Europe: A History of the United Kingdom, 1906–2001,* 5th edition (Oxford: Oxford University Press, 2002), Table 6, 532.

References

A Woman to Women. 1918. *Important Matters before Parliament and the Women's Vote.* Conservative Party Archive. Oxford University. (hereafter referred to as CPA) 1918/55.

A Word to Women by a Man. 1944. *Onlooker* (July): 7. CPA 1944/15.

Ask Your Wife. 1910. National Union of Conservative and Unionist Associations (hereafter referred to as NU) Pamphlet no. 1349. CPA 1910/127.

Barnett, Correlli. 1995. *The Lost Victory: British Dreams, British Realities, 1945–1950.* London and Basingstoke: Pan Books.

Broad, Richard, and Suzie Fleming, eds. 1981. *Nella Last's War: A Mother's Diary, 1939–1945.* Bristol: Falling Wall.

Brookes, Pamela. 1967. *Women at Westminster: An Account of Women in the British Parliament, 1918–1966.* London: Peter Davies.

Cain, P. J. 1999. Economics and Empire: The Metropolitan Context. In *The Oxford History of the British Empire Volume III—The Nineteenth Century,* ed. Andrew Porter, 31–52. Oxford and New York: Oxford University Press.

Canning, Kathleen, and Sonya O. Rose. 2002. Gender, Citizenship and Subjectivity: Some Historical and Theoretical Considerations. In *Gender, Citizenships and Subjectivities: Gender and History Special Issue,* ed. Kathleen Canning and Sonya O. Rose, 1–17. Oxford: Blackwell.

Cards and Coupons. 1918. CPA 1918/15.

Editor. 1917. The New Elector. *Primrose League Gazette* 25, no. 9 (December): 5.

———. 1918. The New Franchise Act. *Primrose League Gazette* 26, no. 101 (March): 5.

Egerton, Joan. 1944. What's the Kitchen Like? *Onlooker* 7 (August). CPA 1944/6.

Eking out the Rations. 1941. *Onlooker* 7 (May). CPA 1941/5.

Fieldhouse, D. K. 1999. The Metropolitan Economics of Empire. In *The Oxford History of the British Empire Volume IV—The Twentieth Century,* ed. Judith M. Brown and Wm. Roger Louis, 88–113. Oxford and New York: Oxford University Press.

Gamble, Andrew. 1980. Economic Policy. In *Conservative Party Politics,* ed. Zig Layton-Henry, 26–49. London and Basingstoke: Macmillan.

General Purposes Committee. *Report to the Grand Council 7th June 1917.* Oxford University: Bodleian Library. Primrose League Papers. MSS Primrose League 6/1, no. 16. 1914–32. Leaves 218–20.

Gilmour, David. 1995. *Curzon.* London: Macmillan.

Gorham, Deborah. 1982. *The Victorian Girl and the Feminine Ideal.* London and Canberra: Croom Helm.

Green, E. H. H. 1994. *The Crisis of Conservatism: The Politics, Economy and Ideology of the British Conservative Party, 1880–1914.* London and New York: Routledge.

Hendley, Matthew. 1996. Constructing the Citizen: The Primrose League and the Definition of Citizenship in the Age of Mass Democracy in Great Britain, 1918–1928. *Journal of the Canadian Historical Association* (7): 125–51.

———. 2004. Women and the Nation: The Right and Projections of Feminized Political Images in Great Britain, 1900–1918. In *The Culture of Fascism: Visions of the Far Right in Britain,* ed. Julie Gottlieb and Thomas Linehan, 13–26. London and New York: I. B. Tauris.

Home on Leave: Some Ideas for a Snack Supper. 1942. *Onlooker* (January): 7. CPA 1941/1.

How to Beat the Coupon: Some Useful Hints to Mothers. 1941. *Onlooker* (July): 7. CPA 1941/8.

Howe, Anthony. 1997. *Free Trade and Liberal England 1846–1946*. Oxford: Clarendon.

Jarvis, David. 1994. Mrs. Maggs and Betty: The Conservative Appeal to Women Voters in the 1920s. *Twentieth Century British History* 5 (2): 129–52.

———. 1996. The Conservative Party and the Politics of Gender, 1900–1939. In *The Conservatives and British Society, 1880–1980*, ed. Martin Francis and Ina Zweiniger-Bargielowska, 172–93. Cardiff: University of Wales Press.

———. 2001. "Behind Every Great Party": Women and Conservatism in Twentieth Century Britain. In *Women, Privilege and Power: British Politics, 1750 to the Present*, ed. Amanda Vickery, 289–314. Stanford, CA: Stanford University Press.

Jersey, Dowager Countess of. 1918. The Primrose League and the New Electorate. *Primrose League Gazette* 26, no. 110 (December): 9.

Lloyd, T. O. 2002. *Empire, Welfare State, Europe: A History of the United Kingdom, 1906–2001*. 5th ed. Table 6. 532. Oxford: Oxford University Press.

Maguire, G. E. 1998. *Conservative Women: A History of Women and the Conservative Party, 1874–1997*. Basingstoke, United Kingdom: Macmillan.

Marshall, T. H. 1965. Citizenship and Social Class. In *Class, Citizenship and Social Development*, ed. Seymour Martin, 65–122. Garden City, NY: Anchor Books.

McCrillis, Neal R. 1998. *The British Conservative Party in the Age of Universal Suffrage*. Columbus: Ohio University Press.

"Meal Time Substitutes." 1942. *Onlooker* (June): 7. CPA 1942/7.

"Our Letter Box: Should There be a Women's Party?" 1918. *Primrose League Gazette* 26, no. 100 (February): 4.

Phillips, Anne. 1991. *Engendering Democracy*. University Park, PA: Pennsylvania State University Press.

Politics in the Co-op Shop—Women of All Parties are Welcome, But—. 1944. *Onlooker* (January): 7. CPA 1944/5.

Potatoes to the Rescue. 1941. *Onlooker* (April): 7. CPA 1941/4.

Pugh, Martin. 2001. *The Pankhursts*. London: Penguin.

Ramsden, John. 1978. *A History of the Conservative Party Volume Three—The Age of Balfour and Baldwin, 1902–1940*. London and New York: Longman.

———. 1998. *An Appetite for Power: A History of the Conservative Party since 1830*. London: Harper Collins.

Rose, Sonya O. 2003. *Which People's War? National Identity and Citizenship in Britain, 1939–1945*. Oxford and New York: Oxford University Press.

Ross, Ellen.1986. Labour and Love: Rediscovering London's Working Class Mothers, 1870–1918. In *Labour and Love: Women's Experience of Home and Family, 1850–1940*, ed. Jane Lewis, 74–96. Oxford: Basil Blackwell.

The Dear Loaf Lie—An Exposure. 1910. NU Pamphlet no. 1296. CPA 1910/76.

The Vote and What It Means. 1918. *Primrose League Gazette* 26, no. 101 (March): 6.

The Woman and the Canvasser. 1910. NU no. 1261. CPA 1910/44.

The Woman's Vote—A Simple Guide. 1918. CPA 1918/54.

This Controls Question. 1945. CPA 1945/36.

To Women Voters. 1918. NU 1878. CPA 1918/53.

Trentmann, Frank. 1996. The Strange Death of Free Trade: The Erosion of the "Liberal Consensus" in Great Britain, c. 1903–1932. In *Citizenship and Community: Liberals, Radicals and Collective Identities in the British Isles, 1865–1931,* ed. Eugenio F. Biagini, 219–50. Cambridge: Cambridge University Press.

———. 2008. *Free Trade Nation: Commerce, Consumption and Civil Society in Modern Britain.* Oxford: Oxford University Press.

Trustees for the Silent—A Word to Women. 1918. NU no. 1827. CPA 1918/4.

Turner, John. 1992. *British Politics and the Great War: Coalition and Conflict, 1915–1918.* New Haven and London: Yale University Press.

What Bolshevist Socialism Has Done for Russia It Would Like to Do for You. 1918. CPA 1918/21.

Wilson, Keith, ed. 1988. *The Rasp of War: The Letters of H. A. Gwynne to the Countess Bathurst 1914–1918.* London: Sidgwick and Jackson.

Women and the Peace. 1945. CPA 1945/4.

Zweiniger-Bargielowska, Ina. 1993. Bread Rationing in Britain, July 1946–July 1948. *Twentieth Century British History* 4 (1993): 57–85.

———. 2000. *Austerity in Britain: Rationing, Controls and Consumption, 1939–1955.* Oxford and New York: Oxford University Press.

PART III

Boundaries

CHAPTER 8

Capoeira and Globalization

Joshua M. Rosenthal

Introduction

Capoeira, a cultural African expression consisting of martial arts and dance, is set to music. In Brazil, it is generally understood as a mix of a dance and a fight, although in some way, it is simultaneously both and neither.[1] Instantly recognizable as a product of the Black Atlantic, a cousin to the religious practices of Candomble and the music of samba, capoeira's adaptation and survival reflect globalization. For viewers, even the uninitiated with no knowledge of the art, it is a dramatic spectacle, pulsating, physically improbable, menacing, funny, inverted, and uplifting. For those who practice capoeira, it is, to use the words of Robert Farris Thompson, a "flash of the spirit" (Thompson 1984). Capoeira, as a game, is played in a circle composed of other capoeiristas that is called a *roda*. In some styles a capoeirista may join a game in progress by entering the circle to "buy the game," a kind of cutting in where one of the pair in play exits the roda, thereby leaving the new pair to their game. As presently practiced, capoeira is always played to music. The instruments usually include a drumhead tambourine or *pandeiro*, a drum called an *atabaque*, and most importantly, a *berimbau* (a tonal percussive bow) or several berimbaus.

Capoeira varies tremendously depending on the style involved and a range of factors. What is universal is that to begin a game, two capoeiristas enter the roda and begin the *ginga*, a rhythmic, side-to-side back step, though different schools, styles, and varying abilities produce enormous variations in what a ginga looks like. From the ginga, capoeiristas unleash circular kicks that are evaded rather than blocked. From these evasions, more kicks and movements—acrobatic, funky, and ritualized—flow, creating a fluid dialogue between the two capoeiristas. Jokes, quick rejoinders, naked aggression, reminders of old slights, bravado, technical prowess, wit, and memory are expressed in this body play. As a spectacle, there are few sights that equal capoeira. When played by capoeiristas—who possess grace, cunning, and knowledge—the game transcends physical dexterity. The intoxicating charisma of twisted, inverted bodies moving to rhythm and song offers an affirmation of the culture that has endured and even thrived across the Atlantic over the last five centuries. The game varies depending on the rhythm chosen by the musicians, the style favored by those playing, or the balance between aggression and playfulness, but it remains itself, simultaneously a trifling pastime and an art form wherein genius can shine forth. Capoeira defies the dichotomies that characterize Western culture: the oppositional understanding of physical and intellectual pursuits, high and low culture, dance and fight.

The history of capoeira and the debates over this history are grounded in the history of the Black Atlantic and the African diaspora and therefore fit into the rubric of cultural globalization. This essay will consider how Atlantic history, capoeira, and globalization are interrelated. Globalization shaped capoeira as a tradition, and the art form reflects a microcosm of modernity shaped by the ongoing process of contemporary globalization. The practice of capoeira moves people, ideas, and services around the world; with the transit of these people, their ideas, and the culture they represent, the world is changed. In this discussion I am particularly concerned with how global infrastructures facilitate the dissemination of lived memory.

Early Globalization of Capoeira

Where should this discussion begin? Historians often debate when to mark the beginning of a historical era like the Industrial Revolution or globalization. The precise beginning of globalization is fraught with historical debate. For example, in a course on world history, the Pax Mongolica of the thirteenth century might be termed the "first era" of globalization, although the trade networks and ecological exchanges in question were confined to the Old World (Marks 2006). Historians of the Black Atlantic might favor the fifteenth century, with the 1440s as a fair starting point; the first decade that Portuguese traders brought slave cargos to Lisbon (Thornton 1998). Other choices are 1493, the year Columbus returned to Europe with news of his successful Atlantic venture, and 1571, the year Spain established its colony at Manila, connected Mexican silver production to Chinese demand via the Philippines, and created a global commodity network (Marichal 2006). Whatever one's preference, it is beyond dispute that by the sixteenth century, the interacting economic, political, technological, social, and cultural forces of the African and the Lusophone (or Portuguese-speaking)

Atlantic reflected globalization. In this chapter, this dynamic, the playing out of the various interchanges and exchanges across the Atlantic and its generously defined littoral, will be termed "Atlantic globalization." Atlantic globalization reflects the causal factors in the process of early modern globalization. That is to say, Atlantic globalization's environmental, commercial, and cultural exchanges accelerated the pace of worldwide globalization, a process that feeds back into ongoing changes in the Atlantic World.

At some point, long before it was written about or depicted in drawings, capoeira became part of this Atlantic. There is, however, no agreement on when or how it originated in this world. The debate on this point is at the center of how capoeira and its history are understood. According to one view, Africans transported to America from Angola continued to develop the art as an act of defiance, a form of cultural survival, and an expression of resistance (Desch-Obi 2001, 2008). In this perspective, capoeira actually preceded Atlantic globalization. An alternate view of capoeira depicts its genesis as having occured after the disembarkation of enslaved Africans in the Americas (Talmon-Chvaicer 2007). For those who argue in favor of an American genesis, the development of capoeira was a creative act of resistance and defiance.[2]

Those who favor an African origin point out that the insistence on the American origin of capoeira plays into the pan-American racist tendency to deny and underestimate African contributions to New World culture, a tendency especially evident in the way in which the relationship between dance and national culture is understood (Chasteen 2004). This critique views with suspicion the documentary records of slaveholding societies in the Americas, which cannot be relied on for accuracy given the legal and political cultures' investiture in dehumanizing and exploiting African captives. Without disputing the logic or the veracity of this objection, I see the existing historical record as a useful place for considering capoeira's past. The first known references to the game of capoeira under that name appear just before Brazil gained its independence, breaking from Portugal to form the Empire of Brazil (1822–1889). From this point, there are an increasing number of references to capoeira. The most famous are in the works of the German painter Johann Moritz Rugendas, who toured Brazil in the 1820s and whose illustrations, collected in *Viagem Pitoresca através do Brasil*, included a depiction of two Africans in the *jogo de capoeira*. The picture, both a document of what capoeira looked like as it emerged into the historical record and a visual icon, is now extensively reproduced.

Brazil and Capoeira

The site for most of the nineteenth-century references to capoeira was the city of Rio de Janeiro, which was transformed by the political and economic changes of the Independence era. The catalyst for this transformation was Napoleon's invasion of Portugal in 1807. Rather than oppose the powerful French army, the Portuguese royal family and court fled from Lisbon to Brazil. Rio was temporarily turned into the capital of a diminishing yet still global empire. In the following fifteen years, Rio grew in size and in importance. When King João VI returned to Portugal, his heir, Pedro, remained in the Americas, joining the relatively bloodless movement for independence and, in time, was crowned Dom Pedro I, the monarch of the newly declared Empire of Brazil. At the moment of Rugendas' tour and drawings, the new Brazilian government faced a number of challenges. While some were typical for a newly independent state, others were specific to a society where the ruling elite sought to control a population in which the majority were Africans and people of African ancestry, whether enslaved or free. The Brazilian leaders worked to ensure that the radical changes implicit in the break with Portugal were not manifest in a challenge to fundamental social hierarchies.

Customs and traditions like capoeira received greater, and unfriendly, scrutiny from the security apparatus of the new regime even as the practice of capoeira changed. During the Imperial era, the art transformed from a social activity engaged in mainly by Africans to the criminal behavior category. In Imperial Rio, the word "capoeira" described not only the practice of capoeira, but also the people who practiced capoeira, and the gangs, or *maltas*, associated with the art. Thus *capoeiragam* (an anachronism meaning capoeirista, or simply one who does or even is capoeira) were detained simply for who they were, for being members of maltas, gangs that specialized in the art. Arrest records from the period show that capoeiragam came to include not only African bondsmen and freedmen, but also Brazilian-born blacks, free people of color, and members of other ethnic and socioeconomic groups (Talmon-Chvaicer 2002; Holloway 1989; Soares 2001, 1998). In this conflicted and repressed atmosphere, capoeira endured and thrived. Although declared criminal, it gained prominence in public life in Rio as maltas formed alliances with politicians, who valued the capoeiras as street toughs who could intimidate opposition voters. In this context, the changes in capoeira were a response to various factors and a crucial part in the development of a distinct African Brazilian culture (Sweet 2003; Karasch 1987; Kiddy 2005; Matory 2005).

Still, capoeira's imperial changes did not occur in some kind of Brazilian isolation. The commercial and intellectual world of the greater Atlantic firmly linked nineteenth-century Rio to the establishment of the capoeira culture. Rio was a point of disembarkation for slaves from the Congo/Angola region until the middle of the century, which meant that capoeira continued to draw directly on African cultural traditions even after its recorded documentation.

The Empire ended in 1889, a year after the final abolition of slavery. The newly established republic came to be referred to as the "old Republic." Just as its imperial predecessor had struggled to claim the mantle of legitimacy, the republican state that took power worked to establish the basis of its rule. The end of slavery and the loss of the implicit hierarchy of a monarchical society exacerbated the elite's perennial concern over Brazil's population of color. As in the previous regime change, the impulses toward political reform that had helped usher in a new era were subordinated to the need for control. In the eyes of the state, there was an even greater need for social order than in the Imperial era. Tellingly, it was at this point that the modern Brazilian flag adorned with the motto "order and progress" was created.

The Imperial government had repressed capoeira largely through intimidation and harassment. The government of the newly established Republic went further when it formally outlawed the art (Taborn 2000). In the face of legal prohibition and intense repression, the art dwindled in Rio de Janeiro. It survived mainly, though not exclusively, in Salvador da Bahia, a major port city in Brazil's northeast that had long-standing commercial and cultural ties with West Africa. Salvador had been in economic decline for some time but remained one of the Black Atlantic's most important cultural centers as well as a city where international forces shaped local political debates (Graden 2006). Even during this period of repression, some writers touted capoeira as a genuine product of Brazilian culture that was worth supporting. There were also elites who maintained the tradition of studying the art despite its outlaw status, but such attitudes were in the minority.

During this era, the martial qualities of capoeira, which were always disguised by the standard of European combat sports, were further disguised (Assunção 2005; Taylor 2005, 2007; Abreu 1999; Downey 2005, 2002). Tracking these changes is difficult. The open martial display documented by Rugendas was reshaped into something more covert; the blows were more disguised, and the art's secret qualities were enhanced. The rise of the *berimbau* as the irreplaceable instrument of capoeira (the one that guides the action through rhythm) probably occurred in this era. The bond between capoeira and resistance, forged during slavery, was renewed by a repressed urban population under the watch of an increasingly powerful state security apparatus. Though the changes in the art were secretive, they did not take place in Atlantic isolation. There was continued contact between Brazil and Africa, the worship of Orixas—African deities that were also venerated in the Americas—ensuring that the exchanges of the southern Atlantic continued into the twentieth century (Parés 2004; Butler 1998). Whatever capoeira's exact global origins, there was ample opportunity for capoeiristas to place the practice within a broader African cultural world.

When capoeira emerged into the public eye in the 1930s after the fall of the old Republic when the rhetoric of racial democracy was taking hold in Brazil, the pioneers who reinserted capoeira into public life were Mestre (Master) Bimba (Manuel dos Reis Machado 1900–1974) and Mestre Pastinha (Vicente Ferreira Pastinha 1889–1981). A simplified version of the histories of these two towering figures runs as follows. Both men apprenticed under African masters and were accomplished capoeiristas. Bimba, the son of a champion of the Afro-Brazilian art of batuque (a kind of dance with combat implications) opened his Academia de Luta Regional da Bahia, creating what is now commonly, though not universally, called capoeira Regional (Abreu 1999). Though deeply immersed in Brazil's African cultures, he wanted to emphasize that capoeira was a combat form equal to other martial arts. He also created a structured pedagogy and offered instruction to white and middle-class students. The result was a capoeira practice that was lauded by the populist authoritarian President Getulio Vargas as genuinely "Brazilian," and also seemed to reflect the celebration of racial democracy associated with his government and the era.

This quasi-official recognition of Bimba's work led to accusations that he tacitly endorsed the myth that Brazil was, in fact, a racial democracy, thereby facilitating the racist appropriations of the era and the overall whitening of "capoeira." (Lund 2006; Twine 1997). Pastinha, an experienced capoeirista who ran in the intellectual Afrocentric circles of Bahia, mourned the changes he saw taking place in his beloved art.[3] To combat this adulteration he opened an academy where he taught what he deemed traditional capoeira, which he called capoeira Angola.[4] Anecdotally, those who practice capoeira Angola today are more likely to argue that capoeira was developed in Africa. Some Angoleros maintain that their art is fundamentally different from capoeira Regional. In this view, Angola and Regional are not two variants of a single encompassing art, capoeira. Rather they are two different arts—capoeira Angola and capoeira Regional (though in this chapter, I will continue to refer to a single capoeira at various points). The tension between these two points of view runs through the debates about the art's history, practice, and even its meaning.

For all of these different opinions over history and meaning articulated in the divide between Angola and Regional, the innovations of Bimba and Pastinha mark the beginning of capoeira's modern era. In one sense, their pioneering work was informed by the endogenous forces of a modernizing Brazil and by the dialogue between Vargas' government's populist rhetoric of racial democracy and currents of Afro-Brazilian political culture. The idea of racial democracy held that Brazilian society was built on African, Portuguese, and indigenous cultures and that it did not have the same deeply rooted patterns of racism that were evident in the United States. In this view, arts like capoeira were simply Brazilian, a label that in the end aided the ongoing economic and cultural marginalization of the Afro-Brazilian population even as it paid lip service toward recognizing African contributions. While this dynamic is essentially Brazilian, global currents were also in play in this era.

Bimba's opinion that capoeira needed to be reinvented, or perhaps returned to its original incarnation as an effective fighting form, was in part a response to its place within the world of martial arts, particularly the Asian forms that were increasingly popular in Brazil, the home of a large Japanese community and a destination for touring martial artists. The most famous product of that intersection is Brazilian *jiu-jitsu* (see the Gracie Jiu-Jitsu Web site). The full history of this martial art requires its own complex discussion touching on the nature and history of Japanese immigration to Brazil and its cultural ramifications. In most tellings of the stories, the Gracie family studied jiu-jitsu and, by the middle of the twentieth century, had established academies and developed a distinctive approach to the art. They not only tested their skills in open competitions and challenge matches, some met Bimba, but they developed a system of grappling from the ground. As in capoeira, Gracie jiu-jitsu, or Brazilian jiu-jitsu, uses a position of apparent weakness—a fighter often grapples on their back—as a position for offense by placing their opponent in submission holds. Thus, a Japanese martial art was reinvented as another postcolonial inversion of dominant and submissive roles in a moment of conflict.

Moving Beyond Brazil

Brazilian jiu-jitsu and mixed martial arts competitions initially reached public consciousness in the United States with the first Ultimate Fighting Championship (UFC) pay per view television broadcasts in 1993. Members of the Gracie family, who helped organize the first event, were no doubt expecting their own Royce Gracie, a moderately sized man, to win this competition. But in the United States, where sports culture is obsessed with size and brute force, his victory was a revelation. As mixed martial arts spread in the United States, grappling was all the rage. The UFC is now a corporation, brand, and reality television show that has drawn on various mixed martial arts to develop a distinct look and style, one that contains few explicit references to the key role of Brazil in its genesis (Downey 2006). In the collective memory of this aggressively marketed sport, the Brazilian contribution has been diminished.

Martial arts leagues have mushroomed on television. In May 2008, the CBS television network broadcast the first such competition on network television. The role of Brazil and the African invention of inverted attacks, and even the role of the Gracies, have become less important. Many of the celebrated champions of mixed martial arts in the United States, whether in the UFC or rival organizations, are of European ancestry. This stands in marked contrast to boxing, whose popularity is at a historic low in the United States. In boxing, African Americans, Latinos, Latin Americans, and Filipinos hold—with the exception of Eastern Europeans who have won a few very visible heavyweight titles—the majority of titles. The whitening of popular American martial arts is not merely a phenomenon of the previous centuries.

Public memory and countering the tendency to whiten capoeira were on Pastinha's mind when he championed capoeira Angola as a product of African culture. His concern with history is captured in a photo from 1966, where he stands posed with his students, who are wearing jackets and ties, on the steps of the airplane that will take them to the first International Festival de Artes Negras in Dakar, Senegal (Capoeira-Infos). I see this date as the beginning of capoeira's contemporary globalization, and the significance of Pastinha bringing his students to Africa should not be under-estimated. Faced by modern globalization and in defiance of the Brazilian knack for downplaying African cultural traditions by embracing them as American, Pastinha emphasized capoeira's African provenance.

The conscious internationalism of capoeiristas touring to share their art was shaped in part by the development of the commercial aviation industry in the decades following the Second World War. Just as technology and nau-tical knowledge allowed Europeans to sail the world's oceans in the fifteenth century, and railroads linked spaces in continental interiors that produced bulky commodities to the world market, the airplane revolutionized the speed and ease of travel. For capoeiristas, travel came with the art for centu-ries, and in the case of capoeria in Brazil, constant movement shaped the tradition. Capeoira songs celebrate the sea, sailors, and games on the docks. The sea carried capoeira or its predecessors from Africa to the Americas, and the association between capoeira and the littoral remains strong to this day. Air travel did not bring a fundamental change just because it opened up continental interiors. Rail travel and buses had done this long ago. Nestor Capoeira emphasizes the art's reach throughout Brazil beyond the cities of Rio, Bahia, and Recife in the 1960s, a growth that did not rely on air travel (Lopes 1999). But commercial aviation made quick transcontinental travel possible and made it relatively easy to go and return.

By the 1970s, recognized *mestres* were teaching outside Brazil. Nestor Capoiera first performed and taught in Europe in 1971, Jelon Viera settled in New York in 1975, and Mestre Accordeón (Bira Almeida) began teaching in San Francisco shortly thereafter (Capoeira 2002, 2005, and 2006). A factor that may have encouraged the emigration of instructors was the rule of a right-wing military dictatorship in Brazil (1964–1985). This government was the first, though not the most vicious, of the southern cone's Cold War military regimes, an example of how global politics shaped domestic life in Latin America (Rose 2006). No instructor claimed that the repressive atmosphere of Brazilian life led to teaching abroad, but no one appears to have asked these pioneering mestres about this possibility. The explanations that are given for the travel that diffused capoeira focus on pull factors and the viability of earning a living solely by teaching capoeira. The specter of poverty and obscurity was significant for anyone dedicating their life to the art. For all of the lip service paid to capoeira by the Brazilian state, Pastinha died impoverished in Bahia. Bimba, who had left Bahia for Goiânia in part because he hoped to earn a better living, died poor as well (Mestre Itapoan 2006). Nestor Capoeira also points out that wanderlust played a role in spreading capoeira too. He mentions that his own desire for adventure led to foreign travel, and he also describes how Mestre Camisa, who joined the seminal Grupo Senzala and then founded ABADÁ-capoeira, stayed in Rio after a brief visit because he was simply drawn to the city.

At some point in the 1980s, the exodus of teachers combined with cultural forces, fashion, and economics as capoeira reached a critical mass outside Brazil. Audiences across the world became interested in performances, and many people wanted to study the art rather than simply view it. The first countries outside Brazil with settled schools were in Western Europe and the United States. These societies have vast disposable wealth and long-standing interest in practices deemed exotic or culturally authentic. Brazil's sizable middle- and upper-class population was historically disinclined to embrace capoeira because of its associations with the street and blackness, although this has changed somewhat in the last decade. I have observed that people across the socioeconomic and ethnic spectrums embraced the art abroad. Further, the combination of leisure time, disposable income, and the insistence on enduring youth has produced student cohorts in the United States and Western Europe that are older and in control of more discretionary income. This is not a claim that there is more capoeira outside Brazil than in it, or that the art is more popular abroad than at home. This is simply not the case. But the lack of existing prejudice against capoeira as a practice with a criminal past facilitated its international expansion. Abroad, it had no link to a history of marginalization or criminality, and its African roots were just as likely to be celebrated as they were to be denigrated.

The international rise of capoeira begun in the 1970s continues to this day, although even after three decades of international growth, competition for students among instructors remains less outside Brazil. The supply of viable capoeira instructors in Brazil far outruns the demand for their services, at least in terms of their ability to earn a living by teaching. This is not to discount the challenges of teaching capoeira abroad. There are daunting legal and cultural obstacles for instructors hoping to settle permanently outside Brazil. If the challenges of language, culture, the increasingly difficult laws regarding residency, and alien climates are overcome, many potential students interested in paying for lessons can be recruited. Population centers and universities are ripe for settlement by driven and charismatic instructors who want to start an academy. Further, as knowledge of capoeira spreads, the demand for instruction increases. The Web site capoeirista.com lists schools in ninety countries.[5] There are large cities around the globe with no capoeira instructors, but each year such places are becoming fewer and fewer.

The first mestres to establish themselves abroad were not limited to teaching capoeira. Jelon Viera, who settled in New York in 1975, is also the director of Dance Brazil, an internationally known company.[6] Mestre Accordeón, who still teaches in the San Francisco Bay area, wrote a number of books and is one of the most influential teachers in the Anglophone world (Almeida 1999, 1986). He is also one of the guardians of Mestre Bimba's legacy. Both mestres settled in international centers and worked to expand capoeira beyond the roda, broadening the context for capoeira and winning more attention for the art. Urban centers, including New York and the San Francisco Bay Area, not only provide a place for practices such as capoeira, they also depend on such practices to maintain their cosmopolitan identities. They are loci of globalization, places that maintain their status as "world cities" by attracting people, goods, and arts from around the world. Like international cuisine and art movies, capoeira is now a standard part of the repertoire of such cities.

For students, capoeira can prove to be a life-changing experience, even a globalizing one, in addition to being a physical discipline. Studying capoeira brings international contacts and a place within a network that extends into Brazil (or indeed any place with an affiliated academy) or other countries. There is an excitement to the initial arrival in a forbidding foreign city to be greeted by people as brothers because of the common experiences of capoeira. There is also an excitement to being a practitioner of this art form outside Brazil. A synergy exists between the intensely physically demanding pursuit of learning capoeira and the display of that knowledge and ability in a space where it is unusual. Barbara Browning describes the novelty of the experience, "Capoeirista in New York—that was me, too, and I played the part: my friends and I used to stride through the park leonine and muscular, feeling the mechanism of our bodies walking, and the material presence of the sun on our shoulders" (Browning 1995, 1987).

How is that particular physical awareness a reflection of and a part of globalization? My sketching of an answer is grounded in my own experience and my understanding of the relationship between Brazil and the United States—a long-running link that serves as a reminder of the deep roots of contemporary globalization. These two pigmentocracies have parallel, yet distinct, histories. Both were societies ruled by those of European ancestry that grappled with issues of citizenship and the cultural practices of those of African descent (Holston 2007). Brazilians of all ethnicities and classes have acknowledged African contributions to their national culture, but identifying practices as "Brazilian," as opposed to Afro-Brazilian, deemphasized the role of Africans in creating that culture. Historically, there has been less recognition of African contributions to the national culture in the United States than in Brazil. Thus, historical representation resonates differently in the two countries. To say capoeira was Brazilian in the United States, where many see all Brazilians as people of color, is an implicit recognition that Africans had played a part in its creation. What registered as a marginalization of African contributions in Brazil was still a greater acknowledgement of African tradition than is usually the case for U.S. cultural forms. Both views play into the distinct racist patterns and practices of each country.

The divide between capoeira Regional and capoeira Angola complicates the dynamics of this cultural transmission. For some U.S. students, capoeira Regional offers entry into an authentic non-white cultural practice because it is Brazilian. But for some Angoleros in the United States and Brazil, Regional is a creolized art that is based on the negation of African contributions. In emphasizing capoeira Angola's African roots, that it comes from the Dance of the Zebra, some groups move toward a discourse that the art is a direct product of the Atlantic diaspora, almost eliding Brazil's role as capoeira's incubator from the history (a participant's observation). Both schools of thought have found followers, defenders, and advocates outside Brazil. As a result, debates that began in the 1930s over the art's origins and meaning have been taken up with great passion in the United States and Europe.

During the last few years, an international wave of scholarly publications on capoeira's history, in particular the works of T. J. Desch-Obi, Maya Talmon-Chvaicer, Matthias Röhrig Assunção, and Carlos Eugênio Líbano Soares (all cited above), have brought scholarly rigor to the debate over history. Tucked inside these works, sometimes in footnotes, are pointed arguments about capoeira's origins and the work of other scholars. While these studies engage in these debates in a manner appropriate for academic conversation, the arguments often reflect the fundamental division between Regional and Angola. The debate also occurs in more popular venues. The comments section under videos posted to YouTube come from people arguing the origins and purposes of capoeira. Here, globalization has increased the frequency and intensity of disputes over capoeira rather than diminished them. The context for these arguments, both the physical practice and historical understanding, expanded with the art.

Beyond the extension of the preexisting debates, capoeira's dissemination has also affected those who teach the art. On the one hand, the rewards of international teaching and the recognition of capoeira abroad, which are taken seriously in Brazil, have added to the prestige and rewards of instruction. To cite the most notable example, Mestre João Grande, one of Pastinha's most important students and among the most important living capoeiristas in the world, now teaches in New York City. Mindful that Pastinha had lived his final years in poverty, he retired as an instructor in Brazil when he was persuaded to travel to the United States to take up active instruction (personal communication with C. Dan Dawson). In this case, U.S. interest in capoeira added immeasurably to the art by ensuring that a living treasure continued to share his knowledge. In contrast, the possibility of international employment does not ensure a high level of instruction. In settings where capoeira is relatively unknown, people may claim the mestres' status and open academies.

There is no set path to obtaining the formal status of mestre; however, most generally agree that the process takes decades of study, and demands contributions to capoeira as an art, a culture, and a community; physical skill alone is not enough to gain this rank. Most regional groups award cords indicating status and recalling capoeira tradition. The red mestre cord of Grupo Senzala, for example, imitates the scarf given to students by Mestre Bimba upon completion of training. In other words, there are mestres and there *are* mestres. Simply possessing a certain cord does not automatically earn the respect of a community. Without such respect, the proclamation of mestre status rings hollow. In places without a community of practitioners, it is difficult to assess claims relating to status or lineage, always an important point. Where communities exist, one's training and teachers is a matter of public knowledge, but where capoeira is unknown or exotic, few checks on the claims of "would-be" mestres exist. If capoeira is a novelty, who can judge an instructor's ability or understand that there is more to being a mestre than eye-catching movements? When referring to instructors who exaggerate their status after leaving Brazil, people say that they earned their mestres' cords "on the plane." Here globalization contains a threat: second-rate teachers will be free to spread imperfect, thoughtless capoeira.

The threat of second-rate instruction is not merely that the capoeira taught will be poor but also that the thread of the art's history will be broken. There is a tendency to conflate lineage with history and knowledge of history, as if those not taught by famous mestres do not have equal access to the past. The issues of history and historical consciousness are fundamental ones for capoeira. The past is venerated in song, symbols of African defiance such as the *quilombo* of Palmares—an independent state in northeastern Brazil established by escaped slaves that defied Portuguese forces for most of the seventeenth century—are celebrated as fresh points of inspiration, and photos of Pastinha and Bimba decorate many studios. This consciousness is not simply a matter of knowing about historical events and practices. As Greg Downey has discussed extensively, capoeiristas seek to embody the past, to remember and live history through movement. Innovation is admired, but to have *raiz* (roots), to play a game that demonstrates that one is rooted in the past, is better. It is difficult to achieve this sort of mastery without the high level of guidance usually offered by known mestres.

In the United States, the practice of revering the history and memory of African descent dovetails with long-held practices, from black pride to cultural appropriation. Something essential, if conflicted, about capoeira has traveled to the United States more or less intact from Brazil. But as capoeira spreads beyond places with deep links to Atlantic slavery, what will its history mean? Leaving out the rest of the Americas and the parts of Western Europe that also benefited from the slave trade, how will lived history be embodied in Poland, Bogotá, Mexico City, Manila, Maputo, or Russia? There is no answer to that question at present. In a few years, it will be a point to return to for continued examination. My guess is that the manner of capoeira's transmission beyond the parameters of the Atlantic world depends on the method of its transmission. As long as the engine of growth is the teaching done by migrating Brazilian instructors, the central traditions of the art are likely to hold strong.

The alternate possibility stems from capoeira's long history of autodidactism. How long people have been teaching themselves capoeira is a mystery but *Capoeira sem Mestre* (capoeira without a master) was published in 1962, and the practice has continued since then despite the inherent conflict between individual study and the importance of community (Da Costa 1962). After all, Grupo Senzala of Rio de Janeiro, arguably the most important single force in spreading and shaping capoeira Regional after mestre Bimba and now very respectable, were originally autodidacts who began by training by themselves.[7]

This practice could damage capoeira because the dissemination of information about and representations of the art surpass the availability of instruction. Movies and television have been partly responsible for spreading this knowledge but the Internet is now the most important source of readily available information on capoeira. Before the Internet era, knowledge of capoeira outside of Brazil was limited. Now there are an overwhelming number of resources, albeit of varying quality, available to anyone who can go online. How this dynamic particularly affects the unreliable nature of the information about capoeira is hard to assess as the Internet changes with such rapidity (Gleick 2002). When I originally considered this topic a few years ago, stories of people who had trained by imitating clips online seemed like apocryphal tales of ethnographic science fiction. This was before YouTube or social networking sites like MySpace or Facebook became popular. It was also before I had seen a Latin American Internet café where every monitor had a digital camera and streaming video.

In the decreasing but significant parts of the world where access to instruction is difficult, can one learn capoeira from the Web? Movement can be imitated and it is not hard to imagine someone successfully imitating a great deal of the physical aspects of capoeira. But learning this art does not involve a straightforward process of mimesis nor is it an art that is learned individually. The nature of play in the roda, the essential link between the game and music, is a communal affair. Virilio (2000) and Apolito (2005) raise the question of how it is possible to reconcile these realities and practices with the Web, which fluctuates wildly between fostering democratic, egalitarian connections and isolated, passive voyeurism. Can the cultural knowledge needed to become a capoeirista be transmitted in such a fashion? My feeling is that the answer is no; I think personal instruction is necessary. And yet it is not inevitable that globalization, with all of its threats of diluted cultures and information technology, will weaken capoeira culture. In part, this is because globalization has also brought an infrastructure that permits travel to Brazil in a fashion unimaginable only a few decades ago. Instructors and senior students who are not from Brazil can, and do, travel there with great frequency.

Conclusions

Globalization has also been good for capoeira. It has provided a living for many capoeiristas and helped the art gain greater recognition as an important element of cultural life in Brazil. For example, beginning in 2006, the Brazilian Ministry of Culture, working with the Fundação Gregório de Mattos and the sponsorship of the state-owned oil company Petrobras, has worked to support projects to develop capoeira as a constituent part of Brazilian cultural patrimony (Capoeira Viva). The international prestige of the art and its practitioners has helped make such programs possible and desirable in Brazil. The perils of globalization, as articulated on the Internet or the threat of an ahistorical capoeira practice, have yet to materialize. Incorrect and ignorant capoeira is practiced around the globe, but that was probably true in Brazil in earlier eras as well. One could say that the presence of mestres and qualified teachers outside Brazil outweighs other factors. Further, the ease of air travel allows serious practitioners from around the world to travel to Brazil, thus maintaining the art. It is too soon to say that great teachers will not die in obscurity and poverty or that capoeira will remain profoundly unchanged. Globalization, for all its many dangers, has not produced a capoeira that has lost its essence or not enough of it to threaten the capoeira that stirs the heart. Because of travel and video, foreigners who play tepid versions of the games are well aware of where their skills stand in relation to their Brazilian counterparts. Even as the art is on the verge of becoming truly global, the debate over history, meaning, and practice rages on as it has for at least three quarters of a century. If nothing else, the fervor of this debate is a sign of health and vitality in a globalizing world.

Notes

1. I have made every effort to present full and accurate citations in this essay. However, at various points, often involving chronology, I am unable to provide more than generic references. A great deal of my knowledge about capoeira, and to a lesser extent, Brazilian Jiu-Jitsu, has been garnered in continuing conversations with different people and in various settings: class, encounters, workshops, social events, and other venues. Capoeira knowledge is still a product of oral culture and personal contact. There are many mestres, teachers, and thinkers who have shared their time and understanding with me on these matters. For their generosity and patience, I would like to thank Mestre Caxias; Mestres Boneco, Paulão, and Paulinho Sabiá, all of Grupo Capoeira Brasil; Mestre Jelon Vieira of Grupo Capoeira Luanda; Mestre Efraim Silva who teaches in New Haven, CT; Mestre Acordeon; Mestre Itapoan; Mestre Ramos of Grupo Senzala; Mestre Preguiça and Instructor Marola of Omulu Guanabara; and the incomparable scholar, thinker, and talker C. Daniel Dawson. I would also like to thank my cousin Alexander Liss, a student of Taekwondo who was the first to show me footage of mixed martial arts competitions, and Thomas Beal who listened to and supported my ideas for writing about capoeira. There are perhaps hundreds of people I have not mentioned who also shared their understanding of these matters with me. I am only sorry that space prevents me from naming them all. The credit for what is of value in this piece belongs to those named and unnamed here; the responsibility for errors or poor thinking is mine alone. Thanks finally to Amber Douglas for enduring countless conversations about capoeira and more than her share of events over the last dozen years, to Zeke who has a fine esquiva, and to Samara who is more fun than a dozen rodas.

2. An elaboration of this view is that capoeira was created in settlements of fugitive bondsmen, called *quilombos* in Brazil, as a weapon against reenslavement. This story is sometimes discussed and then dismissed as unrealistic, but it is also presented uncritically; see, for example, the beginning of Letícia Vidor de Sousa Reis, *O mundo de pernas para o ar. A Capoeira no Brasil* (São Paulo: Publisher Brasil, 1997). For a more public linkage between quilombos and capoeira's history, see the Web site of the Santa Cruz California chapter of the capoeira group ABADÁ-Capoeira (Associação Brasileira de Apoioe Desenvolvimento da Arte-Capoeira), www.bnbcomp.net/Capoeira/.

3. To name the most famous members of these circles, Pastinha was familiar with Jorge Amado, one of Brazil's most successful and important novelists; Edison Carneiro, a singular force for the serious study of African cultures in Bahia; and Pierre Verger. Among Carneiro's many works is *Capoeira* (Rio de Janeiro: Cadernos de Folclore, 1975). Verger was a French photographer and ethnographer who wrote on and documented life in Africa, in the Caribbean, and across the Americas. He is the author of various works, but the place to begin to consider his work is his photography. A foundation dedicated to his work contains a number of images though it has become strict in allowing access to enlarged versions of these photos, http://www.pierreverger.org/br/index.htm. Before restrictions were imposed, a search for capoeira in the database returned sixty-eight photographs of capoeira. To get a sense of this intellectual current, see Kristin Mann, "Africa in the Reinvention of Nineteenth-Century Afro-Bahian Identity," *Rethinking the African Diaspora. The Making of a Black Atlantic World in the Light of Benin and Brazil*, ed. Kristin Mann and Edna G. Bay (London and Portland, OR: Frank Cass, 2001), 135–54.

4. For Pastinha's views, see his own work *Capoeira Angola,* which, according to WorldCat, can only be found in two library collections in the United States, at the Smithsonian and at Harvard, and an interview with Finnish anthropologists, translated and available, courtesy of the International Capoeira Angola Foundation (FICA), at somaie.capu.vilabol.uol.com.br/entrevistamp. html. See also essays reprinted in a packet sold by Mestre Cobra Mansa's academy, including Kenneth Dossar, "Capoeira Angola: Dancing between Two Worlds," *Afro-Hispanic Review: Publication of the Afro-Hispanic Institute* 11, nos. 1–3 (1992): 9; Kaira Lingo, *The Politics of Race and Power in Capoeira. A Cultural Thermostat or Thermomoter?* (Stanford University: Department of Anthropology Honors Thesis). For more on capoeira Angola, see the writing of C. Daniel Dawson; excerpts from his piece "Capoeira Angola and Mestre João Grande" are at http://www.joaogrande.org/mestre.htm. Also see the liner notes in *Capoeira Angola from Salvador, Brazil* (Washington, DC: Smithsonian/Folkways Recordings, 1996).

5. This figure should be taken as simply descriptive. The list is intended to help those seeking instruction, and the schools listed are self-selecting and self-described; it is not necessarily accurate or comprehensive. The fact that there are 545 schools listed for the United States and only 287 in Brazil implies that there

are more capoeira academies in the United States, but this is not the case. There are many more places to learn capoeira in Brazil, probably more than in the rest of the world combined, but the Web simply does not reflect that fact accurately. See http://www.capoeirista.com/schools.html.

6. By 1977, the Capoeiras of Bahia were mentioned in the cultural calendar of the *New York Times* as a dance company. See *New York Times*, July 22, 1978 (Arts, 10:3). From that point on, there are steady references to the company in the Arts section of that paper.

7. On the capoeira that did survive in Rio during this era, see Antonio Rodrigues and Joseph R. Svinth, "Many Things at Once: An Introduction to Capoeira," *Journal of Combative Sport* (August 2000), though there is little indication that this tradition had a direct link with the founders of Grupo Senzala.

References

Abreu, Frederico J. 1999. *Bimba é bamba, a capoeira no ringue*. Bahia: Instituto Jair Moura.

Almeida, Bira. 1986. *Capoeira: A Brazilian Art Form. History, Philosophy, and Practice*. Berkeley, CA: North Atlantic Books.

———. 1999. *Água de beber, camará. Um bate-papo de Capoeira (Em memória de Mestre Bimba, capoeirista, educador e uma das mais expressivas manifestações do pensamento afro-brasileiro na Bahia)*. Bahia: Empresa Gráfica da Bahia.

Apolito, Paola. 2005. *The Internet and the Madonna. Religious Visionary Experience on the Web*. Translated by Antony Shugar. Chicago: University of Chicago Press.

Assunção, Matthias Röhrig. 2005. *Capoeira: The History of an Afro-Brazilian Martial Art*. New York: Routledge.

Browning, Barbara. 1995. *Samba, Resistance in Motion*. Bloomington and Indianapolis: Indiana University Press.

Butler, Kim D. 1998. *Freedoms Given, Freedoms Won. Afro-Brazilians in Post Abolition São Paulo and Salvador*. New Brunswick, NJ: Rutgers University Press.

Capoeira, Nestor. 2002. *Capoeira: Roots of the Dance-Fight Game*. Berkeley, CA: Blue Snake Books.

———. 2005. *The Little Capoeira Book*. 2nd ed. Berkeley: Blue Snake Books.

———. 2006. *A Street-Smart Song. Capoeira Philosophy and Inner Life*. Berkeley: Blue Snake Books.

Capoeira-Infos. *Histoire: Expansion & Globalisation*. http://www.capoeira-infos.org/histoire/expansion/index.html (accessed in December 2008).

Capoeira Viva. http://www.capoeiraviva.org.br (accessed in December 2008).

Chasteen, John Charles. 2004. National Rhythms, African Roots: The Deep History of Latin American Popular Dance. *Dialogos*, series ed. Lyman Johnson. Albuquerque: University of New Mexico Press.

Costa Lima, Paulo. Apresentação. *Capoeira Viva*. http://www.capoeiraviva.org/br/apre.htm (accessed in December 2008).

Da Costa, Lamartine Pereira. 1962. *Capoeira sem mestre*. Rio de Janeiro: Edições de Ouro.

Desch-Obi, T. J. 2001. Combat and the Crossing of the *Kalunga*. In *Central Africans and Cultural Transformations in the American Diaspora*, ed. Linda M. Heywood, 253–70. New York: Cambridge University Press.

———. 2008. *Fighting for Honor. The History of African Martial Arts Traditions in the Atlantic World*. Columbia: University of South Carolina Press.

Downey, Greg. 2002. Domesticating an Urban Menace: Reforming Capoeira as a Brazilian National Sport. *International Journal of the History of Sport* 19(4): 1–32.

———. 2005. *Learning Capoeira: Lessons in Cunning from an Afro-Brazilian Art*. New York: Oxford University Press.

———. 2006. The Information Economy in No-Holds-Barred Fighting. In *Frontiers of Capital: Ethnographic Reflections on the New Economy*, ed. Melissa Fisher and Greg Downey, 108–32. Durham, NC, and London: Duke University Press.

Gleick, James. 2002. *What Just Happened: A Chronicle from the Information Frontier*. New York: Pantheon.

Gracie, Jiu-Jitsu. *Gracie Jiu-Jitsu Academy*. http://www.gracieacademy.com (accessed in December 2008).

Graden, Dale Torston. 2006. *From Slavery to Freedom in Brazil. Bahia, 1835–1900*. Albuquerque: University of New Mexico Press.

Holloway, Thomas. 1989. "A Healthy Terror": Police Repression of *Capoeiras* in Nineteenth-Century Rio de Janeiro. *Hispanic American Historical Review* 69(4): 637–76.

———. 1993. *Policing Rio de Janeiro: Repression and Resistance in a Nineteenth-Century City*. Stanford, CA: Stanford University Press.

Holston, James. 2007. *Insurgent Citizenship: Disjunctions of Democracy and Modernity in Brazil*. Princeton, NJ: Princeton University Press.

Itapoan, Cesar. 2006. *The Saga of Mestre Bimba*. Trans. Cynthia Mellon. North Arlington, NJ: Capoeira Legados.

Karasch, Mary C. 1987. *Slave Life in Rio de Janeiro, 1808–1850*. Princeton, NJ: Princeton University Press.

Kiddy, Elizabeth W. 2005. *Blacks of the Rosary. Memory and History in Minas Gerais, Brazil*. University Park: Penn State University Press.

Lopes, André Luiz Lacé. 1999. *A volta do Mundo da Capoeira*. Brasil: Coregráfica editora e Gráfica.

Lund, Joshua. 2006. *The Impure Imagination. Toward a Critical Hybridity in Latin American Writing*. Minneapolis: University of Minnesota Press.

Marichal, Carlos. 2006. The Spanish-American Silver Peso Export Commodity and Global Money of the Ancien Regime, 1550–1800. In *From Silver to Cocaine. Latin American Commodity Chains and the Building of the World Economy, 1500–2000*, ed. Steven Topic, Carlos Marichal, and Zephyr Frank, 25–52. Durham, NC: Duke University Press.

Marks, Robert B. 2006. *The Origins of the Modern World: A Global and Ecological Narrative from the Fifteenth to the Twenty-first Century*. 2nd ed. New York: Rowman and Littlefield.

Matory, J. Lorand. 2005. *Black Atlantic Religion: Tradition, Transnationalism, and Matriarchy in the Afro-Brazilian Candomble*. Princeton, NJ: Princeton University Press.

Parés, Luis Nicolau. 2004. The "Nagôization" Process in Bahian Candomblé. In *The Yoruba Diaspora in the Atlantic World*, ed. Toyin Falola and Matt D. Childs, 185–208. Bloomington: Indiana University Press.

Rose, R. S. 2006. *The Unpast: Elite Violence and Social Control in Brazil, 1954–2000*. Athens, Ohio: Ohio University Press.

Soares, Carlos Eugênio Líbano. 1998. *A negredada instituição. Os Capoeiras no Rio de Janeiro*. Rio de Janeiro: Coleçao Biblioteca Carioca.

———. 2001. *A Capoeira escrava. E outras tradições rebeldes no Rio de Janeiro (1808–1850)*. Rio de Janeiro: Editora da Unicamp.

Sweet, James H. 2003. *Recreating Africa: Culture, Kinship, and Religion in the African-Portuguese World, 1441–1700*. Chapel Hill: University of North Carolina Press.

Taborn, Karen. 2000. A Summary of History, Ethnomusicology and Acquired Afrocentric Brazilian Philosophies Research Regarding Capoeira! Raízes do Brazil Capoeira—New York. http://www.capoeiranyc.com/study.html (accessed in December 2008).

Talmon-Chvaicer, Maya. 2002. The Criminalization of Capoeira in Nineteenth-Century Brazil. *Hispanic American Historical Review* 82(3): 525–47.

———. 2007. *The Hidden History of Capoeira: A Collision of Cultures in the Brazilian Battle Dance*. Austin: University of Texas Press.

Taylor, Gerard. 2005 and 2007. *Capoeira. The Jogo de Angola from Luanda to Cyberspace*, volume 1 (Berkeley, CA: North Atlantic Books, 2005) and volume 2 (Berkeley, CA: Blue Snake Books, 2007).

Thompson, Robert Farris. 1984. *Flash of the Spirit: African and Afro-American Art and Philosophy*. New York: Vintage.

Thornton, John. 1998. *Africa and Africans in the Making of the Atlantic World*. 2nd ed. New York: Cambridge.

Twine, France Winddance. 1997. *Racism in a Racial Democracy: The Maintenance of White Supremacy in Brazil*. New Jersey: Rutgers University Press.

Virilio, Paul. 2000. *The Information Bomb*. Translated by Chris Turner. New York: Verso.

CHAPTER 9

Immigration and Indigenization in the Mexican Diaspora in the Southwestern United States

Brian D. Haley

Many observers of globalization have commented on the impact that global processes appear to be having on group identities. The changing loci of capital accumulation and power, the greater global flows of goods, labor, culture, and information, and the new global political and rhetorical conventions accompanying these changes, are having significant repercussions for forms of social organization, including identity. This should come as no surprise, given our current understanding of ethnic, national, and other identities as products of social relationships and not simply of cultural inheritance. The anthropologist Jonathan Friedman, one observer of these matters, has explained how globalization should be expected to affect identity (Friedman 1999a, 1999b, 2000). Friedman has focused on two primary tendencies relating to identity: a hybridization and cosmopolitanization of identity among class and cultural elites, and an indigenization of identity among lower and middle classes. I have engaged briefly with Friedman's ideas on the indigenization of identity (Haley and Wilcoxon 2005) to support his contention that people not considered indigenous by standard definitions are now asserting indigenous identities, and to suggest that their reason for doing so may not be to seek territory and autonomy from a weakened state, as Friedman proposes. Here I wish to expand my engagement with Friedman's ideas on the indigenization of identity by once again taking a look at the Mexican diaspora in the southwestern United States, but widening the discussion this time to address three distinct waves of migration rather than just one. The three waves of migration I will address include one begun under preindustrial Spanish colonialism (1769–1820), the refugee and labor migration of the maturing diversified capitalism in the early twentieth century (1910–1930), and the ongoing late capitalist labor migration (1960s to the present). Most of my data are drawn from California, but are not always unique to that region.

Friedman's model

Friedman proposes that globalization is a dual process. He posits a decline in the centrality or hegemony in the world system, with a weakening of nation-states in the former centers and weakest regions of the periphery.[1] This first process reflects a mobility of capital: the rise of new centers of hegemony where capital is accumulating, and the decline of older centers where capital accumulation is being eclipsed.[2] He also speculates that the cycles of rise and decline may have so shortened in length of time that a continuous state of globalization may be emerging. Friedman's second process of globalization is ethnification. This occurs in response to the decentralization of capital that weakens states, prompting disorder, dislocation, and migration, and the accumulation of capital that gives rise to new or renewed centers. In the new or renewed centers, Friedman sees identity-homogenizing nationalisms and regionalisms growing, and in the declining states, he sees a differentiation of identities and the emergence of cultural politics.

Friedman has focused almost entirely on the declining centers when elaborating the types of identities that appear and the causes for their appearance. In particular, as noted above, he has theorized a growing identity of cosmopolitanism among class and cultural elites, proposing that elites are "very much intertwined with the discourse of globalization" (1999b, 395). They are invested—intellectually, culturally, and financially— in the notion that something evolutionarily new has happened in the world, even as research actually challenges this very assumption. Indeed, Friedman asserts that these elites are "the source of much of the new ideologies of globalization" (2000, 652). Elite cosmopolitans are drawn away from an identity of national homogeneity toward identities of globalized hybridity, multiculturalism, and creolization. They display "an increasing self-consciousness of world position" (2000, 653).

In declining centers of hegemony, Friedman predicts fragmentation of identities, including the rise of indigenous, immigrant, sexual, and other identities, each as a form of "cultural liberation from the perceived homogenizing force of the state" (1999b, 397). As the hegemonic state's influence declines, its ability and desire to promote the nation as synonymous with

the state also diminishes. Globalizing elites who now value multiculturalism push the process along. The once homogeneous nation-state adopts
policies of pluralism or multiculturalism.[3] The conflicts that emerge within
states under these conditions are about group rights and who qualifies for
them. Thus, a politics of difference emerges among the middle and lower
classes, with localized rootedness emerging as a crucial part of a claim to
group rights. Aboriginality or indigeneity provides the most basic way of
claiming local roots, but "lemon nationalisms" (2000, 652)—xenophobic
nationalisms in reaction to high immigration rates—express an alternative
claim of territorial primacy. Indigenization then, according to Friedman,
is not the reemergence of old indigenous groups, but instead is about the
assertion of indigenous identities by "new and strange" groups that are not
indigenous by standard definitions (1999b, 392–393, 408; 2000, 650).
The cultural logic of indigenization, Friedman argues, is that it espouses a
cultural identity related to a territory on which the state is a usurper,
oppressor, and major enemy. He predicts indigenous identities will emerge
when the state is viewed as not representing its people. The purpose of
claiming indigenous identity, Friedman feels, is to gain governmental
autonomy and control over territory.

Friedman acknowledges the complexities, contradictions, and ambiva-
lences of the phenomena about which he is theorizing. He observes, for
example, that although the working-class immigrants have direct firsthand
experience with more than one national culture, they are not drawn to
celebrate this as a cosmopolitan identity as are elites because border crossing
is a dangerous matter for them (1999b, 397). Friedman also questions
whether the end of the nation-state is really at hand, as others have theorized.
He thinks it is more likely that the state is merely separating from the
nation—homogeneity displaced by multiculturalism—as the state's functions
shift from a national to an international focus. As the state becomes associa-
tional rather than national, the nature of its relationship with regional,
immigrant, and indigenous minorities must change, but Friedman does not
tell us how.

Another Logical Opposite for Indigeneity

On this last score, I may be able to offer some ideas. First, following
anthropology's insight that identities thrive only when they are salient to
lived conditions (Barth 1969), we must ask what conditions make
indigenous identities salient. Perry (1996) points out that we associate
indigeneity with the territories of settler nation-states, where the vast majority of the state's population is acknowledged to have come from other

territories. The prime examples of settler nation-states are the United States, Canada, Australia, New Zealand, and South Africa, although there are others as well.[4] Only quite recently has a sustained indigenous political discourse that truly transcends the national arena arisen (Niezen 2003). From a structuralist perspective, one could focus on the logical opposition between indigene and state, as Friedman has, or one could also consider that there is another equally logical contrast present between indigene and settler. Friedman's attention to the state is well-placed, as long as the state and nation are viewed as one. However, historically within some of these settler nation-states, the federal state has not just been an oppressor and enemy, but at times a protector against more dangerous populist, local, or regional forces. With regard to indigenous policy in the United States, more active attention to the protection of indigenous communities began in the 1930s with the Indian Reorganization Act. Even earlier, in 1924, all Native Americans born in the United States were made citizens by an act of Congress. Numerous other policies recognizing specific rights have been enacted since. Indigeneity, then, can activate rights that the state protects. Clearly, in a settler nation-state where most persons are the descendants of settlers or settlers themselves, indigeneity sometimes is wielded against all these people. However, as the shift progresses from homogeneous nation-state to multicultural state, *and* as immigrant labor increases and becomes controversial, indigeneity can have a narrower salience: to differentiate oneself and one's community as members of the state with the strongest claim to citizenship from immigrants and noncitizens. Indigenous identity, then, can be multivalent and, potentially, ambiguous. But with anti-immigrant political agitation running rampant in the United States, indigenous identity's potential salience as a nonimmigrant social category cannot be overlooked.

The following sections explore the usefulness of Friedman's model and my additions to it in reference to three waves of what may be loosely termed the Mexican "diaspora" in the southwestern United States and California more specifically. My use of the phrase "Mexican diaspora" describes people that have or are migrating from what is today the state of Mexico, even though the first wave I shall address arrived before such a state, nationality, or identity existed. I do not mean to imply that the members of these various waves are, or ought to consider themselves, "a people," as that is more appropriately a matter for a scholar to observe than enforce. The first wave consists of those persons who colonized California for the Spanish empire between 1769 and 1820 and their descendant communities. The second wave was much larger, consisting of labor migrants and war refugees arriving between 1910 and 1930 and their descendants, but also conceivably including the smaller number arriving between the U.S.-Mexican War of 1846–1848 and the 1910s, and the few *braceros* (guest workers) from the 1940s to 1964 who managed to stay in the United States. Portions of these first two waves have produced indigenous identity claims in recent decades. The third wave consists of the postbracero labor migrants from the mid-1960s to the present.[5] These migrants are the lightning rod for ongoing and highly visible anti-immigrant political rhetoric and agitation. They are what Friedman (1999b, 397) calls "border-crossers," and are little inclined to assert either indigenous identities or cosmopolitan ones. As this chronology implies, I share the view of many anthropologists and historians (e.g., Wolf 1982; Rosenthal, this volume) that globalization began centuries before the recent popular awareness and scholarly concern with global interdependency emerged. Were we to use the relatively recent self-consciousness of globalization to gauge the existence of global-scale interactions, we would risk overlooking the global political and mercantile concerns that incited the colonization of California on behalf of a European monarchy (Weber 1992). Those concerns were already centuries-old in 1769 (Wolf 1982).

The First Wave

In a recent article, Larry Wilcoxon and I supported Friedman's contention that indigenization concerns identity change rather than a resurgence of standard indigenous groups (Haley and Wilcoxon 2005; Haley 2002).[6] We described how some descendants in Santa Barbara, California (see Figure 9.1), of the soldiers who colonized California for the king of Spain in the late eighteenth to early nineteenth centuries have asserted a local indigenous identity in recent decades, denied their colonial heritage, and gained considerable outside acceptance of these claims locally and regionally with just about everyone except the long-standing local indigenes known as Chumash. We showed that the indigenization of these neo-Chumash is just the latest in a sequence of well-documented identity changes, beginning with the fusion of European-, African-, and American-origin populations into a new population of segmented identities in colonial Mexico, from which the families that colonized California were drawn. We argued that the changes illustrate the process of ethnogenesis—the emergence of new groups and identities through community fission or coalescence—and that they should be considered commonplace, rather than aberrant. We also argued, contra Friedman, that the neo-Chumash did not appear to have the goal of seizing territorial control and governmental autonomy from the state.

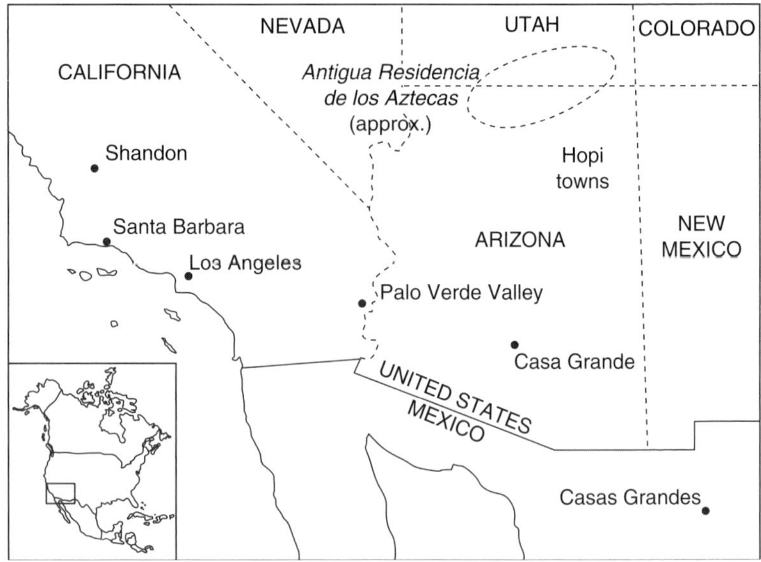

Figure 9.1 Location of places mentioned in the text.

Not only does the neo-Chumash case exemplify Friedman's "new and strange" indigenes, it also occurs in the context he predicts. The neo-Chumash emerged from a marginalized working class that perceived a loss of security and opportunity threatening their social position. Their pre-indigenous position was defined by a Spanish or Californio identity that conformed to the homogeneous state's national myths of European origin, whiteness, and a heroic pioneer past. These identities were never entirely effective and were newly threatened by the 1960s Chicano movement (see next section). Instead of negating this threat by seeking to establish a new nation-state, as Friedman hypothesizes, neo-Chumash indigenous identity claims initially had as goals earning cash land settlement awards, personal transformation and redemption, and gaining access to new economic and political opportunities. The state was their potential ally in this—the enforcer of the policies regarding Indians, archaeology, and the environment that had created new opportunities.

Neo-Chumash indigenization also reinvigorated an old practice of differentiation from the social categories associated with Mexico. The practice began by asserting Californio identity in pointed contrast to Mexican identity during the two-and-a-half decades following Mexican independence (1821–1846), and has continued with an emphasis on distinction from later immigrants for the past century. By asserting local indigenous identity, the neo-Chumash adapt to the Chicano movement's effectiveness in weakening Californio and Spanish identities, yet reject its efforts to erase any remaining social boundary between the first and all subsequent waves of the Mexican diaspora. Identification as local indigenes has the added salience, then, of reemphasizing differentiation from later immigrants just when that category is increasingly attracting negative attention. The advantages of indigenous identity in this context depend upon the continued vitality of the state to enforce existing policies. A homogeneous nation-state would not be conducive to this strategy, but a decline in the authority of a multicultural state would undermine indigenization's value.

The Second Wave

The other case of indigenization of identity that I wish to explore is situated primarily, but a little less precisely, among descendants of the second wave of the Mexican diaspora. This is the interesting assertion that the Southwest is or contains Aztlán, the island in a lake or lagoon to the north or northwest of the Valley of Mexico claimed by Aztec nobles to be the place of Aztec origins and the starting point of their great ancient southward migration. This particular form of indigenization is more widespread across the Southwest than the previous one, yet still is a minority movement among Mexican Americans. Like the neo-Chumash case, it is easily diagnosed as culture-making. But unlike that case, it rejects differentiation from current immigrants in favor of their ideological inclusion. Despite the inclusive ideology, this version of history is subscribed to principally by U.S. citizens descended from persons who arrived in the region between 1848 and 1964, and especially between 1910 and 1930. The large numbers of immigrants at that time provided a critical mass that established a more Mexican-oriented cultural pattern in the Southwest than had been possible previously (McWilliams and Meier 1990, 309–310). Their cultural influences included the *indigenismo* of Mexican revolutionary nationalism.

Indigenismo promotes the idea that Mexican national heritage stems from precolonial indigenous empires that were wrongly stifled in their development by Spanish colonization and later foreign exploitation. Mexican indigenismo originated under the circumstances of declining hegemony and push for autonomy that Friedman outlines. Its origins lie in colonial era "neo-Aztecism" (Keen 1971; Phelan 1960) that began appearing among eighteenth-century Creoles (persons of European ancestry born in the Americas).[7] Although earlier writers, including Torquemada in 1615, began to romanticize and classicize the preconquest Aztecs just as Europeans did with ancient Greece and Rome, Francisco Javier Clavigero's *Historia antigua de México*, first published in 1780–81, established anti-European neo-Aztecism. Clavigero (1731–1787) was a Creole Jesuit priest who had immersed himself in Mexican archives and learned Nahuatl (Ronan 1973). In *Historia antigua*, Clavigero argued against the prejudices of European authors toward Mexico and Mexicans. He asserted that Europe had no exclusive claim to reason, and documented Aztec accomplishments to support his point. To counter the charge that Indians of his time were degenerate and incapable of great accomplishments, he blamed their current demoralization on the effects of Spanish-enforced servitude. He also asserted that a greater fusion of Spanish and native peoples and cultures would have produced a "single and integrated nation," free of the "grave ills" that plagued the caste-based society of the colonies (Clavigero in Phelan 1960, 766). Thus, Clavigero provided three key elements of neo-Aztecism: (1) he framed preconquest Aztec culture as Mexico's classical culture; (2) he asserted that Mexico's Indians would have continued to accomplish great things, had it not been for the Spanish conquest; and (3) he advanced racial amalgamation as a path to nation-building. Subsequent writers supported Mexican independence and nationalism by declaring Aztec heritage as the true heritage of the nation and Spanish heritage as something to be expunged, citing Clavigero as authority. Revolutionaries in 1910 made neo-Aztecism a centerpiece of revolutionary nationalism and an institutional fixture of postrevolutionary Mexico. Thus, when Mexican immigrants entered the U.S. Southwest after independence and especially after the Revolution of 1910, they brought with them the notion that Mexico's heritage—and thus their own—was Aztec rather than Spanish. They brought no collective awareness that Clavigero and other writers had given birth to this idea.

The immigrants of this period came to build railroads, to work in fields or mines, and to flee the Revolution of 1910. Many settled permanently in the United States and formed a growing ethnic minority concentrated in the Southwest. The settlers experienced substantial racial and class oppression before the civil rights era, yet they also formed institutions to protect themselves from prejudice. Gradually after World War II, Mexican Americans made great strides in combating segregation, achieving political representation, and entering the middle class (McWilliams and Meier 1990). The pace of these changes increased during the Chicano movement of the late 1960s and early 1970s. As both a confrontational political strategy and a social movement, the Chicano movement stimulated a new cultural synthesis in ethnic representation, the arts, humanities, and social sciences, and made Chicano identity a viable "third category" alongside Anglo-American and

Mexican identities (Kearney and Nagengast 1989, 6–8). Chicanismo sustained yet transformed neo-Aztecism by turning the Aztlán origin story into a legitimization of the Chicanos' presence in the Southwest. In the poet Alurista's famous vision of the Chicano homeland of Aztlán, Mexican immigrants are merely making their return home by journeying north to the Southwest. The Aztlán story is well-suited to Chicanos' struggle for equality. At the same time, it probably has contributed to conservatives' fear of potential political secession by a Chicano-dominated Southwest (e.g., Sowell 1981). Such fears seem misplaced now, because by the late 1970s, the militancy of the Chicano movement had declined, due largely to the movement's success in penetrating the middle class. The popularity of a Chicano identity has waned in favor of a more integrated Mexican American identity, but the two remain closely intertwined, with Aztlán generally playing a milder symbolic role.

Most anthropologists and historians probably do not accept the idea that the multiethnic Aztec empire had a single point of origin, or even that any of its constituent groups' ethnic identities had a simple linear continuity from the ancient past (e.g., Beekman and Christensen 2003). Recently, linguists have even contested the idea that there was a southward migration of Uto-Aztecan speakers at all (Hill 2001). But for Chicanos or Mexican Americans, the Aztlán question is more personal, even though it provokes a range of views. Although a great many Chicanos and Mexican Americans consider the Aztlán story a metaphorical way of connecting to their current location, for others, questioning its literal truthfulness is considered a sign of disloyalty or racism. While I strongly oppose the prejudice that members of the Mexican diaspora face in the United States, when the need for taking some sort of position on the subject is thrust upon us, a responsible scholar also cannot overlook the research that conflicts with claims of a literal Aztlán in the Southwest. What I seek here is an understanding of an identity process that is sympathetic to the underlying issues that the Aztlán story addresses.

The literalist interpretation is not just a popular perspective on history. Its promoters include college professors, journalists, and community activists. One interesting grassroots quality is that communities in different sectors of the Southwest produce different claims of where Aztlán is located. Usually, it is where that community currently resides—a fine example of establishing local roots through a vision of deep history. One example occurs in the Palo Verde Valley on the lower Colorado River (see Figure 9.1). Under the inspired direction of Alfredo Figueroa, the Palo Verde Chicanos have interpreted the Aztlán story and other evidence as proof that the Palo Verde Valley is La Cuña de Aztlán (the cradle of Aztlán). Figueroa, the son of an immigrant with an impressive personal history of civil rights and labor activism, made investigating the Palo Verde Valley's history as La Cuña de Aztlán his personal project. He has produced a book (Figueroa 2002) and video to convey his beliefs, and helped establish a school where a Southwest Aztlán is included in the curriculum.

Figueroa and others support their arguments with historical maps of the region, ethnolinguistics, ethnographic texts, Mesoamerican codices, local lore, and testimony from what are presumed to be indigenous authorities.[8] Features mentioned by these sources are then associated with points on the landscape and archaeological sites to construct an argument. Aztlán proponents frequently address the conflict between their interpretations and the scholarly mainstream. For example, Figueroa and others note that historians and archaeologists have said that names like Aztec and Montezuma for prominent Southwest archaeological sites originated in nineteenth-century romanticism (Figueroa 2002, 10–12). They point to the presence of the Antigua Residencia de los Aztecas (the ancient residence of the Aztecs) on maps produced between 1804 and 1849 by von Humboldt, Disturnell, and others. The location of the Antigua Residencia de los Aztecas is shown along the Colorado River, northwest of the Hopi villages in Arizona (see Figure 9.1). This is presented as proof that the historians and archaeologists are incorrect; American archaeologists could not be responsible for the names if the United States hadn't even taken the Southwest from Mexico yet.

It is a seductive argument, but ignores scholarship on the introduction of the name of Montezuma—a corruption of Motecuzoma, the name of two Aztec emperors—to the Southwest by the colonizers in the sixteenth and seventeenth centuries. In a fine example of syncretism, Montezuma became conflated with Jesus and the Puebloan culture hero Poseyemu. At times in this culture-making process, Pueblo Indians were known to call all archaeological sites in the region Montezumas. It appears that Mexican leaders, in the years leading up to 1846, promoted Montezuma stories and the idea of an Aztec connection among Pueblos to secure their continued loyalty to Mexico as the threat of U.S. imperialism loomed larger (Bandelier 1892; Parmentier 1979).

In the Southwest, Montezuma stories converged with Clavigero's influence on Alexander von Humboldt, Thomas Jefferson, Albert Gallatin, and other founding figures of the anthropology of the United States and Mexico. Clavigero's *Historia* was first published in English in 1787, in German in 1789, and in the United States in 1804 (Keen 1971; Ronan 1973). Clavigero had declared that the "casas grandes" of the Gila Valley and Chihuahua were products of the Aztec's migration from Aztlán (Fowler 2000, 33). Von Humboldt interpreted this cartographically on his 1804 map of New Spain, placing the first "abode" of the Aztecs northwest of the Hopis (including mention of its "uncertain tradition"), the second at Casa Grande ruins in southern Arizona, and the third at Casas Grandes ruins in northwest Chihuahua (see Figure 9.1). Subsequent mapmakers replicated his markings. For some of the earliest U.S. scholars, Clavigero's association of the large Southwest sites with Aztecs answered the question of whether the Indians living in the region were descendants of the builders of the great ancient sites. The same question was being asked about the origin of earthen mounds in eastern North America (Silverberg 1968). In the latter controversy, Clavigero was used to link an allegedly superior ancient race of Mound Builders to the Toltecs and Aztecs of central Mexico by way of the Southwest (Fowler 2000, 218). If the eastern woodlands and southwestern Indians were a lesser race than the descendants of superior Mound Builders or Aztecs, then they did not deserve the treatment one ought to give to a "civilized" race. Their land, water, and other resources could be justifiably confiscated for more "rational" use by a "higher race" of Euro-Americans, whose "manifest destiny" was invented to help seize this opportunity. It is no accident that the Mound Builder myth grew in popularity when the forced removal of Indians from east of the Mississippi River was being considered. Despite these troubling origins, American anthropology soon revealed the flaws in these racist arguments (Silverberg 1968; Fowler 2000). Nonetheless, belief in the Mound Builders and stories of Montezuma in the Southwest lingered on in Mormonism. All of these influences contributed to the idea of Aztecs in the Southwest. It is clear that Chicanos are not responsible for the invention of all aspects of today's Aztlán story. But it does appear that Friedman's notion of indigenization rather than the reemergence of former indigenes finds more support in this case.

While the history of the idea of the Aztecs in the Southwest recorded by scholars challenges the position of the Aztlán literalists, it also illustrates that to more fully understand a cultural construct, one must understand its salience in context. Thus, to better appreciate the Aztlán story, it is necessary to look at the contexts in which it is salient to the literalists' lived experience. Alfredo Figueroa's book provides many examples, but one will suffice. In its early pages, Figueroa sets the stage for the story of La Cuña de Aztlán by recounting events in his life in the Palo Verde Valley in which he overcame prejudice and discrimination. Figueroa writes, "My political activities in Blythe began in 1956 when that area was known as a 'little Mississippi' because of its racial disorders and the prejudice of its Anglo-dominated powerbrokers toward Chicanos and other minorities." Farther down the page, he notes, "In 1963 I was brutally beaten by a couple of local Anglo police officers at a restaurant in the Mexican section of Blythe.

My case became a cause celebre since I was the first Chicano to sue City Hall and win. Subsequently, I won favorable judgments against a justice of the peace and U.S. Customs for violating my civil rights and those of my brother" (Figueroa 2002, 9). Perhaps the most telling statement of the value and popularity of the Aztlán story comes from the journalistic team of Patrisia Gonzales and Roberto Rodriguez. On their weblog in 1998 under the revealing title, "1847 Map Ends Immigration Debate," Gonzales and Rodriguez addressed the presence of the Antigua Residencia de los Aztecas on the Disturnell treaty map. After reviewing enthusiastic responses from readers, they sum up the map's significance: "To us, it's as if the map has lifted an oppressive aura of 'suspicion' from the psyche of Mexicans/ Central Americans—populations that have been deemed to be illegitimate by some in the U.S. society" (Gonzales and Rodriguez 1998). Both Figueroa's and Gonzales and Rodriguez's respective Aztlán-related statements are claims to the civil rights of full citizens within the multicultural state.

Thus, the indigenization of identity among descendants of the second-wave immigrants revives and transforms earlier ideas that have new meaning and value as anti-immigrant political rhetoric and action swells and threatens the past gains of Mexican Americans. Although anti-immigration speakers complain that the "Aztlanistas" are either a mad fringe or a real national threat, the literalist position is simply all too normal a human reaction to a past experience and threatened resumption of prejudice.[9] Those who disseminate harsh anti-Mexican and anti-immigrant rhetoric fail to see their actions as a factor sustaining Aztlán literalism. The worst of the anti-immigrant rhetoric in the United States today is a thinly disguised resumption of racial prejudice against anyone and everyone who can be linked to the modern territory of Mexico, if not directly, then at least by descent. It is clear that the Aztlán story provides many Chicanos/Mexican Americans with the strength to stand up to this deplorable assault. That said, by adopting this strategy of historical revisionism, the literalists' contribution to the immigration debate has simply been to reverse which party is considered the immigrant who does not belong. Sadly, this means they do not challenge the moral formula that denies rights to immigrants or promote an understanding of the material basis for the occurrence of immigration. But perhaps this supports my point, as it suggests an even closer tie to the existing state than one might understand from just the rhetoric of Aztlán literalism alone. Indeed, one-third of U.S. Immigration Service border guards on the U.S.-Mexican border are Mexican Americans who distinguish themselves and their interests from the current body of immigrants primarily by making a citizen-noncitizen distinction (Heyman 2002).

The Third Wave

Lest I be misconstrued as having argued that indigenization is now rampant among persons whose social histories can be traced to Mexico, I now turn to the type of identity change I have observed and suspect is most common among the post-1960s immigrants. This is the third wave made up of current or recent border crossers who are the main focus of current immigrant loathing. The point here is that not only are Friedman's border crossers not drawn to cosmopolitan identities due to their pragmatic concern with the dangers of border crossing, but that they also don't appear to be drawn to indigenous identities to the same degree as the descendants of earlier immigrants. They are interested in reducing their quite real vulnerability, and achieve this by building roots socially through participating in local affairs and engaging in practices that have preexisting local meaning and value. From 1989 through 1995, I conducted ethnographic research in the small farming town of Shandon, California, located midway between Los Angeles and San Francisco (see Figure 9.1; Haley 2009). Since the 1960s, Shandon's population had changed from nearly all Anglo to one-third Mexican immigrant. The cause of this shift was the California wine boom. Shandon emerged as a wonderful location to grow high quality wine and table grapes, one of many high-value, labor-intensive crops whose expansion in the 1960s triggered the resumption of Mexican immigration to California, Arizona, and Texas (Palerm 1989, 1991; Chavez 1998). Since federal labor programs had been permitted to wither in the 1960s, farm workers who came to California at this time frequently did so without proper immigration papers.

Leo Chavez (1998) draws a contrast between the lives of settler and sojourner immigrants. Settlers gradually become permanent residents of the United States and integrate to a greater degree into local communities, whereas sojourners retain a stronger commitment to family and community in Mexico, where they eventually return. Settlement often emerges as a de facto condition rather than from intentional strategy. Parents' concern for the welfare and happiness of children raised in the United States frequently becomes a major factor in settlement. Perhaps because the difference often emerges gradually, it often goes unnamed or is rendered in quite different terms by local social actors. When a distinction along settler-sojourner lines is made by residents of a host country, it signals that the mobility of people in globalization is received in two different ways depending upon the perceived characteristics of the immigrant group, and that a very real accommodation of one segment of the immigrants is being achieved. A sojourner-settler difference became important for identity formation in

Shandon, because it reproduced a socially important preexisting distinction. For decades previously, Shandon residents had distinguished between farm workers who were considered stable and responsible members of the community and others who were considered unsettled, unreliable, and lower quality people. The former were called "foreman-type" farm workers and the latter were known as "Okie-type" farm workers (Hatch 1979), a category in widespread use in rural California since the 1930s (Gregory 1989). In Shandon, as in other communities, there was no precise relationship between place of origin and the category a farm worker was placed in. The contrasting occupational characteristics and their effect on settlement and community participation provided the basis for distinguishing farm worker types and ethnicizing the lower-status group.

When Mexican workers began coming to Shandon to work in the vineyards, they first fit almost entirely into the low-status category previously considered "Okie." The meaning of Mexican displaced Okie as denoting the lowest status social category. However, the vineyard labor market produced some jobs that were permanent enough to foster family settlement. Workers who could acquire these jobs—tractor driver, irrigator, crew foreman, etc.—made an effort to obtain housing better suited to a family. The larger mass of seasonal workers, because they remained oriented toward home bases in Mexico, sought inexpensive and often temporary housing. There was not a lot available, so group households were the norm and became a public nuisance as they deteriorated under heavy use and inadequate care. Throughout most of the 1980s, tensions grew between Anglos and immigrants as the number of houses occupied by groups of farmworkers increased. Before the end of the decade, however, Anglos had learned that they could get these houses condemned for public health code violations if they complained to the county authorities and a genuine violation was found. Use of this strategy reduced the number of group households, and ethnic tensions eased a bit from the perspectives of both Anglos and Mexican settlers remaining in the town.

Meanwhile, the permanent workers who had obtained single-family houses generally took greater care of their residences and made visible improvements to them. This did not go unnoticed in the community, especially as nonimmigrant workers who commuted to nearby urban areas began to settle in the town and did not always make similar improvements to their homes. These Mexican settlers also placed their children in local schools, which were very small, so children tended to make friends across ethnic lines out of necessity. Because their children were integrated, Anglo and Mexican adults began to know and respect one another as good parents. Mexican parents' participation helped sustain some school and community activities that might not otherwise have gone forward. Lastly, these Mexican parents all took advantage of the amnesty provisions of the 1986 Immigration Reform and Control Act and were in the process of becoming U.S. citizens. They had all decided, then, to be settlers, not sojourners, and they began to voice their common concern for the quality of life in the community in public arenas, through Mexican American intermediaries, if necessary. Anglos perceived this as un-Mexican behavior, since they had come to think of Mexicans as the new Okies. Some Anglos even speculated that the settlers must be from different parts of Mexico unlike the Mexicans they disliked, but that was not the case. Nevertheless, these changes stimulated Anglos to begin differentiating between Mexican sojourners and settlers, usually by distinguishing the former as "migrants" or "Mexicans" and the latter as "Americanized" or "members of the community." The settlers, despite still thinking of themselves as sharing a common Mexican heritage with the sojourners, reinforced their differentiation themselves by asserting a commitment to the local community that the sojourners lacked. In effect, the settlers were making the first step in an identity transition from Mexican to Mexican American, and did so largely socially rather than culturally. The underlying factors behind this improving situation were the combination of stable employment, family housing with modest maintenance and improvements, and children in local schools. These fit the expectations for a preexisting category—stable and respectable members of the community—that had long been valued. Within a few short years, adult settlers obtained U.S. citizenship and asserted an identity as U.S. citizens and local community members in addition to a Mexican one on cultural and ancestral grounds.

Conclusion

The indigenization of identity occurring among some descendants of the first two waves of the Mexican diaspora exemplifies what Jonathan Friedman has described as "new and strange combinations" rather than the reemergence of old indigenes. It also illustrates his predicted lower to middle class contexts for indigenization. The absence of a comparable attraction to indigenization among the current generation of border-crossing labor migrants mirrors their disinterest in a cosmopolitan identity that Friedman has already noted. Presumably, the border crossers have more immediate concerns that can be better addressed through other social strategies. However, the indigenization in the first two cases does not conform to Friedman's claim that the goal of such ethnification is to control territory and gain autonomy from a declining state. Thus, I have appended Friedman's model to accommodate these southwestern cases.

My modification builds upon Friedman's suggestion that the state, in declining centers of hegemony, has changed from a promoter of homogeneity—that is, of the nation—to a protector of multiculturalism. With this shift, indigenous identity is no longer merely opposed to the state, as Friedman proposes, but instead the state is also now a potential ally that can protect civil rights and perhaps provide new opportunities. Asserting indigenous identity becomes a way of differentiating the community from social categories in the same region that do not qualify for state protection, namely, immigrants and noncitizens who are vastly more numerous and socially significant due to the structure of late capitalism. Claiming indigenous identity asserts earlier occupation than the state's in a given territory, with all the moral value that adheres to that argument. But, unlike the settler nation-state, the multicultural state makes such historically deep territorial rootedness an inviolable criterion for citizenship and other potential rights. The cases presented here support the theory that indigenization under the multicultural state is a defense against the xenophobic "lemon nationalisms" (Friedman 2000, 652) of lower and middle classes arising in reaction against increasing international labor migration under late capitalism. The two instances of indigenization given here illustrate two variations within this strategy. Neo-Chumash indigenization announces that the indigenizers are not immigrants, Mexicans, Mexican Americans, or Chicanos. Their claim of primacy is positioned as superior to all others. The Aztlán literalist Chicanos deny they are different from Mexicans and current Mexican immigrants, preferring instead to reverse who occupies the native and immigrant categories. Anglos are refashioned into the real immigrants, taking from them any moral foundation for denying rights to the Mexican diaspora. The logic of indigenous identity claims, therefore, does not merely contrast indigene with state; it also contrasts indigene with immigrant. Given the extreme structural importance of the mobility of labor in late capitalism, this must be considered to be one more reason why the indigenization of identity is occurring during the process of globalization.

Notes

1. Jonathan Friedman's approach has affinities with Eric Wolf's (1982) demonstration of the antiquity and formative effect of mercantilism and capitalism on culture and identity worldwide, David Harvey's (1989) explanation of late capitalism's effect on labor forms and "time-space compression," and Saskia Sassen's (1990) attention to

capital flows and cultural geography. Nevertheless, Friedman mixes these ideas in his own way and makes his own additions to produce a unique model.

2. Friedman suggests that the West, especially Europe, is a declining center, along with the former Soviet Union, and East Asia is the most likely emergent center. Weakened states of the periphery are most apparent in Africa, he argues (Friedman 2000, 648–649).

3. The sort of multicultural state Friedman describes, with repercussions for all ethnic minorities, indigenes, and immigrants, probably begins to come about in the United States during the civil rights era. By now it is at least in its late adolescence, and we are witnessing various reactions to its maturation, not to its original creation.

4. Latin American nation-states may also be placed here, even though many have a much more complex population history, and some, such as Mexico, hold to a national ideology of indigenous origins.

5. The chronology I am using here reflects my data; I am not proposing it as a general chronology for the Mexican diaspora. For example, since I am emphasizing California data, I am not including the earlier wave of colonists who established colonial New Mexico. Although mine may have some broader uses, alternative chronologies are possible, such as Matt Meier's three waves within the twentieth century (McWilliams and Meier 1990, 309–310). *Braceros* were farm workers supplied by Mexico to the United States under a binational guest worker agreement that existed from 1942 to 1964. The end of this program, combined with the passage of the Hart-Cellars Immigration and Nationality Act of 1965, which eliminated race-based national quotas that had hindered Mexican immigration, signals the beginnings of my third wave.

6. A few anthropologists stubbornly resist acknowledging that this is occurring (e.g., Erlandson et al. 1998).

7. Anthony Pagden (1990) treats at length the creole's creative reimagining of the American past, Clavigero's seminal role in that process, and the association of the larger enterprise with the political move toward eventual separation from Spain.

8. Those cited most often are Thomas Banancya and David Monongye, both controversial figures accused by traditional Hopi leaders, Hopi council members, and anthropologists of fabricating Hopi traditions for their own political purposes (Geertz 1994). Coincidently, or perhaps not, they also figured in the transformation of Paul Olivas into Semu Huaute, founder of Chumash Traditionalism and the neo-Chumash movement (Haley and Wilcoxon 1997; Erlandson et al. 1998).

9. Typical extremist rhetoric colors the "Aztlanistas" as "socialist" or "communist" "insurrectionists" who are agitating for a "reconquista" of the U.S. Southwest (e.g., "The Aztlanista Cabal and the Coming Civil War," http://www.rumormill-news.com/cgi-bin/archive.cgi/noframes/read/88093). Media monitors report that on CNN's *Lou Dobbs Tonight* on May 23, 2006, a reporter described the Mexican president Vicente Fox's trip to Utah as a "Mexican military incursion" and "the Vicente Fox Aztlán tour," while an on-screen graphic displayed a map of Aztlán whose source was given as the Council of Conservative Citizens, an

organization observers claim is tied to white supremacists (e.g., http://mediamatters.org/items/20062540011, http://www.huffingtonpost.com/alex-koppelman/cnn-stands-by-lou-dobbs-_b_21617.html). For an informed critique of the misrepresentation of the Aztlán concept by anti-immigrant extremists and the mainstream media alike, see "Reconquista!" (http://dneiwert.blogspot.com/2006/04/reconquista.html).

References

Bandelier, Adolf F. 1892. The "Montezuma" of the Pueblo Indians. *American Anthropologist* 5(4): 319–26.

Barth, Fredrik, ed. 1969. *Ethnic Groups and Boundaries.* Boston: Little, Brown.

Beekman, Christopher S., and Alexander F. Christensen. 2003. Controlling for Doubt and Uncertainty through Multiple Lines of Evidence: A New Look at the Mesoamerican Nahua Migrations. *Journal of Archaeological Method and Theory* 10(2): 111–64.

Chavez, Leo R. 1998. *Shadowed Lives.* 2nd edition. Belmont, CA: Wadsworth/Thomson Learning.

Erlandson, Jon McVey, Chester King, Lillian Robles, Eugene E. Ruyle, Diana Drake Wilson, Robert Winthrop, Chris Wood, Brian D. Haley, and Larry R. Wilcoxon. 1998. CA Forum on Anthropology in Public. The Making of Chumash Tradition: Replies to Haley and Wilcoxon. *Current Anthropology* 39(4): 477–510.

Figueroa, Alfredo Acosta. 2002. *Ancient Footprints of the Colorado River.* National City, CA: Aztec Printing Co.

Fowler, Don D. 2000. *A Laboratory for Anthropology.* Albuquerque: University of New Mexico Press.

Friedman, Jonathan. 1999a. The Hybridization of Roots and the Abhorrence of the Bush. In *Spaces of Culture: City, Nation, World,* ed. Michael Featherstone and Scott Lash, 230–56. London: Sage.

———. 1999b. Indigenous Struggles and the Discreet Charm of the Bourgeoisie. *Journal of World-Systems Research* 5(2): 391–411.

———. 2000. Globalization, Class and Culture in Global Systems. *Journal of World-Systems Research* 6(3): 636–56.

Geertz, Armin. 1994. *The Invention of Hopi Prophecy.* Berkeley: University of California Press.

Gonzales, Patrisia, and Roberto Rodriguez. 1998. Column of the Americas: 1847 Map Ends Immigration Debate. September 25, 1998. Universal Press Syndicate. http://www.voznuestra.com/Americas/_1998/_September/25 (accessed on August 30, 2007).

Gregory, James N. 1989. *American Exodus: The Dust Bowl Migration and Okie Culture in California.* New York: Oxford University Press.

Haley, Brian D. 2002. Going Deeper: Chumash Identity, Scholars, and Spaceports in Radiç and Elsewhere. *Acta Americana* 10(1): 113–23.

———. 2009. *Reimagining the Immigrant: The Accommodation of Mexican Immigrants in Rural America.* New York: Palgrave Macmillan.

Haley, Brian D., and Larry R. Wilcoxon. 1997. Anthropology and the Making of Chumash Tradition. *Current Anthropology* 38(5): 761–94.

———. 2005. How Spaniards Became Chumash and Other Tales of Ethnogenesis. *American Anthropologist* 107(3): 432–45.

Harvey, David. 1989. *The Condition of Post-Modernity.* Oxford: Blackwell.

Hatch, Elvin. 1979. *Biography of a Small Town.* New York: Columbia University Press.

Heyman, Josiah McC. 2002. U.S. Immigration Officers of Mexican Ancestry as Mexican Americans, Citizens, and Immigration Police. *Current Anthropology* 43(3): 479–507.

Hill, Jane H. 2001. Proto-Uto-Aztecan: A Community of Cultivators in Central Mexico? *American Anthropologist* 103(4): 913–34.

Kearney, Michael, and Carole Nagengast. 1989. Anthropological Perspectives on Transnational Communities in Rural California. In *Working Group on Farm Labor and Rural Poverty Working Paper* 3, 1–42. Davis: California Institute for Rural Studies.

Keen, Benjamin. 1971. *The Aztec Image in Western Thought.* New Brunswick, NJ: Rutgers University Press.

McWilliams, Carey, with Matt S. Meier. 1990. *North from Mexico: The Spanish-Speaking People of the United States.* New edition. New York: Praeger.

Niezen, Ronald. 2003. *The Origins of Indigenism.* Berkeley: University of California Press.

Pagden, Anthony. 1990. *Spanish Imperialism and the Political Imagination.* New Haven, CT: Yale University Press.

Palerm, Juan-Vicente. 1989. Latino Settlements in California. In *The Challenge: Latinos in a Changing California,* 125–71. Riverside: University of California Consortium on Mexico and the United States.

———. 1991. Farm Labor Needs and Farm Workers in California 1970 to 1989. In *California Agricultural Studies* 91–2. Sacramento: California Employment Development Department, Labor Market Information Division.

Parmentier, Richard J. 1979. The Mythological Triangle: Poseyemu, Montezuma, and Jesus in the Pueblos. In *Handbook of North American Indians, Volume 9: Southwest,* ed. Alfonso Ortiz, series ed. William Sturtevant, 609–24. Washington, DC: Smithsonian Institution.

Perry, Richard J. 1996. *From Time Immemorial: Indigenous Peoples and State Systems.* Austin: University of Texas Press.

Phelan, John Leddy. 1960. Neo-Aztecism in the Eighteenth Century and the Genesis of Mexican Nationalism. In *Culture in History: Essays in Honor of Paul Radin,* ed. Stanley Diamond, 760–70. New York: Columbia University Press.

Ronan, Charles E., Society of Jesus. 1973. Francisco Javier Clavigero, 1731–1787. In *Handbook of Middle American Indians,* volume 13, part 2, ed. Howard F. Cline, series ed. Robert Wauchope 276–97. Austin: University of Texas Press.

Sassen, Saskia. 1990. *The Global City.* Princeton, NJ: Princeton University Press.
Silverberg, Robert. 1968. *Mound Builders of Ancient America.* Greenwich: New York Graphic Society.
Sowell, Thomas. 1981. *Ethnic America: A History.* New York: Basic Books.
Weber, David J. 1992. *The Spanish Frontier in North America.* New Haven, CT: Yale University Press.
Wolf, Eric. 1982. *Europe and the People without History.* Berkeley: University of California Press.

CHAPTER 10

Construction, Deconstruction, and Reconstruction of State Legitimacy in South Africa and Japan

Robert W. Compton, Jr.

Cape Town to Tokyo: Questions of National Identity

Recently on AM Radio 702 from Cape Town, the host of the show *Cape Talk* noted how little South Africans really know about Africa, and for that matter, about each other within the country. Despite the unprecedented level of globalization realized in the twentieth century, the depiction of the world as increasingly unified and integrated fails to account for the increased degree of emerging xenophobia and insularity. Nationalism requires the psychological labeling of other societies and cultures as "foreign" in order to define its own collective identity. Contrary to the perceptions and cognizance of average national citizens, national identity and nationalism emerge from purposive state action rather than from the seemingly unrelated actions of individuals. Created identities and constructed nationalism provide the state with a mechanism for maintaining legitimacy through the control and channeling of citizens' thought processes about their society and government. In the process of constructing national identity, contradictions and the falsification of history become integral components of the creation and maintenance of nationalism. This chapter explores the creation, maintenance, decay, and the attempts to recreate nationalism in South Africa and Japan. Nationalism in both South Africa and Japan underwent significant transformation in the past century due to internal political and economic developments and the external forces of globalization. By exploring the linkage between external and internal pressures on the state, this chapter will provide a clear explanation for South Africa and Japan's past nationalism and emerging national identity in terms of their similarities and differences.

Over the past twenty years, both South Africa and Japan have experienced unprecedented changes in the foundations of legitimacy and nationalism. Japanese cultural exceptionalism, under the broad umbrella of *Nihonjin-ron* (日本人論), investigates the exclusive cultural sources of the country's origins and continuity, often in light of modernization and globalization. Think tanks, including the Historical Science Society of Japan (Rekishigaku Kenkyu kai, or 歴史学研究会), examine the impact of globalization on Japanese exceptionalism. Yoshio Sugimoto (1999, 23) notes that "[o]f analytical significance is that model of Japaneseness [which] has been constructed by appropriating 'West' as the referential 'other'. "

In South Africa, a vigorous debate centered on what the "new South African" identity should be is colliding with public policy and leadership. Some such as Joe Slovo (a member of the South African Communist Party) and Archbishop Desmond Tutu aspired to a nonracial South Africa, while the former president Thabo Mbeki wanted South Africa to become part of a cultural and economic "African Renaissance" centered on the country affirming its African roots (Halisi 1999). The beneficiaries of the new dispensation (post-1994) and those who now believe they are marginalized in the "new South Africa" derive their affective orientation from the processes and results of cultural construction. These orientations are caused by internal (domestic) social, political, and economic changes intersecting with the processes of globalization. During times of system transformation (South Africa) or protracted economic and political decline (Japan), debates about cultural construction become increasingly de rigueur in public and academic discourse. The present state of cultural redefinition reflects social changes that are underway in these two countries. In South Africa, the "new dispensation" followed the end of apartheid and led to a fundamental change in the political realm and a need for redefining ethnicity-based nationalism. What does the "new South Africa" mean? Clearly, the meaning of postapartheid South Africa differs among ethnic groups and social classes. Beneficiaries of Black Economic Empowerment (BEE), an affirmative action program, benefit from state contracts, stock ownership, and a "transformation" of the executive and board structures of state-owned enterprises (SOE). Nonbeneficiaries have complained that government policies violate the principle of nonracialism enshrined in the Freedom Charter and that only politically well-connected elite are benefiting. William Gumede (2007, 289) states, "The BEE experiment must rank as a huge disappointment."

Meanwhile in Japan, the end of the Cold War, the weakening of the Liberal Democratic Party's (LDP) hegemony, and the long recession that lasted for over a decade after 1989 undermined the legitimacy of the state. Both states have experienced a deconstruction of legitimacy and varying degrees of attempts to reconstruct legitimacy.

Social scientists express concern about the configuration of national identity and its linkage to state legitimacy based on the inordinate number of collapsed or distressed states in the twenty-first century. Tessa Morris-Suzuki's (1995, 776) summary of the writings of the anthropologist Nishikawa Nagao provides insight into this linkage: "The notion of 'national culture' is an ideological construct which, both in Europe and Japan, emerged with the rise of the modern nation state and helped to serve the demands of the state for social integration." Others, including Benedict Anderson (1991) and Eric Hobsbawm (1990), also reflect this Gramscian approach to cultural analysis and denote its link to political power and legitimacy.

Political authorities in every country, including South Africa and Japan, seek to create, maintain, and utilize culture not only for social integration but also for societal control. As noted by P. W. Preston (2000, 11), "It is clear that the notions of the state, nation, and nation-state have to be seen as cultural artifacts created over time and deployed to make sense of the present day." Ongoing Africanization, the new Constitution, and the African Renaissance, as articulated by President Thabo Mbeki in 1997, provide the focal points for recreating and then subsequently replicating political values reflecting the "new" South African national identity. Japanese society's *Gemeinschaft* orientation, as evidenced through the Liberal Democratic Party's (LDP) economic and social policies, reflects traditional values regarding political power. Thus, Japan continuously experiences the agony of social and economic reform because state ideology conflicts with globalization's homogenizing processes.

The cultural legitimatization of power faces opposition, and it remains ensnared by glitches, akin "to computer software design faults," as evidenced through domestic and external resistance. Some people question the orthodoxy that requires constant cultural validation and reification. The cover of *Time* magazine on April 30, 2001, tapped into this deep-seated cognitive dissonance with the phrase, "How the World Sees Japan." Confusion about identity manifests itself in the phenomenon of heightened Japanese obsession with what foreigners think about them. Clearly, external perceptions about a nation impact a citizen's views about his country. Negative external perceptions may magnify a sense of crisis of national identity and nationalism at home that could promote change internally. On other occasions, it can lead to a defensive mechanism of, metaphorically speaking, "circling the wagons" or "expelling the foreigners." The isolation period or *sakoku* (1633–1853) mentality during the Tokugawa era (1603–1868) in Japan and the establishment of the Boer republics (1795–1902) in South Africa signify an attempt to claim national identity and repel globalization by creating a nation-state. Thus constructed, national identity and its twin sister—nationalism—undergo constant reification and recreation through cultural affirmation and rejection. Despite significant cultural and historical differences, the stories of these two societies' experiences of creating, maintaining, and reconfiguring national identity contain striking parallels.

Over the past several decades, both South Africa and Japan have witnessed the states' attempts to strengthen national identity, followed by a sense of crisis in the 1980s and early 1990s. In South Africa, the political transition to majority rule led to the need to completely reconfigure the ideas of national identity, while in Japan, globalization and the economic debacle of the last decade led to massive questions about the configuration of nationalism. Both of these case studies illustrate the impact of globalization and political economy on the changing contours of socially constructed national identity.

This chapter also explores the factors, both international and domestic, that impact the recreation of nationalism based partially on a historical past but also on newly emerging domestic and international pressures. Nationalism, according to the constructivist framework (Gellner 1983; Cohen 1985; Anderson 1991; Hobsbawm 1990), is vital for organizing nation-states and for maintaining political order. However, because nationalism exists as a social construct created and maintained through powerful state-utilized symbols and ideologies, its continuation requires constant re-creation by the state. The cases of South Africa and Japan show resistance to globalization through purposive state action to create exclusivity and to use that to buttress nationalism. However, in both cases, as globalization and domestic changes resulted in pressures for the weakening of national identity, the political elites and the states responded first by emphasizing uniqueness and, then, adaptation and compromise.

South Africa and Japan, more than many societies, relied on socially constructed myths based on notions of exclusivity and external threat to buttress governmental legitimacy. However, the construction of state legitimacy remained much weaker in South Africa than in Japan due to the multifaceted nature (i.e., linguistic, ethnic, and racial bases) of cultural diversity. Contrarily, Japan could use the same symbols with greater potency because of its homogeneity and Tönniesian organic society, which emphasizes kinship (Tönnies, 1957 [1887]). Opponents of Afrikaner-based legitimacy, in contrast to Japan's more loosely organized "essence" of Japanese identity, exerted greater resistance and pressure for weakening the state ideology. Furthermore, international acceptance of the Japanese state was much stronger over the years in contrast to the South African state. South Africa, after the peak of apartheid (1970s), experienced severe deterioration in international acceptance. How did the pressures exerted on nationalism lead to its demise in each respective state? What is the link between the demise of legitimacy and its re-creation? Lastly, to what extent will South Africa and Japan follow parallel developments in the reconstruction of nationalism?

Nationalism and the Nation-State: Exceptionalism and Religion

The genesis of the nation-state in South Africa and Japan shared several common historically grounded themes, including the siege mentality and the need for nationalism as a tool to defeat external and internal threats. At the same time, despite some important parallels, the constructions of Afrikaner and modern Japanese nationalism manifest different existential realities (e.g., relative ethnic homogeneity versus heterogeneity) and external influences (e. g., Asian versus African and European). These respective national ideologies emerged from a history of conflict and resistance to globalization.

Appeals to exclusivity and xenophobia acted strongly to craft nationalism in Japan and South Africa. The sui generis of the Sakoku period in Japan, which began after the rise of the Tokugawa Shogunate in Japan, was based on the need to bring about internal political order by restricting the various *daimyo or warlords* from initiating and maintaining contact with the outside world. Extreme xenophobia forced Christians to renounce their religion during the Tokugawa period. A highly centralized form of government resulted during this time. The Tokugawa Shogunate allowed the "Japanization" of previously imported philosophical and religious ideals (e.g., Buddhism and Confucianism) as a method of strengthening the country's immunity against outside influence. The government constructed and maintained Buddhist temples and subsidized arts. Japan, during this time, experienced an internalized renaissance that resulted in the foundation of Japanese identity and the modern state in the post-Tokugawa period.

The pattern of isolation and indigenization is not unique to Japan. The close-knit and insular orientation of the Boer community began as they moved physically inward to escape the control of the British who had established control over the Cape of Good Hope region by 1806. During the height of Afrikanerdom in the 1970s, the themes of exclusivity and siege expanded, drawing on the history of the Great Trek northward in the 1830s and 1840s. In particular, the defeat of the mighty Zulu in the Battle of Blood River (1838) contributed to the creation of a mythologized invincibility and exclusivity based on Calvinist principles. British imperialism in South Africa, as evidenced through the annexation of the Boer Republics, principally Transvaal (1910), and the subsequent creation of the Union of South Africa that year heightened Afrikaner fears of assimilation into British colonial life (Giliomee 1987, 38). In the 1920s, the influx of Afrikaners into the cities to escape rural economic depression also contributed to the need to maintain the *Gemeinschaft* of Afrikanerdom (Goldberg 1985, 125–6). The symbols of the *volkstaat,* including Calvinist principles of frugality and hard work, the Trek into the inland, and the Reformed Dutch Church became the bond of Afrikaner culture. The Afrikaner ethos became crystallized in the secret *Broederbond* (brotherhood) and reflected in the public policy statements of General James Hertzog who became prime minister in the 1920s. In particular, he wanted the use of the Afrikaans language in schools. In 1939, he advocated South Africa's neutrality during World War II.

Referring to South African nationalism as monolithic, however, creates a misconception that departs from the complex ethnic milieu. Even Afrikaner Christianity was fragmented into three main sects. The largest, the *Nederduitse Gereformeerde Kerk* (NGK), also known as the Dutch Reformed Church, eventually justified separate communion based on racial segregation and became the religious foundation of the Afrikaner state. There were nonsegregationist Dutch Reformed Church sects too. However, in general, Afrikanerism never suggested or encouraged assimilation of cultures, and the Dutch Reformed Church was the "official religion" of the ruling political elite. Therefore, even in apartheid South Africa, other cultures continued to exercise a high degree of subnational dominance with a superimposed control structure set up by the state. These other cultures became the focal points of resistance to the superimposed national political and economic systems organized by and for the benefit of principally Afrikaners. In the geographical periphery and the cultural sub-terrain, the Ndebele, Xhosa, and Shona nations maintained custom-based legal and political legitimacy. With the exception of the colored population and a small group of Asians (Indians), Afrikanerism could not take root among various other ethnicities because of its exclusive propensities. A degree of decentralization at the subnational level existed, and local cultures could work around the confines of the national structure. Furthermore, Afrikanerism was not monolithic as regional and ideological differences existed, primarily between those in the Cape and what is today known as Gauteng. These differences were created largely by the bonds and experiences of those who stayed behind and those who trekked northward and eastward.

Clearly, there was a perceived need to preserve the Boer culture from modernization, urbanization, and British attempts to control and subjugate it. British imperial power was synonymous with globalization and a loss of cultural identity. Exclusivity and exceptionalism became necessary to construct Afrikaner political thought. According to Giliomee (1983, 84), intellectuals after the Boer War saw "themselves as a unique African people in Africa whose strength lay in isolation with freedom to practice with respect to both the English and Africans." This became the foundation of Verwoerd's ideas of Afrikaner nationalism involving separate development and the preservation of culture and anticommunism.

The rise of Japanese nationalism in the post-Tokugawa period did not parallel the ethnic and political complexity of apartheid South Africa. Internally, the post-Tokugawa period was ushered in by the weakening of legitimacy of the shogunate resulting from its inability to address external pressures on Japan to end sakoku. The prospects of colonization led to pandemonium among the Japanese daimyo, and the leadership of the Choshu and Satsuma clans led a coup under the banner of "Expel the barbarians." These clan leaders began a concerted effort to create national identity by differentiating themselves from the non-Japanese. This orientation became crystallized in state Shinto in which the state-led ideologists-cum-nationalists captured Shinto and transformed it into a Japanese religion that emphasized the organic nature of the Japanese people with the emperor as the center of authority (Hardacre 1991). A symbiotic relationship emerged between Shinto and the state, just as in South Africa, where Dutch neo-Calvinism became the religious basis of the new Afrikaner ideology. In South Africa, those like D. F. Malan, a minister and a political and ideological ally of Verwoerd, used the pulpit as a mechanism for advancing ideas of separatism under a religious cloak. Religion and the state formed a mutually supportive bond.

A comparison of the Meiji era in Japan (1868–1911) and the period after the establishment of apartheid as the South African government's official ideology (1948) reveals strikingly similar patterns in terms of their initial successes at forcing acceptance of the new system and converting followers. In both Japan and South Africa, dissent was stifled and the governments began to assemble organic states. In Japan, the samurai resistance was neutralized quickly, and the various local daimyo were brought under central authority control by 1874. By 1900, the complete centralization of administration by national and local governments and through the establishment of a Weberian civil service became the hallmark of Meiji modernization.

Regional attachments were thus subsumed into the national state's ideology through a systematic process of centralization and assimilation of localities. In the 1920s, class conflict between state capitalists and workers became the salient social-political cleavage in Japan. Unions and political parties, including the Communist Party, coalesced around an economic interpretation based on Karl Marx and became the target of state authority. By this time, the *zaibatsu* (large horizontal business conglomerates) and the Japanese governments came to see the importance of labor quiescence as necessary for late modernization.

The rapidity of late industrialization in South Africa and Japan created social confusion among South Africans and the Japanese. Both governments relied on traditional sources of legitimacy to maintain order. It was a type of "legitimacy by results" through economic development (Japan) or preservation and enhancement of white privileges (South Africa). In South Africa, prior to the takeover of power by the unified and hard-line faction of the National Party (NP) in 1948, the British whites and more moderate NP Afrikaners (who together created the United Party) sought to accommodate and ameliorate Boer nationalism by incorporating a soft-line segregationist position.

Once again, global pressures impacted domestic political development. The advent of World War II and the United Party's decision to join the Allies led to the unification of the moderate and radical Afrikaners to form a Reunited National Party. The hard-liner-led Reunited National Party opposed close participation with the Allies and advocated a much stronger sense of Afrikaner nationalism that demanded state intervention to create and protect ethnic privileges. The large influx of blacks into the armaments and mining industry caused by the required military service of white males led to depressed wages for the whites who worked in those economic sectors. Unskilled and semiskilled Afrikaners became vulnerable to declining living standards. The NP platform of national-socialism appealed to both rural and urban Afrikaners. Despite the regional and ideological differences within the Afrikaner community, the NP succeeded in creating a degree of unity among Afrikaners. Even British whites and Asian communities derived significant economic benefits from the exercise of state ideology. The colored population identified culturally with Afrikaners and their language, and sometimes sought to hide its black heritage. They too experienced a trickling down of socioeconomic benefits. State apartheid instituted a complex and segregated social order based on racial hierarchy.

Industrialization and its social effects played an important role in shaping state ideology in Japan too. The appeal of communism during the 1920s and 1930s led to serious attempts by the government to weaken labor-oriented protests through the use of its secret police and the Ministry of Home Affairs. The Japanese Communist Party (JCP), formed in 1922, maintained close links with the Soviet-sponsored Communist International

(COMINTERN). As Japan acquired an empire, thereby adopting a foreign policy based on the globalization of colonization, the JCP was the only political party that opposed the country's involvement in World War II. The Shinto system provided a state-sponsored antidote to the appeal of globalized radical leftism at the height of repressive Japanese industrialization. In South Africa, the apartheid ideology served as a functional equivalent. Thus, not surprisingly, the communist parties in both countries were banned and its leaders imprisoned.

Ethnic homogeneity in Japan, in contrast with the heterogeneity of South Africa, was an environmental difference that shaped resistance to orthodox nationalism. Japan's relative racial homogeneity meant that the ideology of exclusivity was based on a "Japanese versus the rest of the world" outlook. Minorities were presumed not to exist in Japan, a point made erroneously even by Nakasone Yasuhiro, the prime minister from 1982 to 1987. In South Africa, those who were critical of and challenged Afrikaner orthodoxy grew in number. Resistance in South Africa was primarily ethnicity-based. Despite the Freedom Charter's message of nonracialism, very few whites belonged to the African National Congress (ANC). The Xhosa were the most powerful ethnic group in the ANC. The Indian National Congress (INC) was Asian and the Inkatha Freedom Movement (IFM) derived its majority support from the Zulu nation. For the Pan Africanist Congress (PAC), the nonracialism of the ANC was not sufficient; it broke away and became an independent organization. Even the South African Communist Party (SACP) initially started out in 1922 as a group supporting white miners' interests over blacks'. By stratifying society along ethnic lines, the NP succeeded in defining national politics, including resistance, along ethnonational lines.

Resistance to Japanese state ideology came from socialists, Christians, and communists. It reflected a greater degree of class-based opposition that did not find support from the silent Japanese majority. So effective was the official Japanese ideology of organic nationalism that assimilation and homogenization of cultural difference into a singular identity effectively contained the possibility of cultural erosion due to globalization and Westernization. On the contrary, apartheid in South Africa never attempted to create a unified country, but rather an ethnically divided country that preserved minority (i.e., Afrikaner) rights. The ultimate goal during the height of apartheid was the creation of independent homelands, the first of them Transkei, which became "independent" in 1976. The "homelands" essentially became reservations for concentrating black South Africans that would indefinitely prolong Afrikaner privileges while demographic changes led to a relationally smaller white population. In addition, the "homeland" strategy sought to deflect global public opinion against apartheid by creating a modicum of black African self-rule.

From the creation of Broederbond in 1918 to the establishment of the NP in 1948 and the strengthening of apartheid under Prime Minister Hendrik Verwoerd (1958–66) and Prime Minister and, then, President Balthazar Johannes (John) Vorster (1966–79) in the subsequent decades, the ideology of Afrikaner nationalism and separateness remained central. The facts, myths, and rituals regarding the Broederbond, the Great Trek, and the organic "volk" with a common sense of manifest destiny were culturally refined, recreated, and transmitted through state instruments.

In Japan, the period from 1880 to 1940 reflected the prewar height of the emperor system supported by state Shinto. The emperor system refers to a strong organic state centered on the use of authoritarian measures for the purpose of state modernization conducted in the name of the emperor. Power was vested in the hands of a powerful oligarchy consisting of industrialists, military officers, bureaucrats, and elected officials (Compton 2000a, 116–20).

Over time, a close symbiotic partnership between business and the government in both countries, as evidenced through the military industrial and state security complex, strengthened. The Sino-Japanese (1894–5) and Russo-Japanese (1904–5) wars allowed Japanese corporations to become entrenched in East Asia and awarded them valuable military contracts. The two wars strengthened the military's role in the political economy and allowed for the establishment of factories in Korea, Taiwan, and Liaodong Peninsula's Port Arthur region.

Similarly, the apartheid state signed contracts with corporations that specialized in security and military armaments. Rhodesia, in the 1960s and 1970s, purchased South African armaments, while after the independence of Angola and Mozambique in 1976, the South African Defence Forces (SADF) began to fight proxy wars and to direct low-intensity conflicts within the Southern African Development Community (SADC) region. Special forces became involved in "hunt, destroy, and destabilize" missions in the former Southwest Africa, southern Angola, Zambia, and Rhodesia. The engagement of enemies abroad and the quest for national security through the expansion of foreign policy reach reflected internal political pressures and decisions.

The result of Japan's expansionism from the 1890s to the 1940s and South Africa's attempted hegemony over southern Africa from the 1960s to the 1970s benefited the participants in the emperor system and the apartheid system respectively in terms of social status and financial gain. The military-industrial complex and the security apparatus increased their political power. Lastly, the siege mentality and the regional operations of a national security state provided the internal ideological rationale for the continuance and reification of the core ideologies embedded in the emperor system and Afrikanerdom.

How could such strong states based on the notion of the Hobbesian protector decline? External change, brought about by globalization, and internal dislocation caused by identity construction played a major role in deconstructing state legitimacy and national identity.

Domestic Causes of Demise

In comparing the deconstruction of the Afrikaner and the Japanese systems, it becomes apparent that the confluence of domestic and external factors coupled with ideological intransigence accounted for the decline. Despite parallels between the two cases, differences also exist because of the internal and global environments under which each respective regime operated.

The connections between economic performance and political legitimacy in South Africa and Japan are of paramount importance in understanding the construction of legitimacy and its decline. The political-economic system that emerged in Japan after World War II closely resembled the one that existed prior to the war. The expansive literature on the construction of the Japanese political economy takes multiple perspectives on the role of administration, leadership, and culture as an explanation for the country's economic success. For example, some assert that administrative modernization accounted for Japan's rapid rise (Johnson 1982; Katz 1999). According to this logic, the creation of a modern state and its commitment to Weberian bureaucracy accounted for the country's rise after the Meiji Restoration. Hofheinz and Calder (1982) point to cultural values, as derived from Confucianism, among other sources, as the main factors that brought about industrialization. Johnson (1982, 1995) and Compton (2000a, 2000b) address the importance of leadership in the developmental state. Despite these differences in terms of the role of culture, leadership, and institutions, all three perspectives agree on one salient point—the state and economy coexisted in a collusive rather than in an adversarial manner.

In South Africa, the study of the intricate connections between economy and politics from the multifaceted approach encompassing leadership, administration, and culture have not emanated from the scholarship. Instead, most research shows that the cultural identity of the Afrikaners contributed to the formation of the modern South African state. During the 1950s and the 1960s, the state in South Africa became more entrenched in the economic realm for national security purposes and the promotion of Afrikaner welfare. In Japan, the state's inability to continuously deliver the type of economic growth characteristic of the 1960s and early 1970s into the latter half of that decade and into the 1980s reduced the legitimacy of the LDP government that controlled the state and contributed to increased internal pressures for system modification. Meanwhile, external pressures also mounted as the United States and Europe expected Japan to internationalize and become more open, both economically and culturally.

Significant research exists that shows that the decline of economic performance and souring perceptions about the economy undermined the legitimacy of the apartheid system (Manzo and McGowan 1992; Giliomee 1995). In the 1980s, economic growth averaged 1.5 percent due to international sanctions, lack of foreign direct investment (FDI), a skills shortage, and drought (Lowenberg 1997). The value of the rand dropped precipitously during the 1980s. In fact, the core of the system could have endured, had it not been for the economic stagnation and the persistence of resistance. Manzo and McGowan's (1992, 8–10) research further shows that Afrikaner elite public opinion had not become liberal, but the sheer desire to survive motivated them to seek dialogue with the ANC.

Robust economic performance formed the modern foundation for state legitimacy in both Japan and South Africa. Furthermore, traditional *Gemeinschaft*-based nationalism established antiglobalization bases for legitimacy while reinforcing modern legitimacy. In other words, the essence of Japanese and South African participation in the global society derived from an antiglobalization culture.

Both countries benefited from the Cold War's international constellation. Japan received significant economic aid and contracts from the United States during both the Korean and Vietnam wars. The Treaty of Mutual Cooperation and Security between the United States and Japan (1960) and its predecessor, the Security Treaty (1951), provided the Japanese government with international protection. The regional stabilization achieved through U.S. hegemony contributed to the legitimacy of the conservative Liberal government but also weakened the political left. The political left sought to "Finlandize" and neutralize Japan by distancing the country from the U.S. sphere of influence and opposed any security treaty with the United States. After the treaty was signed, the opposition sought its abrogation. Not surprisingly, the U.S. policies during the latter years of occupation and after the signing of the Treaty of San Francisco (1951) favored the conservative Liberal Party, which joined with the Democratic Party to form the Liberal Democratic Party (LDP) in 1955. The occupation's Reverse Course (1947–1952) ended the emphases on democratization and instituted a policy of economic reconsolidation. It was within this context that the Meiji and Taisho eras' oligarchic structures and significant elements of political culture were recreated.

The United States created a bulwark against communism, and the Japanese political elite delighted in the Reverse Course because it empowered them by embracing a Japanese economic model. The economic model weakened independent labor unions and rested on a foundation of traditional cultural values that harkened back to the Meiji Restoration and Nihonjin-ron philosophies. In essence, the ideological basis of the reconstituted political economy system conformed to an attitude and ideology of anticommunism. Anticommunism can be traced back to the basic political thinking among Japanese elites prior to World War II. As Yanaga (1949, 34) notes, "The anti-communist attitude can be said to form an immutable part of Japanese political thinking. The strong reverence for the emperor system makes communism not merely incompatible but inadmissible."

Therefore, World War II did not destroy completely the Japanese nationalist sentiments among the political elite. The early postwar actions of the Japanese conservatives held over from the war and American acquiescence reconstructed the emperor system. While the military and the emperor emerged as clear losers in the new configuration of elites based on bureaucratic corporate leadership, the basic social, political, and economic foundation of the new Japan resembled the old Meiji system. The Reverse Course resulted in the partial success of democratization in postwar Japan and the dominance of corporate Japan, supported by bureaucratic planning and a dominant party system headed by the LDP. The LDP buttressed the traditional notions of Japanese nationalism by constructing a consumer-based economic philosophy of modernity in which successful government policies enabled a better material life for all Japanese (Gluck 1987 and Garon 1998). Japan remained xenophobic, self-centered, and a *Gemeinschaft*-oriented society that embraced modernization and globalization reluctantly. Japanese leaders knew that their country was poor in natural resources and that they needed to develop international economic ties, especially with the West, in order to redevelop their economy. This was part of the siege mentality. As Japan needed to catch up with the West, economic nationalism and cultural conservatism became its postwar foundation. The state played a major role in the inculcation of national values through the curriculum approval process and a variety of economic slogans, such as the Double Your Income program.

Both South Africa and Japan derived legitimacy through economic policies, and economic crises would lead to a significant weakening of support for orthodox ideology. During the 1950s, the passive protests of the ANC, known as the Defiance Campaign, led to arrests and bans. The Sharpeville Massacre (1960) transformed ANC tactics from nonviolence to armed resistance. For the next fifteen years, the South African government contained the resistance through force and extolled the virtues of apartheid. The next turning point came after the Soweto Uprising in 1976 and the independence of the Portuguese colonies of Mozambique and Angola. Sensing the rise of solidarity with the ANC from abroad, especially from African states, the new president, John Vorster, sought to develop diplomatic relations with friendly or conciliatory black governments abroad (e.g., Liberia, Malawi, and Zaire). On the home front, South Africa became a police state besieged by hostile forces with external black African state support.

From 1975 to 1978, the economy grew at less than 2 percent, and then from 1982 to 1992, the economy contracted six years (USDA International Macroeconomic Data Set). Some whites fled South Africa, taking with them technical skills and financial assets despite tough government controls. But the economic downturn preempted a possible loosening of apartheid, and instead brought out the xenophobic mentality as evidenced by the common reactionary phrase "Total [African] Onslaught," which symbolized the need for Afrikaners to once again circle their wagons.

The economic crisis transformed the political landscape of South African politics. Declining living standards meant a series of strikes that the government could not contain. The more the government used force, the greater the resistance and the coalescing of black antiapartheid protests into a Black Consciousness Movement. P. W. Botha instituted a "Total Strategy" by engaging so-called anticommunist guerilla armies in Angola and Mozambique and sending troops into the townships. The Umkhonto we Sizwe (MK) or "The Spear of the Nation," responded by making the townships ungovernable. In the 1980s, the pressures of economic and diplomatic isolation negatively affected the regime's legitimacy precisely at a time when many countries were integrating into a new global economic order that came to fruition after the collapse of the Soviet bloc. The economic costs of isolation, declining gold prices, and the expenditures associated with maintaining the police state led to a fiscal crisis in which government spending greatly exceeded revenue receipts.

The pullout of Cuban troops from Angola and its independence and the demise of the Soviet Union contributed to F. W. De Klerk's decision to release Nelson Mandela from prison and unban the ANC, PAC, and the SACP. De Klerk decided to negotiate out of a possible bloody civil war and intensified negotiations for a settlement through Codesa (Congress on Democratic South Africa). The Afrikaner system of government was replaced in 1994 by a government of national unity (GNU) headed by the ANC. With that, a new political culture and national identity needed construction.

Japan also experienced challenges to its economic growth. In the 1970s and early 1980s, the Japanese economy continued to grow rapidly, albeit slowed by the successive oil shocks at that time. With growth rates exceeding 5 percent annually, the LDP remained in firm control, and Japan emerged as the world's most formidable exporting nation and the second-largest economy.

The student protests of the 1960s and the 1970s subsided considerably by the 1980s. In the latter half of the 1980s, Japan experienced considerable growth caused by the development of a "bubble economy" centered on real estate and a strong yen. At the same time, Japanese exporters continued to increase their competitiveness but the domestic economy began to show distortions and severe inefficiencies during that decade.

During the 1990s, Japan experienced unprecedented economic difficulties with previously unseen levels of bankruptcies, growing unemployment, and the virtual collapse of the banking sector. Overall, the economy entered into a vicious deflationary cycle. Despite the strong export sector, the Japanese economy had firmly become a dual economy with weak internal markets (Katz 1999). Due to the hegemony of the LDP and its collusion with bureaucracies and corporations, reform could not be implemented readily or speedily. The troubled economy cost the LDP its legitimacy, and it was temporarily swept out of power for the first time in postwar Japan in 1993 for ten months. The opposition was fragmented and led by those who defected from the LDP. Numerous electoral reforms were enacted, but the LDP managed to return to power, albeit in coalition with the Socialist Party and the Komei-to.

What external factors influenced political development in South Africa and Japan? The demise of the Soviet Union directly affected the environment under which the political and economic systems of both countries operated. While some of the consequences have been noted previously, one important point needs discussion. The collapse of the Soviet Union led policy makers in the United States to adopt a much harder line on Japan's closed economy. Such pressures began to mount in earnest from the mid-1980s and accelerated in the late and early 1990s (Gao 2001). Faced with the paradox of record trade and budget deficits and the emergence of the United States as the world's only superpower, American ideology consisting of "free trade" and "democracy" became the *de rigueur* of U.S. foreign policy. Thus, the United States applied immense pressure to open up the Japanese market, while the Japanese domestic economy simultaneously became acutely vulnerable to implosion caused by corruption, inefficiency, and a massive real estate bubble. Japan had identified its socioeconomic system as preferable to the U.S. market system, but the recession that lasted for more than a decade and unprecedented political corruption during the growth years destroyed the political system's legitimacy. Increasingly, national identity and purpose became fragmented. The invincible Japanese economy experienced stagnation and people became unemployed. Jobs were lost to China and manufacturing hollowed out as a result. The Japanese model and its cultural foundation were not impregnable after all.

Challenges of Reconstructing State Legitimacy

Once the notion of the Hobbesian protector in both societies melted away and the governments' legitimacy waned, a new legitimacy needed construction. In order to reconstruct legitimacy, the redefinition of national identity is required. Because Japan experienced a gradual decline in domestic political legitimacy, it lacks the clear demarcation that South Africa (1994) experienced. In other words, South African national identity required a complete overhaul, whereas in the case of Japan, a greater degree of continuity could be maintained. What are the main challenges and problems of creating a new national identity as the basis of legitimacy? To what degree have these two countries succeeded in this reconstruction? A government can craft legitimacy through the use of specific policies and symbols. Due to the democratic transition in South Africa, a completely new system needed construction. It needed to address economic issues, including growth and redistribution, and political and cultural issues, including that of crafting a "new" South Africa, which required a transformed political and cultural framework. In Japan, a general consensus exists that the current politico-economic situation has failed, but few demand a new dispensation (Pempel 1998). Thus, legitimacy in South Africa and Japan, while culturally constructed in both places, is being transformed in very different ways. In South Africa, the changes are almost revolutionary on several fronts, but in Japan it is at best evolutionary. The newer Japanese elite are still beholden to a political structure and culture that evolved from the Meiji era, whereas in South Africa, the new elite has moved in to make the primary political and cultural decisions. Reforms in South Africa and Japan have centered on the economic, political, and social sectors. Briefly, I will now compare and contrast the similarities and differences in these reform areas as they relate to the reconstruction of national identity and legitimacy.

In the area of economic legitimization, South Africa and Japan must both seek to increase growth. Over the past thirteen years, deflation and rising unemployment have characterized the economic situation in Japan. On the other hand, in South Africa, the reintegration of the country into the global economy created both positive and negative outcomes. Upon taking power, the ANC could not resort to wholesale socialism. The world in 1994 became a very different place than it was in the previous decades. The uneven progress of the South African economy since Nelson Mandela reflects the double-edged sword of globalization. While globalization assisted in dismantling apartheid, the pressures of global economic integration led to a weakening of the political will and ability to implement the radical redistribution of wealth, contributing to persistently high unemployment and income inequality.

ANC elites faced a dilemma. On the one hand, rising expectations from its core supporters demanded the rapid redistribution of wealth commensurate with political power. At the same time, such a strategy would have damaged the economy by thwarting foreign investment and leading to the flight of financial and human capital. Dialogue resulting from the 1990 Discussion Document on Economic Policy reflected the degree to which economic policy makers were aware of the trade-offs between redistribution and economic growth (Nattras 1994, 346–7). Some of the discussion centered on the need for strategic Asian-style developmental state intervention in the economy. Upon taking office, the ANC, as the senior partner in the GNU, embarked on an ambitious Reconstruction and Development Program (RDP) that contained economic and social elements. One major component of the RDP was the need to create an integrated community spirit that would help decentralized small-scale enterprises to thrive. During the RDP, 1.1 million basic homes were constructed, 1.75 million households were connected to electricity, and 2.5 million people gained access to clean drinking water (Lodge 2002, 57–8). However, given the poor quality of the homes, the inability of residents to pay for water and electricity, and the extremely low threshold of government rations provided at no cost, there were many critics of the social programs. At the same time, the government established minimum wage provisions and affirmative action policies for previously disadvantaged groups. Under the system that emerged, "black" control over the economy would take place in an evolutionary rather than in a revolutionary manner.

Despite the emergence of a large number of black middle managers in both the public and private sectors, the record of economic-policy-based legitimacy creation is mixed. Unemployment over the past ten years has increased and wages have stagnated. The informal sector employs a large number of people. The percentage of the labor force that is employed by the formal sector has actually decreased. According to research conducted by the Human Sciences Research Council (HSRC), South Africa, and published by the Southern African Regional Poverty Network (SARPN), 57 percent of South Africans lived in poverty and "poor households sunk deeper into poverty" in 2001 (Southern African Regional Poverty Network 2004).

Clearly, the spirit of the ANC government could not match the rising expectations of the rank-and-file members of the ANC or those people living in rural areas (Glaser 1997). Thus, the size and number of informal settlements without basic amenities has increased and not decreased since the beginning of majority rule. This has been caused by the end of restrictions on mobility and the large number of sub-Saharan Africans who have fled their respective countries to escape even more egregious conditions there.

Despite some degree of success in the area of redistribution and social policies, the problems at hand are intractable. Drought, AIDS, and the costs of training, compensating, and maintaining a service-oriented civil service come at a high price. There is a serious imbalance between the required costs of program implementation and revenue raised by the government. Thus, black South Africans demand more, but their white counterparts often complain about the costs of these programs and its associated economic burden being shifted onto them. The current economic program known as GEAR (Growth, Employment, and Redistribution), which was instituted in 1996, emphasizes growth rather than redistribution. While the monetary climate has stabilized and inflation has declined from the highs of several years ago, employment growth remains elusive. Giliomee (1995, 99) notes that in 1995, less than 1.8 percent of Africans operated their own business, and that 70 percent of black Africans lived below the minimum subsistence level. By the late 1990s, statistics showed greater deterioration in employment, earnings, and life expectancy. The United Nations Development Program's annual *Human Development Report* based on the Human Development Index (HDI), which consists of life expectancy, literacy, educational attainment, and the Gross Domestic Product (GDP) per capita, showed virtually no improvement from 1975 to 2005. The HDI the index stood relatively unchanged at 0.65 and 0.674 for 1975 and 2005, respectively.

After 1994, urban integration and the creation of political and social space became one of the most important developments in the new South Africa. The rush toward the cities coupled with the transition created major dislocations in service delivery, law and order, and governmental authority. White flight and the departure of middle-income and mobile blacks to the suburbs led to urban blight. The vicious cycle of blight and flight then created fiscal crises in the cities.

Despite these problems, cities have begun to adjust to new realities by regulating crime and seeking new identities through the annexation of suburbs. Thus new identities, such as eTekwini (Durban), Tshwane (Pretoria), and Polokwane (Pietersburg), reflect more than African names. Crime control through the use of foot- and horse-based patrol, supplemented by the use of street cameras, as in Cape Town, reflect new and innovative strategies toward crime control. Meanwhile, townships are now constituent parts of integrated development plans. The townships have experienced significant investment through RDP in the form of basic infrastructure construction. Each municipality, working through the Department of Provincial and Local Government, has created an integrated development plan that could provide greater coordination and structure to political participation and authority (Tomlinson et al. 2003). As municipalities learn to work with various new and more established associations and nongovernmental organizations (NGOs), new South African political spaces are being created. One such example is the creation of recognized hawkers and taxation of commuter omnibus associations in Johannesburg (Gotz and Simone 2003, 123–47). At the national level, patterns of interactions between Congress of South African Trade Unions (COSATU), South African National Civic Organization (SANCO), and other NGOs create new patterns of state-society interactions (Heller 2003).

At the same time, bifurcated patterns, rather than systematic integration, exist in South Africa today. Pockets of white affluence in suburbs like Sandton are far removed from the ocean of poverty and associated poverty in places like Hillbrow and Yeoville. The new South African identity on the macro level consists of Africanization but on the micro level, the persistence of race and the emergence of class reflects day-to-day reality (Moodley and Adam 2000). As noted by Ramutsindela (2001, 76–8), South African politics is experiencing a reracialization on one level and the expression of strong subidentities (Cornelissen and Horstmeir 2002).

Perhaps the greatest success of the new South African government consists of its use of cultural and symbolic tools of legitimization. A vast array of symbols, including the new flag, the constitution, and the coats of arms, and the presence of black and other previously disadvantaged groups in Parliament and the changing ethnic composition of the judiciary point to the governments' orientation toward the black majority. Slogans or phrases (e.g., the new South Africa, the Rainbow Nation, and ubuntu) point to a dramatic shift from the old cultural regime. The new South Africa, as evidenced in Thabo Mbeki's term "African Renaissance," reflects a more positive attempt to engage in the affairs of the continent and the world by a more open method. Despite the successes in this area, the economic picture, in regard to equality, is so poor that gains in other areas such as culture, legality, and increased social equality could be potentially undermined. Implementation of economic and social policies remains the Achilles' heel of the new regime's legitimization scheme.

Despite the decline of the Japanese economy and the rising levels of political dissatisfaction in the country, Japanese leaders have failed miserably to increase political legitimacy. Japan's economic stagnation has resulted from years of inefficiency and policies that sought to protect domestic economic actors unable to compete internationally. In particular, agricultural subsidies, protection for small-scale businesses, and pork barrel projects for the construction industry have created powerful interests seeking the public trough.

Given the lack of political will created by weak leadership and entrenched special interests, the Japanese economy has grown slowly. According to the Ministry of Finance (MoF), the deficit spending from 1990 to 2000 averaged about 21 percent of the national budget. Annual growth averaged below 2 percent (2001). Caught between the economic pressures of globalization and the need to maintain a traditional social contract of full employment forged in the 1960s, the Japanese economy has drifted and limped along since its bubble burst (Carlile 1998).

Given the defeat of Japan in World War II, the Japanese political elite does not have multiple tools of legitimization unlike the government in South Africa. Thus, the Japanese are much more reliant on economic growth and the *Gemeinschaft* orientation toward the economy as sources of legitimacy. A *sakoku* mentality and notions of exclusivity remain entrenched in Japan's quest for internationalization. Even in the higher education realm, foreign professors must confront pervasive discrimination against outside professors (Hall 1997). In contrast, South Africa, given the relatively new nature of the current dispensation, is experiencing a honeymoon period in which significant policy changes remain possible.

Conclusion

Both Japan and South Africa emerged as constructed societies in which numerous and sometimes conflicting symbols (both modern and traditional), ideologies, and economic systems coexisted. In particular, both countries became modern states based on the principle of exclusivity and internal and external siege, while managing to confront globalization. The role of traditional values, as defined by both modern governments, played a critical role in the modernization of both societies. In Japan, the Shinto religion and the emperor system operated, while in South Africa, the Boer culture emphasized traditional Calvinist values.

However, while the Japanese embarked on the process of constructing a monolithic culture based on the existing relative homogeneity, the Afrikaners in South Africa sought separate development because of the heterogeneity that existed in that country. This environmental factor had a major impact on the construction, deconstruction, and reconstruction of political legitimacy in South Africa and allowed for a cleaner break from the old system. In contrast, the Japanese are currently experiencing an inability to design legitimating systems. The Afrikaner government ultimately failed to retain power, and other cultural and political groups, especially the ANC, dominate politics today. Unlike Japan, South Africa's break with the old system is clear, and the country is beginning to create a new political culture. This political culture, with the revolutionary armed struggle and Africanization as its core, dominates the national level, but significant subnational variations exist. Clearly, the gamut of what constitutes government legitimacy and national identity differs vastly from one group to another.

Japan, in contrast to South Africa, has not yet experienced a reconstruction of political legitimacy. Furthermore, unlike South Africa, Japan has not experienced a meltdown of legitimacy structures. Instead of an acute crisis of legitimacy, Japan has experienced a slow, creeping demise of the power of its myths, symbols, and identity. Thus, Japan remains trapped in a failed system of exclusivity and xenophobia. South Africa's future is far from certain. It remains in a purgatory of conflicting and overlapping identities. A much more pluralistic culture presents centrifugal tendencies that could lead to declining central government authority.

Despite the differences between Japan and South Africa, both countries must now contend with the problem of recreating legitimacy. South Africa's transition will require leadership that can mobilize disparate culture groups that coexist in a democratic framework. Meanwhile, Japanese leaders will need to rely on traditional symbols that must now be adapted to the era of globalization. Japanese identity and globalization are, to a large degree, mutually exclusive, if the latter means that Japan needs to abandon an ideology of Japanese uniqueness. Lastly, while both South Africa and Japan remain "works in progress," they are no longer on convergent paths. The countries' systems are more different than more similar now.

References

Anderson, Benedict. 1991. *Imagined Communities: Reflections on the Origin and Spread of Nationalism.* New York: Verso.

Calder, Kent E. 1991. *Crisis and Compensation: Public Policy and Political Stability in Japan.* Princeton, NJ: Princeton University Press.

Carlile, Lonny E. 1998. *Is Japan Really Changing Its Ways?: Regulatory Reform and the Japanese Economy.* Brookings Institute: Washington, D.C.

Cohen, Anthony. 1985. *The Symbolic Construction of Community.* New York: Methuen Drama.

Compton, Robert. 2000a. *East Asian Democratization: Impact of Globalization, Culture, and Economy.* Westport, CT: Praeger.

———. 2000b. Reconstructing Political Legitimacy in Asia: Globalization and Political Development. *International Journal on World Peace* 17: 19–39.

Cornelissen, Scarlett, and Steffen Horstmeier. 2002. The Social and Political Construction of Identities in the New South Africa: An Analysis of the Western Cape Province. *Journal of Modern African Studies* 40: 55–82.

Gao, Bai. 2001. *Japan's Economic Dilemma: The Institutional Origins of Prosperity and Stagnation.* New York: Cambridge University Press.

Garon, Sheldon. 1998. *Molding Japanese Minds: The State in Everyday Life.* Princeton, NJ: Princeton University Press.

Gellner, Ernest. 1983. *Nations and Nationalism.* Ithaca, NY: Cornell University Press.

Glaser, Daryl. 1997. South Africa and the Limits of Civil Society." *Journal of Southern African Studies* 23: 5–25.

Giliomee, Hermann. 1983. Constructing Afrikaner Nationalism. *Journal of Asian and African Studies* 18: 83–98.

———. 1987. Western Cape Farmers and the Beginnings of Afrikaner Nationalism, 1870–1915. *Journal of South African Studies* 14: 38–63.

———. 1995. Democratization in South Africa. *Political Science Quarterly* 110: 83–104.

Gluck, Carol. 1987. *Japan's Modern Myths.* Princeton, NJ: Princeton University Press.

Goldberg, Melvin. 1985. The Nature of Afrikaner Nationalism. *Journal of Modern African Studies* 23: 125–31.

Gotz, Graeme, and Aboumaliq Simone. 2003. On Belonging and Becoming African Cities. In *Emerging Johannesburg: Perspectives on a Postapartheid City,* ed. Richard Tomlinson, Robert A. Beauregard, Lindsay Bremner, and Xolela Mangcu, 123–47. London: Routledge.

Gumede, William Mervin. 2007. *Thabo Mbeki and the Battle for the Soul of the ANC.* London: Zed.

Halisi, C. R. D. 1999. *Black Political Thought in the Making of South African Democracy.* Bloomington: Indiana University Press.

Hall, Ivan. 1997. *Cartels of the Mind: Japan's Intellectual Closed Shop.* New York: W.W. Norton.

Hardacre, Helen. 1991. *Shinto and the State, 1868–1988.* Princeton, NJ: Princeton University Press.

Heller, Patrick. 2003. Reclaiming Democratic Spaces. In *Emerging Johannesburg: Perspectives on a Postapartheid City,* ed. Richard Tomlinson et al., 155–84. London: Routledge.

Hobsbawm, Eric. 1990. *Nations and Nationalism since 1780: Programme, Myth, and Reality.* Cambridge: Cambridge University Press.

Hofheinz, Roy, and Kent Calder. 1982. *The Eastasia Edge.* New York: Basic Books.

Johnson, Chalmers. 1982. *MITI and the Japanese Miracle: The Growth of Industrial Policy, 1925–1975.* Berkeley: University of California Press.

———. 1995. *Japan: Who Governs? The Rise of the Developmental State.* New York: W.W. Norton.

Katz, Richard. 1999. *Japan, the System That Soured: The Rise and Fall of the Japanese Economic Miracle.* Armonk, NY: M. E. Sharpe.

Lodge, Tom. 2002. *Politics in South Africa: From Mandela to Mbeki.* Cape Town: New Africa Books.

Lowenberg, Anton. 1997. Why South Africa's Apartheid Economy Failed. *Contemporary Economic Policy* 15: 62–72.

Manzo, Kate, and Pat McGowan. 1992. Afrikaner Fears and the Politics of Despair: Understanding Change in South Africa. *International Studies Quarterly* 36: 1–24.

Ministry of Finance Statistics. 2001. Tokyo: Monthly Policy Research Institute, Ministry of Finance.

Moodley, Kogila, and Heribert Adam. 2000. Race and Nation in the Post-Apartheid South Africa: Patriotism, Nationalism, and Non-Racialism. *Current Sociology* 48: 51–59.

Morris-Suzuki, Tessa. 1995. The Invention and Reinvention of Japanese Culture. *Journal of Asian Studies* 54: 759–80.

Nattrass, Nicoli. 1994. Politics and Economics in ANC Economic Policy. *African Affairs* 93: 343–59.

Pempel, T. J. 1998. *Regime Shift: Comparative Dynamics of the Japanese Political Economy.* Ithaca, NY: Cornell University Press.

Preston, P. W. 2000. *Understanding Modern Japan: A Political Economy of Development, Culture, and Global Power.* London: Sage.

Ramutsindela, Maano F. 2001. Down the Post-Colonial Road: Reconstructing the Post-Apartheid State in South Africa. *Political Geography* 20: 57–84.

Southern African Regional Poverty Network [SARPN]. 2004. Fact Sheet Poverty in South Africa. Fact Sheet No.1. Retrieved from http://www.sarpn.org.za/documents/d0000990/ (accessed on June 10, 2003).

Sugimoto, Yoshio. 1999. Making Sense of *Nihonjin-ron. Thesis Eleven* 57: 81–96.

Tomlinson, Richard, Robert A. Beauregard, Lindsay Bremner, and Xolela Mangcu. 2003. The Struggle for an Integrated Johannesburg. In *Emerging Johannesburg, Perspectives on the Postapartheid City,* ed. Richard Tomlinson, Robert A. Beauregard, Lindsay Bremner, and Xolela Mangcu, 3–20. London: Routledge.

Tönnies, Ferdinand. 1887. *Gemeinschaft und Gesellschaft, Grundbegriffe der Reinen.* Trans. Charles Loomiis. 1957. New York: Harper and Row.

United States Department of Agriculture (USDA). *International Macroeconomic Data Set.* Economic Research Service (ERS). Available at http://www.ers.usda.gov/Data/Macroeconomics/ (accessed on June 10, 2003).

Yanaga, Chitoshi. 1949. *Japan since Perry.* New York: McGraw-Hill.

CHAPTER 11

Searching for Semantics in Music: A Global Discourse

Orlando Legname

Introduction

Music is an activity that is found in almost any culture or period in history. From this perspective, music might be considered universal, but to what extent? Is it possible to find a set of universal values that could be applied to any culture or period? These are metaphysical questions that have been asked by many scholars and philosophers in history. The search for answers to these questions reveals even more profound dichotomies in the Western view of the universe.

We live in a constantly changing world. At the brink in the third millennium, our perceived national boundaries are becoming less apparent as a new "global" concept of the planet on which we live takes their place. In this world, one might ask how universal values could be found among all cultures. We are all members of the same species, after all. Is there a universal set of rules that can be drawn up, either by reason, as Plato thought, or by a more sophisticated aesthetic experience?

Globalization is integrating the political, economic, and cultural aspects of society in a new international order. The world is becoming smaller; distances are shorter, and information travels at the speed of light. Even though that is the case, the world has many cultures; each one has its own language, values, and aesthetics that make up its identity. If the world is gradually becoming one small place, is it our future to be one human race not defined by national, racial, or religious boundaries? If yes, how universal will culture be? We express ourselves in many different ways, and the language we speak is directly related to the way we think. A language is much more than a set of symbols and sounds arbitrarily determined throughout history for the purpose of communication. Language is a door to a culture and to the way a particular people think. A culture's view of a human being's place in the universe is reflected in its language.

Art is the aesthetic way we express ourselves, and music, a unique kind of language, is an art that has the power to invade a listener's world even when they do not want it. One might consciously decide not to look at a particular work of art or not to read a poem, but it is very difficult not to listen to a piece of music playing in a public place. Music communicates messages using a system of sounds and silence according to certain aesthetic principles that vary across cultures and historical periods. Furthermore, in music, as in any human activity, the only constant phenomenon is change.

The other question one may ask is whether music is capable of transmitting information about the world outside the realm of sounds. Some think that there is a universal "translation" of certain sounds or sound structures to places, events, or even emotions. This leads to a discussion of whether musical language has a semantic or denotation level. There have been many attempts in history to establish a semantic level of music. Yet we shall see that there is a relationship between the level of denotation and the universality of a particular type of music.

This theoretical question leads to the discussion of two historical cases that illustrate this phenomenon. One is the "universal" characteristic of the nationalism in Brazil at the beginning of the twentieth century, as for instance, in the *anthropophagite* movement. Nationalism, at least in music, was a movement that reinforced the traditional roots of particular countries. In most cases, very old traditions were brought back, and influences of other countries or cultures were denied. To reinforce national values, one needed to expose the differences between those roots. Each country needed to have its own identity, and the difference with other countries needed to be clear. From a nationalist perspective, a nation's culture is not universal; the culture is a unique component of the people, the place, and the nation that sets it apart from other peoples, other places, and other nations.

This chapter will also provide another case study on Japan. In contrast with Brazil, Japan is far more culturally and ethnically homogeneous. Japan is considered a very traditional society. However, Japan's ancient culture, willingly and unwillingly, incorporates Western influences and experiences—the consequences of global capitalism. This chapter will examine to what extent Western pop music in the twentieth century had a profound impact on ancient cultures such as Japan, where national values are changing drastically.

Musical Semiotics

Music is an Art, which makes use of a system of sound signs, or a language as a means of expression.

Hans-Joachim Koellreutter

The study of music as a language has engaged the attention of many musicologists, and it is now known as the science of musical semiotics. Jean-Jacques Nattiez (1975) and Eero Tarasti (1994) introduced the formal concepts, which would be elaborated by Raymond Monelle (2000), who investigated "musical meaning."

Hans-Joachim Koellreutter was a composer and a professor who constantly revolutionized the music in the country he adopted as his own—Brazil. He taught many generations of musicians, and one of his pedagogic methods involved the use of semiotics in musical analysis along with a phenomenological approach.

Many musicologists consider music to be a language. Koellreutter conceptualized music as an art that uses a system of sound signs, or a language, as a means of expression.[1] Music itself is not a language per se, but uses one to transmit aesthetical ideas.

Another way to examine music as a language is to analyze musical events as signs that have three levels: syntactic, semantic, and pragmatic. The syntactic is the level of structure and deals with relationships between the signs. In music, the syntax pertains to the idiom, which, in Western music, can be modal, tonal, atonal, or elemental.[2] The semantic is the level that deals with the relationship between the signs and the external world; it is the level of denotation and pertains to the meanings of the signs. The pragmatic is the level that deals with the relationship between the signs and the interpreter; it is the level of connotation. It pertains to the interpretation of the signs, and it is subjected to the experience, culture, and other elements related to the interpreter.

Umberto Eco (1968) argues in *La Struttura Assente* that music is a system with denotation and not connotation. Koellreutter argues contrarily that music is a system without denotation. He further argues that musical signs have no semantic level or signification, but they may have sense. Some musical signs do not have either sense or signification. Koellreutter (1990, 116) defines musical sense as the phenomenological result of the syntactic relationship of musical signs.

A denotation level in music would mean that musical signs could be understood in terms of extramusical elements. Music would have a "translation," and musical signs such as notes, chords, or musical phrases would have an exact meaning for everybody, everywhere at any given time in history.

There have been many attempts in history to attribute a denotation to music, and we shall see that religious or political forces in general drove them. In some periods, music tended to be universal without being limited to cultural boundaries, and in other periods, music was related to particular cultures or nations. Considering that music does not have a semantic level, we should state that the attempts to establish musical denotation have variable levels, depending on the historical period. This point can be equally applied to the question of how "universal" or "local" the music was in a particular period. Examining the relationship between these concepts, this chapter analyzes how semantics is, in mathematical terms, inversely proportional to universality. In other words, whenever music has a high level of universality in history, there is no attempt to establish a denotation level of music. Whenever music is not "universal" but "local," there is an attempt to establish a denotation level of music. The level of the attempt to establish a musical denotation varies with the inverse of the level of musical universality.

Western History as a Conflict between Two Traditions

Western culture and thinking have been shaped by two different traditions. Hubert Dreyfus (2006) calls them the Greek, or Philosophical, and the Judeo-Christian traditions. Greek tradition, which was developed by the ancient philosophers Socrates, Plato, and Aristotle, laid out rational thinking and a particular view of the universe. The philosophy developed by the Greeks is divided into three categories: the theory of knowledge or epistemology, ethics, and metaphysics. For the Greeks, knowledge was achieved by reason and its principles are universal and timeless; ethics searches for universal truths about how one should live and how they could be applied to everybody; and metaphysics is concerned with the nature of what is real. In the philosophical view, what is real is universal, eternal, and achieved by reason.

Dreyfus continues by stating that the Judeo-Christian tradition is by origin religious, and says that the truth is achieved not by reasoning but by doing God's will and by being involved and committed to Him. Truth is not universal, but personal. It can be different for each person, depending on what God plans for him or her. Truth is not timeless but local and historical. The creation took place in a certain place and at a particular time, and then a series of events occurred to divide history into two eras—before and after Christ (in the Christian tradition).

Table 11.1 summarizes the main characteristics of the two traditions according to Dreyfus.

Throughout history, there have been many attempts to reconcile these two tendencies. Dreyfus considers the Gospel of John to be the first. In the fourth

Table 11.1 The characteristics of the Greek and Judeo traditions

Greek-philosophical	*Judeo-Christian*
Detached	Involved, committed
Disembodied	Embodied
Timeless	Historical
Universal	Local
Rational	Spiritual

century, St. Augustine, in *De Doctrina Christiana,* attempted to interpret Christian doctrines in Platonic terms. Almost one thousand years later, St. Thomas Aquinas (thirteenth century) published his most influential work—*Summa Theologiae* (2006), in which he applied the philosophy of Aristotle to theology. Dante Alighieri (fourteenth century) put St. Thomas Aquinas's view in a poetic form in *La Divina Commedia* (1972). At the end of the Renaissance, starting modern philosophy, Rene Descartes (1637 [1998]) viewed God from a rational perspective. One generation later, according to Dreyfus (2006), Pascal (1966) had a paradoxical view of the human condition and questioned Descartes' view from an existentialist perspective. More than a century later, Hegel (1807 [1977]) developed a concept of the universe in which he tried to reconcile reason, history, and Christianity.

The Danish philosopher and religious thinker Søren Kierkegaard (1843 [1994]), the first existential philosopher, was a strong critic of Hegel. Kierkegaard's solution to the dichotomy of Western civilization is an unconditional commitment to someone or something, such as an ideology or a cause. Kierkegaard's *Fear and Trembling* has a subtitle—*A Dialectical Lyric.* Dreyfus (2006) calls attention to the paradox of something being dialectical or philosophical and, at the same time, being lyrical or poetic.

Also in the nineteenth century, another existentialist, Friedrich Nietzsche, developed a concept of life and its possible meaning as an aesthetic experience. In *The Birth of Tragedy,* Nietzsche (1872 [2006]) describes ancient Greek culture as a conflict between two tendencies: Apollonian and Dionysian, based on the two Greek deities. Solomon (1996, 233) states that "Dionysus, the god of wine, sexuality, and revelry, represents the dynamic flux of being, the acceptance of fate, the chaos of creativity . . . Apollo, the sun god, by contrast, reflects the Athenian fascination with beauty and order." Greek tragedy was their way to reconcile these two tendencies.

Western history oscillates between periods dominated by rational Platonic values and periods characterized by introspection and emotionalism. Art and music always reflect this dichotomy. In periods when reason dominates, music is universal and usually does not attempt to describe anything outside the music itself. In periods when thought is dominated by emotion and romanticism, music is idiosyncratic and representative, and composers attempt to create a musical denotation level. The following is a discussion of music history with the perspective of each period described in terms of the level of the attempt to create a denotation of music and the level of universality of that music. It attempts to resolve the conflict between denotation and universality in music as the dichotomy depicted by the concepts of the Apollonian and the Dionysian.

Music Denotation in a Historical Perspective

During the Middle Ages, between 500 CE and 1450 CE, music was used mainly for religious purposes, and many thought that it could only be used in the name of God. This is a fine example of music denotation. In the twelfth and thirteenth centuries, secular music started to flourish in many parts of Europe. In southern France, the troubadours were poets and musicians who sang monophonic songs about love. They wrote in the vernacular tongue Old Provencal, and it reached a larger audience. Their counterparts in northern France were called Trouvers, and in Germany, Minnesingers.

Vocal music in the church, such as the Gregorian chant, had a very specific function of setting the listener's mind in the spirit of prayer and within the context of his relationship to God. The music was not meant to call attention to itself. The parishioners were not supposed to pay attention to the music because they would forget what they were doing in the church. There was an attempt to establish a musical denotation by setting a purpose and a meaning to music. This attempt was driven by religious purposes.

The fall of Constantinople occurred in 1453, the same year in which Copernicus developed the first heliocentric system and took the earth, and consequently the human being, out of the center of the universe with his *De Revolutionibus Orbium Coelestium*. The Renaissance, between the years 1450 and 1600, began with the revival of the classical and humanistic values of ancient Rome and Greece. The spirituality of the Middle Ages gave way to an increased interest in this world. The Apollonian concepts of beauty, clarity, and perfection dominated the arts.

In the Renaissance, religious music aimed at perfection. The church musician Giovanni Pierluigi da Palestrina followed strict rules to compose complex and beautiful music and, at the same time, to achieve the function of religious spirit in the medieval period. The music was perfect; all the dissonances were carefully prepared and resolved to keep the flow and prevent the listeners' minds from straying away from the spiritual purpose.

This is one of the periods in history when there was a conflict between the attempt for a denotation level of music and its universality.

Toward the end of the sixteenth century, several composers were concerned with how music would reflect a text, and they developed a style called *Musica Reservata*. It was a style that used chromaticism, ornaments, and other new techniques of the period to reinforce the text being sung. Around 1570 in Florence, a group of nobles, later called *Camerata*, started to meet in Giovanni Bardi's palace to discuss arts and science and to listen to new music. They were concerned with the way in which the ancient Greeks had achieved "powerful effects with their music" (Grout 1988). Plato theorizes in *The Republic* that the modes in which melodies are composed determine what emotions or states they incite in the listener.[3] Plato also thought that melodies could imitate a person's exclamation and thus incite that particular emotion in the listener. The philosopher Peter Kivy states that the *Camerata* "argued that the power of music to arouse the human emotions lay in the representations, by melody of human speaking voice when expressing the various emotions" (2002, 17).

The scientific and philosophic thinking of the end of the Renaissance opened the path for the art of the Baroque period (between 1600 and 1750). Galileo Galilei (1564–1642) developed the scientific method that would shape science from that point on. René Descartes started modern philosophy with *Discours de la Methode,* and in 1649, Descartes published *Les passions de l'âme*, where he described the "six basic emotions" as he understood them. At the end of the seventeenth century, Isaac Newton published *Philosophiae Naturalis Principia Mathematica,* demonstrating how he developed mathematical functions that can predict occurrences based on observation of phenomena. These changes in human thinking were reflected in the transformation that occurred in the music of the Baroque period and the tonal music of the next centuries.

The Baroque period started with changes, such as the establishment of tonality, instrumental music, and opera. Tonal music dominated music for the next 300 years and most of the popular music in the twentieth century. Instrumental music and opera became the music for entertainment of the courts and the people.

Composers believed that music could be translated into emotions and developed the Doctrine of Affects, probably the strongest example of an attempt to establish a musical denotation. It started with Musica Reservata in the previous century and became a practice among baroque composers. The theory was published by many during the eighteenth century, with precise "translations" of musical signs and techniques for "affections." This is one of the clearest attempts to create a denotation of music, and at the same time, the music was not intended to be universal. The composers intended to convey certain affections to the listeners, and expected the listeners to receive the same messages. Each culture had its own style.

With the rise of scientific thinking after Isaac Newton, Europe started a new age based on reason called the Enlightenment. It merged in England with the philosophers Locke and Hume. It quickly moved to France with Montesquieu and Voltaire and culminated with the French Revolution in 1789. Thinkers of the time believed in secularism, empiricism, and rationalism. National borders were ignored in a new "cosmopolitan" age. Values and truth were universal and thought was progressive and liberal.

This period, known as the Age of Classicism (1750–1810), reflected the Enlightenment way of thinking. According to Grout (1988, 547), the ideal music of the period might be described as follows:

> [I]ts language should be universal, not limited by national boundaries; it should be noble as well as entertaining; it should be expressive within the boundaries of decorum; it should be 'natural', in the sense of being free of needless technical complications and capable of immediately pleasing any normally sensitive listener.

Composers valued balance, perfection, form, and objective expression. Art was within the reach of everybody, and the same music entertained the courts and the people. Opera was very popular, and composers such as Mozart wrote for both the court and the people's theater. In the Classical period, music was to be perfect, without a denotation level, and universal.

The nineteenth century was a period of conflicts and a dualistic way of thinking. The Industrial Revolution brought prosperity and helped cities to grow. The French Revolution changed the general view of the world order of the Enlightenment and nationalism emerged. Charles Darwin published *The Origin of Species,* which challenged the place in the universe held by human beings. This new view of the world and the conflicting and dualistic ideas of the time were reflected in art, which had to be personal and super-expressive. The universality of the previous period did not have a place. Each composer would have his or her own way of expressing emotions. Classicism gave way to a period called *Romanticism* (1810–1910). Romantic music is idiosyncratic and subjective. Grout (1988, 658) says that "against classic ideas of order, equilibrium, control, and perfection within acknowledged limits, Romanticism cherishes freedom, movement, passion, and endless pursuit of the unattainable."

Based on the theories of Immanuel Kant, the German philosopher Arthur Schopenhauer (1958) developed the concept of the *Will* as the ultimate reality and inner driving force in humans. The philosopher believed that music was the representation of the will itself. Schopenhauer's ideas influenced Richard Wagner (1983, 510), who, in his autobiography, refers to the philosopher's work *The World as Will and Idea*, writing that:

> through it, I was able to judge things which I had previously grasped only instinctively, and it gave me more or less the equivalent of what I had gained musically from the close study of the principles of counterpoint. ... all my subsequent occasional writings about artistic matters of special interest to me clearly demonstrate the impact of my study of Schopenhauer and what I had gained by it.

The interest in Schopenhauer's work was one of the first reasons that Wagner got close to Friedrich Nietzsche, who became a frequent guest at the composer's house in Tribschen. Nietzsche wrote about Wagner with admiration initially. Later, however, Nietzsche became disappointed with the composer's ideas, the banality of his performances, and his anti-Semitism. Although he still valued the composer's music, he completely distanced himself from the family and wrote the essay *Nietzsche Contra Wagner*.

Composers from the Romantic period did not believe that music could be translated into "affections" as the Baroque ones did, but they frequently tried to represent extramusical elements with their music. This idea started with Beethoven, the transitional composer, with his Pastoral Symphony. Later, several new genres developed, such as Liszt's "symphonic poems" and Berlioz's "program symphonies." This new attempt sought to develop a denotation level of music, while recognizing that music was not universal. Romantic music is Dionysian, with personal elements, and idiosyncratic. As in the Baroque period, Romanticism had a high level of denotation with a low level of universality.

The Impressionist period (from the late nineteenth century to the middle of the twentieth century) overlaps in time with the Romantic and late Romantic periods. Claude Debussy and the French painters of the period were influenced by Eastern art. Debussy's music was a turning point for tonality, and his temporal concept started to transcend the rational, going toward a greater "relative perception of time."

Albert Einstein changed this concept with his *Theory of Special Relativity*, published in 1905. The concept of the steady and universal flow of time that had been accepted since Newton was no longer absolute. Time was now relative to the observer, and it could stretch and contract depending on the observer's reference point. The change in this concept, believed to be one of the most basic in nature, changed the human view of the universe, and this was reflected in all areas, including the arts.

The combination of the Impressionist influence, the new relativistic concept of time, and primitive Russian rhythms resulted in Stravinsky's music and the famous riot at the premiere of *Le Sacre du Printemps*. Einstein's concept of time influenced Stravinsky's music all his life. The beginning of *Le Sacre du Printemps* uses several musical techniques that make the listener lose his or her sense of measured time. The regular pulse of traditional music could not be perceived, and the music would flow freely in time. Pablo Picasso changed the way time was represented in painting with his cubism. A figure could be seen from several angles at the same time. James Joyce (1998) introduced a new concept of time in writing, describing one day in the life of the character Leopold Bloom in *Ulysses*.

At the same time, Arnold Schoenberg was not concerned with the concept of time but with the expansion of tonality. Schoenberg broke the barrier of the tonal system with the twelve-tone technique. The focal point of tonality disappears, giving all twelve notes the same hierarchical importance. The abstract painter Wassily Kandinsky's revolutionary style of painting and its relation to traditional painting correspond to the revolutionary musical insights of Schoenberg. Kandinsky was very impressed with Schoenberg's music, and the two exchanged a series of letters.

Schoenberg had two disciples: Alban Berg and Anton Webern. The three composers, known as the second Viennese school, exemplified Expressionist music, which impacted profoundly the subsequent twentieth-century music. Art music became more intellectual and drifted away from the general public. Their music was meant for universality and objectivity. Throughout the twentieth century, this distance increased although there were and still are many attempts to bring music back to tonality and closer to the general public.

During the nineteenth century, the nation-state concept was strong and nationalism reached its peak at the beginning of the 1900s. Extreme nationalism led to the rediscovery of folk music. Nationalist composers reacted to the intellectual and avant-garde music of Schoenberg and turned to the roots of their country's musical identity. Nationalism in music, then, became both a reactionary and conservative movement. The idea was perfect for the purposes of governments who needed to reinforce the country's identity with important means such as music. Nationalist music happened almost everywhere in the world and in a few countries, such as Germany and Spain, it was used as a means to disseminate sociopolitical ideologies.

Nationalism was a politically driven attempt to establish a musical denotation. Nationalist music has to be local and historical, not universal. The two concepts of denotation and universality came together one more time in the exact opposite way. In both the Baroque and the Nationalist periods, there were attempts to create a denotation level of music, but in the Baroque period, the reference to emotions was the main goal, whereas for the nationalists, the aim was a low level of universality. In other words, denotation was used as a reference to a particular culture in the Nationalist period.

Grout (1988, 657) compares the cyclic oscillation between two tendencies in history, saying that:

> romantic art differs from classic art by its greater emphasis on the qualities of remoteness and strangeness, with all that such emphasis may imply as to choice and treatment of material. Romanticism, in this general sense, is not a phenomenon of any one period, but has occurred at various times in various forms. It is possible to see in the history of music, and of the other arts, alternations of classicism and romanticism. Thus the Baroque period may be considered romantic in comparison with the Renaissance in somewhat the same way the nineteenth century is romantic in comparison with the classicism of the eighteenth century.

One might argue that in this historical perspective, music shifts between Apollonian and Dionysian periods. During Apollonian periods, such as those of the Renaissance and Classicism, music is objective and universal, and values perfection, balance, and form. During Dionysian periods such as those of Baroque and Romanticism, music is subjective and idiosyncratic and represents human conflicts. Table 11.2 summarizes the main characteristics of the two tendencies.

Further, during Apollonian periods, music is universal and does not try to represent extramusical concepts. During Dionysian periods, music is not universal, and there is always an attempt to establish a denotation level by creating external references. Figure 11.1 shows that the level of universality is always the opposite of the level of music denotation.

The attempts that develop and resolve the dichotomy of denotation and universality in music discussed above mainly took place in West European

Table 11.2 Contrasts between Apollonian and Dionysian periods

Apollonian	*Dionysian*
Renaissance, Classicism, Expressionism	*Baroque, Romanticism, Nationalism*
Music is:	Music is:
Objective	Subjective
Universal	Idiosyncratic
Emphasis on:	Emphasis on:
Perfection	Expression
Balance	Conflict
Form	Imagination
Connotation	Denotation

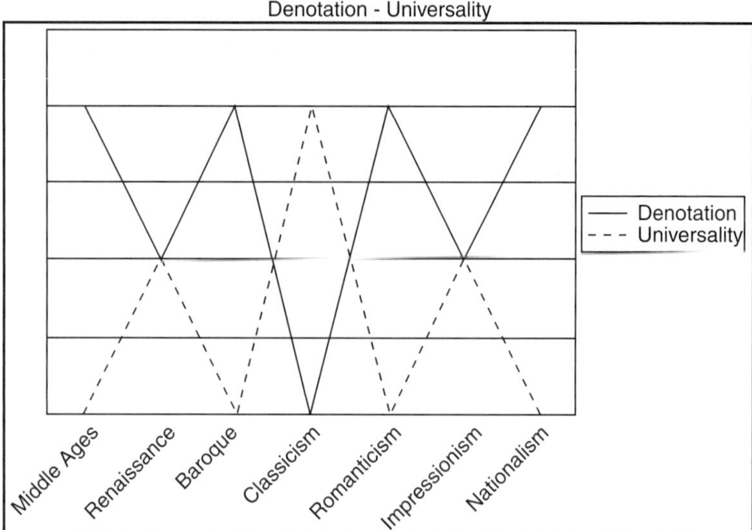

Figure 11.1 Relationship between denotation and universality in several historic periods.

states, which have been influenced, at least historically, by relatively similar cultural, philosophical, and religious backgrounds. It is intriguing to examine how Brazil and Japan, which are located in different continents, with different cultural formations and nationalisms, developed music in the modern and contemporary eras, and this music emphasizes the influence of globalization.

Anthropophagite Manifesto

Nationalism in Brazil had very distinctive characteristics. The return to the roots of the native Indian people combined with an avant-garde movement. In 1922 a group of artists organized the Week of Modern Art at the Municipal Theatre in São Paulo, which was a defining moment for the establishment of Brazilian cultural identity. After a century of independence from Portugal, the influence of natives and artists who had lived and studied in Paris resulted in this progressive movement. This new Brazilian art was divided into two groups, the Nationalists, who wanted art to be free of foreign influences, and the *Anthropophagics,* who wanted to digest all the influences and create something new. The only modern Brazilian composer invited to participate was Heitor Villa-Lobos.

The central figure of the Anthropophagic movement was the poet, writer, and dramatist Oswald de Andrade. In 1924 Andrade published *Manifesto Pau-Brazil* along with his future wife, the painter Tarsila do Amaral, reinforcing the need for a Brazilian art based on the country's Indian roots and at the same time critically incorporating European avant-gardism in a parodic tone. Pau-Brasil is the name of redwood trees that were abundant during the first century of the country's discovery in 1500 and that almost vanished due to unsustainable harvesting and export to Europe. The term *pau-brasil* was used by de Andrade and do Amaral to refer to the idea of Brazilian poetry as an export product.

The two artists went further in 1928 when they published a newspaper entitled *Anthropophagite Manifesto*, a humorous reference to the cannibalism among some Brazilian native tribes. They used the word "anthropophagite," or cannibal, to say that the only way the people would develop a true Brazilian art would be by "devouring" the European influence instead of copying it or reacting to it by being conservative nationalists. That was the difference between the Brazilian and most other nationalist movements of the period—the idea that a national art of a multicultural country like Brazil should be based on the country's roots and "incorporate" European influences, not simply deny them. This concept is clear in statements of the *Anthropophagite Manifesto* such as "we want the Carahiba revolution. Bigger than the French Revolution.... We made Christ be born in Bahia. Or in Belém do Pará." In the manifesto, revolutionary ideas were always presented with humor: "Before the Portuguese discovered Brazil, Brazil had discovered happiness" and "Happiness is the proof of the pudding."

De Andrade and do Amaral insist on the influence of Brazilian roots with reference to one of the native languages, the Tupy, in the famous quote: "Tupy or not Tupy, that is the question." They express their disgust at repression, with the proposal of a Brazilian utopia based on completely different elements, "against social reality, dressed and oppressive, registered by Freud-reality without complexes, without madness, without prostitutions and without the prisons of the matriarchy of Pindorama."

Another humorous fact is that the author signed the article as "Oswald de Andrade, In Piratininga [the original Indian name of the city of Sao Paulo] Year 374 of the swallowing of the Bispo Sardinha." Bispo Sardinha was the first Brazilian Bishop who, in 1556, was killed and devoured by the Indian Caetes.

The idea of nationalism in Brazil was to "digest" European influence and incorporate it into the local tradition. This led to a nationalism that had a "global" characteristic that exhibited hybridization of different cultures. Brazilian culture was formed by the combination of several

European influences, such as Portuguese, Italian, Spanish, and German, with native roots, and its nationalism was a paradox. It had both local and universal components.

Brazilian nationalism in music shows one of the consequences of some nations expressing their identities after becoming independent of colonial power, which played a significant role in facilitating willing and unwilling global cultural exchange. Although many colonies became independent, particularly after the Second World War, the former colonial powers' economic, political, and cultural influence did not necessarily wither. Many might argue that the current globalization phenomenon is an extended form of colonial imperialism, Americanization, or Westernization, which continue to dominate technological advancement. The rapid technological changes in recent decades have brought the world cultures close to each other by facilitating the flow of people, ideas, and materials at an unprecedented speed. Although the debate over whether the global exchange between the West and the rest is more one-directional or reciprocal is beyond the scope of this chapter, the Western influence on other world cultures continues. That is undeniable.

Other than Brazil, another intriguing case is that of Japan, which closed its borders with the hope of fending off outside influence. Yet it failed to do so, at least in the field of music. In this case, Japanese pop music will be used to show the impact of globalization on Japan. Before any further discussion, the impact of technology on music should be explored.

The Postwar Music Trends

In the second part of the twentieth century, art music, which is most commonly called classical music, became more experimental and even more elitist than it had been earlier. On the other hand, popular music became more easily available, and it grew into a huge business. Television and radio sped up the transfer of information but did not really "globalize" the world as many had thought it would. The invention of the long-playing record (LP) gave more people access to music and changed the way people would listen to music.

Since the 1960s, art music included noises (*musique concrète*), graphic scores with the participation of the performer as a co-composer. The development of electronic music added a completely new range of sounds for composers. Rock music became more elaborate, and the use of electronic devices became more popular. The progressive rock movement mixed rock with classical and contemporary music. These musicians were trained in classical music and they "consciously" mixed the genres. After the 1970s, computers became more accessible, giving artists and musicians new tools with a better technology.

During the 1970s, an urban phenomenon gave birth to a new style of pop music, the hip-hop. The style uses more electronic music, but unlike progressive rock musicians, hip-hop artistes were not necessarily conscious of electronic music.

In the 1980s, the concept of world music was coined to designate non-mainstream music that incorporates an ethnic element. Many of the world music artists also mix genres and influences to create the crossover style.

The last two decades of the twentieth century saw the growth of a technology that would revolutionize the world of communications, the Internet. Now, people can get information or chat with somebody anytime, anywhere, on the other side of world, many time zones away.

This led to the development of a specific language, which is a low-level English. Most people can have access and even publish their own Web sites with anything they want for very little money. Music downloading has become an integral part of our world culture. The iTunes Music Store, which started in 2003, had sold over 3 billion songs by July 2007.

Over the last few decades, mainstream music has become part of the corporate world and the dominance of Western culture, via means of communication, has caused an impact on cultures all over the world. This influence is seen clearly in the millenary culture of Japan. A brief analysis of the differences between Western and Eastern cultures will help one to understand this impact.

Eastern and Western Cultures and Globalization

Hans-Joachim Koellreutter was always interested in Eastern cultures and that influenced his music significantly. He was the director of the *German Cultural Institute* in Tokyo and regional representative of *Goethe Institute* between 1970 and 1974. During this period, he exchanged letters with the Japanese scholar and German teacher Satoshi Tanaka. In a series of twelve letters, Koellreutter (1983) and Tanaka discussed the differences between Western and Eastern cultures. According to Tanaka, twentieth century physics, which included relativity and quantum mechanics, brought a view of the universe to Western civilization that is close to the Eastern view. Scholars agree that Japanese thinking considers everything to be relative; opposing concepts are complementary, and expression is introverted, intuitive, and global. Western thinking is dependent on the concept of the "absolute;" opposing concepts are contradictory, and expression is extroverted, analytic, and rational.

Despite the differences between Eastern and Western music, the encounter of the two types of music during the colonial eras induced musical diffusion. Japan had been a tribal society and had lived in relative isolation over a thousand of years of its history. The problems posed by internal conflict with regional regional daimyo who gained political power through international trade and the arrival of Portuguese missionaries and traders in the sixteenth century led Japan to decide to completely seal itself off from the outside world by closing its ports. Between 1635 and 1853, known as the Tokugawa era, Japan lived in isolation again, except for contact with a few foreign traders from Korea, China, and Holland.

The ports were only reopened again in 1853 for American trade under the pressure of the presence of the American Navy led by Commodore Perry. In about 1868, the Meiji emperor restored his supreme power by overthrowing the Tokugawa shogun, and started a version of modernization, which safeguarded itself from European colonization. Yet Meiji Japan incorporated Western models such as the navy of the British, the army of France, and the education system of the United States, and introduced Western music—a word *ongaku* was devised to designate music as separate from the other arts. In contrast, Japanese music before this period had been considered part of the arts and with specific functions.

An interesting incident helps illustrate the reciprocal influence of Western and Eastern music. All Impressionist artists, including Debussy, were influenced by Eastern music and art at the turn of the century. In the same way, the Japanese composer Toru Takemitsu (1930–1996) was among the most important figures who wrote music in the Western tradition. However, he preserved a fundamental Japanese identity despite being influenced by Debussy.

Tanaka argued in the early 1970s that the Japanese should be able to incorporate Western culture without jeopardizing their own traditions. Perhaps, in a similar way, the *Anthropophagite* tried to absorb external influences without losing the Brazilian identity. In the last decades though, the influence of Western culture has changed completely the way Eastern cultures view their own traditions, including those of Japan. Western culture reaches them in a global manner, making their scale of values obscure. What is important or valuable is relative to one's perception and what is presented to a person. The result is seen in examples such as the current Japanese pop music, which is completely Americanized. A millenary culture and tradition might be in danger because of the power and the values of the global mass media phenomenon.

Koellreutter wrote to Tanaka in 1976 that he was convinced that in the technological era, the human race would have to change and humans would become global beings who were not part of a national group or religion. In a world without "*vis-à-vis*,"[4] one would feel at home in all cultural fields. The exchange of experiences and ideas would lead to a different dynamic, producing new forces and possibilities. Koellreutter knew that we would have to give up part of our traditions in favor of a new view that would incorporate and open our consciousness to universal values.

The concept of globalization, as we know today, developed a decade before Koellreutter wrote about his view of the future world. At the beginning of the twenty-first century, the perception of our own identity is challenged by global influences due to the increasingly rapid flow of people, ideologies, images, and commodities mediated by advanced technological media. Even though geographic and political boundaries are well defined on maps, they are blurred by the mass media and what is presented as important to the people within that boundary.

Koellreutter did not live to see the global world that is developing, and maybe, many of us are giving up some of our traditions in favor of other values. The problem is that the extension of our consciousness takes shape as a supranational understanding of universal relations. If only one dominant culture determines the future values of the whole world, we are not incorporating, assimilating, or extending our consciousness toward universal values.

The development of art music at the turn of this century might be going in the direction Koellreutter wanted. Art music composed today is closer to Koellreutter's conception than it ever was in history. Now, music might be universal, not in the Apollonian sense, but in the sense that we are incorporating all traditions, tendencies, and the reality of our technological world. Art music is becoming universal but the audience is still elite. Since the beginning of the twentieth century, the distance between art music and the general public has increased. Paradoxically, art music is being suffocated by other universal values—the ones dictated by commercial music.

Popular music was one of the many great cultural developments of the twentieth century. Jazz and rock have crossed over the boundaries of pop and classical music. But at the end of the last century, pop music became more of a business than an art. A global commercial music emerges as a product of a culture that is neither national nor supranational, it is borderless. In the global world, major corporations no longer have a country, but function all over the world. The result blurs national boundaries even further, and consequently, leads to a less defined sense of identity.

In a world without "vis-à-vis," people would transcend local values without surpassing them. The human race would have to incorporate and assimilate all cultural influences, integrating them creatively. Humanity, as a whole, would experience an organic growth, leading to sociocultural equilibrium. Koellreutter sees the inevitable construction of a universal culture as the only alternative to destruction. The development of this global culture, a world without "vis-à-vis" (without barriers), requires a continuous rediscovery of our own identity, because each rediscovery deepens the awareness process that enlarges, enriches, and frees this identity. A world without "vis-à-vis," Koellreutter continues, is fatal necessity, but only part of the way. It is not a final purpose, because each obtained goal merely creates a new challenge.

Notes

1. Koellreutter defined music as a language in his book about musical terminology, but later, he changed his concept. He considered music an art that uses a system of sound signs. This concept was never published, and it is from a personal account of the author.
2. Koellreutter described elemental as simple, essential, and fundamental and also as a new emergent musical idiom that uses silence and noise as well as pitches; the tempo is free from a pulse or beat.
3. Greek music was based on a system of scales called modes. They were based on the position of the half-steps in the scale and were later used in medieval music.
4. "Vis-à-vis," from the French, means "face-to-face." Koellreutter uses it as a reference to the conflict between cultures as "opposing" forces. He refers to this term as "barriers."

References

Alighieri, Dante. 1972. *La Divina Commedia*. Cambridge: Harvard University Press.

Andrade, Oswald. 1924. Manifesto Pau-Brasil. *Correio da Manhã* (March 18, Rio de Janeiro).

———. 1928. Manifesto Antropófago. *Revista de Antropofagia* (May).

Aquinas, Saint Thomas. 2006. *Summa Theologia*. Cambridge, United Kingdom: Cambridge University Press.

Descartes, Rene. 1998. *Discourse on Method and Meditations on First Philosophy*. Indianapolis: Hackett.

Dreyfus, Hubert. 2006. *Phil 7—Existentialism in Literature and Film*. Podcast. University of California, Berkeley. <http://webcast.berkeley.edu/course_details.php?seriesid=1906978306> (accessed between January 16, 2006, and August 5, 2006).

Eco, Umberto. 1968. *La Struttura Assente. La Ricera Semiotica e il Metodo Strutturale*. Milan: Bompiani.

Grout, Donald J., and Claude V. Palisca. 1988. *A History of Western Music*. New York: W. W. Norton.

Hegel, Georg W. F. 1977. *Phenomenology of Spirit*. Oxford: Clarendon.

Joyce, James. 1998. *Ulysses*. London: Folio Society.

Kierkegaard, Søren. 1994. *Fear and Trembling and the Book of Adler*. London: Everyman's Library.

Kivy, Peter. 2002. *Introduction to a Philosophy of Music*. New York: Oxford.

Koellreutter, Hans-Joachim. 1983. *Estética*. Trans. Saloméa Gandelman. São Paulo: Novas Metas.

———. 1987. *Introdução à Estética e à Composição Musical Contemporânea*. Porto Alegre, Brazil: Editora Movimento.

———. 1990. *Terminologia de uma Nova Estética da Música*. Porto Alegre: Editora Movimento.

Monelle, R. 2000. *The Sense of Music*. Princeton, NJ: Princeton University Press.

Nattiez, Jean-Jacques. 1975. *Fondements d'une Sémiologie de la Musique*. Paris: Union Générale.

Nietzsche, F. 2006. *The Birth of Tragedy*. Trans. Ronald Speirs. Cambridge: Cambridge University Press.

Pascal, Blaise. 1966. *Pensées*. Baltimore: Penguin.

Schopenhauer, A. 1958. *The World as Will and Representation*. New York: Dover.

Solomon, Robert, and Kathleen Higgins. 1996. *A Short History of Philosophy*. New York: Oxford University Press.

Tarasti, E. 1994. *A Theory of Musical Semiotics*. Bloomington: Indiana Univ. Press.

———. 2002. *Signs of Music: A Guide to Musical Semiotics*. New York: Mouton de Gruyter.

Wagner, R. 1983. *My Life*. Trans. Andrew Gray. Cambridge: Cambridge University Press.

CHAPTER 12

Human Movements: Consequences to Global Biogeography

Thomas Horvath

The examples discussed throughout this book show that globalization influences modern society's social, political, and economic structures. However, globalization also impacts the biological and scientific environments. Lewellen's definition that "contemporary globalization is the increasing flow of trade, finance, culture, ideas and people brought about by the sophisticated technology of communications and travel and by the worldwide spread of neoliberal capitalism and it is the local and regional adaptations to and resistances against these flows" (2002, 8–9) misses the accidental movements of nonhuman species. Although many of the trends in increased globalization have been going on since the beginning of trade itself, the scale has grown substantially in the past fifty years. The latter half of the twentieth century has seen an exponential increase in the number of species being transported between distinct geographically based ecosystems as a result of advances in technology, especially transportation. These technological advances are the direct result of globalization.[1] As the number of multinational corporations has increased in the latter half of the twentieth century (Gabel and Bruner 2003, 3), so has the total tonnage of materials being moved between continents by these corporations. Additionally, Gabel and Bruner observe, "The transportation revolution led to shrinking the time it takes to get people and materials from here to there" (2003, 9). For nonhuman "hitchhikers," this shrinking of time has greatly increased the number of species that can now take part in colonization processes. Time is money when transporting materials from place to place. Shorter transport times mean higher profits, but it also enhances the survival of accidental stowaways by minimizing their exposure to unnatural conditions inside containers, ships, or airplanes. Functionally, more species are now able to successfully colonize distant habitats than ever before. What does this mean for the natural borders of plants, animals, and other nonhuman species?

This chapter looks at how the natural borders of nonhuman species are becoming less and less meaningful. This is not because species have decided to ignore their natural surroundings and gone off in search of greener pastures; instead, this is rather closely linked to many of the social aspects related to globalization. In essence, humans have decided either consciously or unconsciously to disregard natural borders. We have altered the mobility processes in a natural environment, and we continue to disregard nature despite many of the economic consequences realized most recently. Thus, due to human behaviors, especially within the past few hundred years, what has been witnessed is an unprecedented increase in the rate of the movement of people and goods with deleterious consequences for the natural organization of ecological communities.

I am defining natural borders as geographic barriers or environmental conditions that prevent or have prevented species from moving from one area to another. Benedict Anderson (1991), in *Imagined Communities*, maintains that political communities with their finite boundaries are imaginary spaces. We manifest these spaces as lines drawn on geopolitical maps rather than ecological maps. Natural borders are not arbitrary lines drawn by political action. Rather, environmental conditions determined prior to the arrival of modern humans created these boundaries. For example, one area may be too dry, thus excluding certain species from that area. Natural borders based on environmental conditions often have gradual transitions, with a few individuals from a species living on the extreme edge of borders imposed by environmental conditions. These geographic features may also keep a species from crossing over into an area that could theoretically support it. Natural borders and boundaries do share some similarities with those that are constructed by political entities. Oceans were once a barrier to human populations, and they often compose the borders of countries. Mountain ranges have long kept populations of humans from significant amounts of interactions. For example, mountain barriers have led to the development of separate dialects of the German language within Germany itself (König 1978). Later in the chapter, I will give examples of how species have used human systems as transport mechanisms over inhospitable terrains in search of new habitable environments.

An Introduction to Biogeography

Biogeography, a branch of science, attempts to define and explain the natural boundaries of species and patterns of species distributions. A species range is the geographic area in which the species is found exclusively. This term is not without contradictions, however, because many species are quite mobile. Think of a migrating bird, such as the American robin. It is found in Northern Canada and throughout the continental United States. This is its breeding range, which correlates to its wintering range. At certain times of the year, it is also found as far south as Mexico, which is its wintering range. Looking through any bird field guide will enable one to learn about species ranges.

Biologists and naturalists have long been interested in describing the habitation patterns of flora and fauna. For example, Alexander von Humboldt wrote numerous volumes on the distribution of plants around the world in the eighteenth and nineteenth centuries. One of the most influential works describing ecological borders, *The Geographical Distribution of Animals* (two volumes, 1876), was written by Alfred Russell Wallace. On the basis of his observations and data collected on the distribution of plants and animals (primarily birds), Wallace defined eight distinct realms within which species shared a common evolutionary starting point (see Figure 12.1). The geographical realms possessed natural barriers (e.g., mountain ranges, deserts, or ocean expanses) that prevented large-scale movements. In essence, the realms were separated from each other for extended periods of time, with only occasional transgressions, thus allowing the development of unique flora and fauna. As a result, two landscape pictures, one populated with koala bears and kangaroos, the other with black bears and bison, are immediately recognizable as those of Australia and North America (or Australian and Nearctic in Wallace's terms). Even

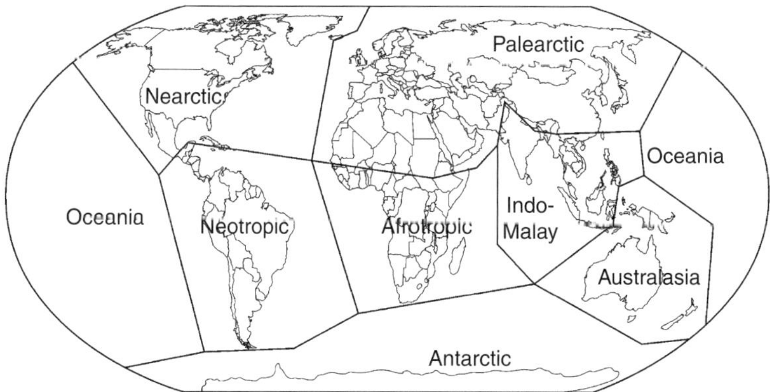

Figure 12.1 Biogeographic borders.

The lines in the figure above approximate the biogeographic zones originally proposed by Alfred Russell Wallace. The lines demarcate natural boundaries that define zones of common evolution. Before human time, these lines were rarely crossed by natural movement patterns of plants and animals.

within a context, smaller-scale boundaries exist to restrict species movement and habitation. Olson et al. (2001) describe fourteen biogeographic regions, and nested in those are 867 ecoregions. The ecoregion concept, now widely accepted as being ecologically relevant, influences many environmental protection policies.

Despite all of this, natural borders are never stationary or static as they exhibit expansion and contraction over long geologic time frames. For example, as global climates have changed, so too has the distribution of plants and animals. Ice ages would have greatly restricted the northern ranges of many species. But as the ice masses retreated, species expanded back into the regions. Such expansions are now occurring as the global climate warms. For example, a model of plant and animal habitation of the Glacier National Park in Montana shows an expected gain of close to forty species due to expanded northward and higher altitude species movement caused by changes in global temperature (Burns et al. 2003).

Natural boundaries do exist, but they can also be crossed. If a species makes a successful jump from one region to another, the geographic barriers that define the regions must be overcome. Biological colonization is not as simple as just crossing from one region to another as many successive steps must take place. Each is fraught with difficulties.

The process of colonization has been well studied in biology, and a few important steps have been outlined. First, individuals from a population must find a way to disperse into an area beyond their original range. Many different methods have arisen among species to aid in their dispersal. Take, for example, the airborne seeds of the common flowering plant, the dandelion. A familiar sight during the spring and summer months are the tiny dandelion seeds connected to a white "parachute" called a pappus, dispersing themselves across fields, often aided by children puffing the seeds free from the flower. These seeds can travel many kilometers under proper wind conditions (Tackenberg et al. 2003). In the animal world, spiders are known to be very successful dispersers. In a process called ballooning or kiting, a spider will expel silk threads that act as an air foil by carrying the spider on air currents. Some spiders have been collected from airplanes as high as 5,000 feet (Glick 1939). Of course, only arriving at a new locale does not constitute colonization. The differences between environments often bring new challenges that need to be overcome. The new environment must have conditions suitable for the dispersed specimen. If the dandelion seed or the ballooning spider falls in the middle of an interstate highway, it will not find conditions that would allow it to survive. Arriving in an environment full of predators or superior species (i.e., competition) usually means a reduction of the chances of survival. Once you arrive and survive, then there is the problem of reproducing. For many asexual species, this is less of a problem because they can produce new individuals on their own. But members of sexually reproducing species must find a mate and manage to successfully produce the next generation. Enough individual processes must work in collaboration in order to establish a self-sustaining colony. During any of the steps in the colonization process, chance events can negate colonization. As an example, spiders may arrive on a volcanic island and successfully reproduce. But what happens if the volcano then erupts and covers the island in a new layer of lava? The spider colonization process was for naught.[2] It is not an easy process to increase your survival chances given all of the potential pitfalls. Most species stay somewhat restricted to their geographic area and make only small-scale changes in their range, expanding and contracting their range over time. An analogy can be drawn with the expansion of the human range. Some cultures and nationalities have expanded and contracted over time. These were not necessarily easy processes either, and were often achieved only through direct conflict with indigenous or neighboring peoples. Many cultures were lost or subsumed into the larger conquering cultures as a result.

However, a few species seem to be very successful at managing the steps of colonization as they have become established in many biogeographical regions. A pan-global species is one found naturally in many of the biogeographical regions. As a rule, very few pan-global species exist. Humans are the obvious example.

Human Influences on Natural Borders

The human species have been incredibly successful in conquering natural borders. It seems no mountain was either high enough or any ocean wide enough to prevent us from colonizing new biogeographical regions. In fact, even our predecessor, *Homo erectus*, was able to move into new territories, leaving the warm environments of the African continent and venturing out to colonize Europe, Asia, and Indo-Asia. Each successive hominid species took their turn moving out of Africa to replace existing hominids throughout the world. Little, if any, evidence suggests that early hominids brought much with them in terms of other species. These early hunter-gatherer societies tended to move themselves to find the resources they needed to survive, rather than move their resources to themselves. However, as human populations increased, especially after the arrival of modern humans, *Homo sapiens*, the impact on the species they encountered was severe. Strong evidence suggests that as humans began expanding their range and occupying new lands, mass extinctions followed. For example, as humans moved from Asia into North America and continued southward (100,000 years before the present), North America lost over 70 percent of its large mammal species, and South America lost almost 80 percent. When humans arrived on the Australian continent about 50,000 years before the present, the continent lost all large mammals, except kangaroos, and half of its flightless bird species. So we have certainly had an impact on species ranges in terms of contractions. However, we have also had a hand in many range expansions.

Human movements significantly impacted plants and animals, including microscopic organisms. Clearly, as a species, we are directly responsible for expansions and contractions of other species. In other words, we have decided to ignore the natural borders that nature has long been observing. Globalization exacerbated the transportation of species beyond natural borders leading to ecological destabilization.

The earliest examples of humans changing the natural boundaries of plants and animals come from agricultural practices. Plants have long been a favorite item of humans and accompany them during relocation. It makes sense that people should want to have familiar plants that serve as food, when moving to a new location, especially if they were not sure what to expect in the new land. The domestication of plants probably started around 8000 BCE and harbingered the agricultural revolution, when some hunter-gatherer societies decided to stay in areas year-round and cultivate their foods. Humans have a long tradition of intentionally moving cereal grains or other staples for their diet. Since the advent of agricultural societies, wheat, rice, and corn have become some of the most widely distributed plants in the world. They no longer have any particular natural border. For example, corn was found only in small regions in modern-day Mexico but now it is common throughout the world. These plants undoubtedly would never have made the cross-continental jumps without human intervention. However, these particular species and others similar to them require intensive cultivation for them to survive outside of their once native ranges. Without irrigation, fertilizer, and pesticide practices, many of these crop species would disappear from most of the areas they now occupy. Thus, humans have altered the natural process of colonization for many species. A few of these cultivated species have "escaped" the fields and become acclimatized to the point of being self-sustaining. One would find it odd to encounter a corn plant in the middle of a forest. Speaking of forests, tree species make up a notable exception. In tropical regions, tree plantations are populated primarily by pine, acacia, and eucalypt species. In numerous examples, these species are spreading off the plantations and establishing themselves in forest areas. A good example is the apple we know from grocery stores and fruit stands. It is not native to North America.[3] Modern apples are probably descendants of those native to Asia in the regions of Afghanistan and

Kazakhstan. In the northeastern United States, it is not uncommon to run into apple trees in forests. If we could look back in time, we would probably find farm fields nearby, where these apples were once cultivated. They have been able to tolerate the climate and are still able to hold their own against native species in the abandoned farm fields that are reverting to being wild forests.

As with domesticated plants, the agricultural revolution also saw the expansion of animals near and dear to humans. Cattle, sheep, horses, goats, and pigs are as common in agricultural landscapes worldwide as corn, rice, and wheat. Domestic animals, unlike their plant companions, seem to have more ability to "escape" the barnyard and colonize the new lands. During the age of exploration, it was quite common for ships to carry loads of livestock on board with the intention of starting new homesteads. Often enough, these ships would end up docking along the way to pick up provisions, and accidental exchanges of animals took place at these ports. One animal that seems particularly well-suited to using humans to help increase its own range is the rat. Rats are now found on nearly every land mass. Although not intentionally carried on these ships, they were stowaways in grain and bedding for the animals.

The aquatic habitats also provide examples of how humans have expanded animal species' ranges, especially in the aquaculture and sport fisheries industries. The Great Lakes of North America are dominated by large salmonid species (salmon and trout) introduced for fisheries purposes. A native salmonid, the lake trout, is now a minority in the Great Lakes. Lake Victoria, in the Rift Valley of Africa, is an impending natural disaster partly because the Nile perch, a large and voracious predator fish, was introduced in the mid-1950s by the Uganda Game and Fisheries Department as a supplement to sport and commercial fisheries and to "weed out" the smaller fish (Pringle 2005). The result was the loss of an estimated 200 species of fish native only to the lake (Ogutu-Ohwayo 1990).

Although the above examples support the idea that humans have changed the natural borders of species, they may not be directly related to transnational connectivity associated with globalization. More germane to globalization is the establishment of transnational trade routes and the consequences such connectivity has on species distributions. An early example can be found in the Silk Route, which had established regular movements between Europe, Asia, and parts of Africa as early as the first century CE. Even though this well-traveled route was traveled by very few individuals, it impacted biogeography significantly. Rats from the Orient became established along the route, and some of them carried the fleas containing microbes that cause bubonic plague. Data suggest that it took less than twenty years for the Black Death or the Plague to overtake Europe from its origin in the Orient.[4] The result was an estimated 10 percent decrease in human population size and up to a third reduction in European population totals.

The colonial and empire building era of the eighteenth and nineteenth centuries brought about an increase in travel between continents, which may be the first real mass movements of humans back and forth over long distances. As European nations set up colonies in Africa, Asia, and North and South America, it was imperative that goods and people be moved from one end of an empire to the other. Shipping routes were developed, and the shipping industry became a symbol of early globalization. Colonies spread out widely among continents received a constant stream of visitors and goods from far-off lands. These visitors brought with them a host of species, some intentionally but others unintentionally.

The world is increasingly concerned about the consequences of species being delivered as unintentional cargo, especially via the exchange of ballast in global shipping practice (for example, see Ruiz et al. 2000). Ballast, material carried inside the hulls of ships, helps stabilize them while they are in the water. For example, ships light on cargo would have to take on additional ballast to improve their height in the water, and heavier ships would have to offload ballast. Until very recently, ballast was composed of soils, rocks, wood, and anything else that was readily available. So ballast, along with goods, was transferred all over the colonial world. Many species, especially plants, were accidentally carried all over the known world in the ballast of ships. One can imagine the number of seeds that could be picked up while loading ballast. Ballast technology has changed with solid ballast being all but replaced by liquid ballast. Modern ships pump as much water into huge ballast tanks (some as large as 200,000 cubic meters) as needed. They also dump that water into the ports of destination when the ballast is no longer needed. Thus, major port areas now have become almost homogeneous in terms of what species of marine life are found. For example, the San Francisco Bay and Delta is now home to over 300 species of nonnative marine organisms. These accidental species now far outnumber the native species. As a response to the ecological consequences of ballast-water dumping, nations and international organizations are drafting guidelines for regulating ballast exchange.

The technology involved with moving people and goods from continent to continent has made large leaps forward. The invention of the steamship greatly reduced the time it took to cover cross-ocean voyages. Prior to steam travel, it would have taken about fifty-three days to travel from Norway to New York in a sailing vessel, for example. Early steam boats made the trip in eight to twelve days (Norway Heritage). Today, ocean-going vessels do it in three to five days. The reduced travel time is important for the survival of many plant and animal (and microbial life) species being carried in the ballast. Shorter time in the inhospitable confines of a ship hull improves survival. Also, as ships became larger, they required more ballast, thus simultaneously increasing the overall magnitude of plants and animals in accidental transport. Additionally, transoceanic ship traffic has increased, and new shipping routes continue to be developed. There were over 46,000 registered trading ships with a combined freight of 600 million tons in 2005 (Lloyds Register Fairplay 2006). The Automated Mutual-Assistance Vessel Rescue System (AMVER), originally known as the Atlantic Merchant Vessel Emergency Reporting System, is a voluntary program administered by the U.S. Coast Guard to track international shipping traffic. AMVER produces density plots,[5] which can illustrate the most heavily traveled shipping routes. Particularly heavy traffic exists between Europe and North America, as does intracontinental trade along the East Asian coasts. These are areas experiencing increased pressure due to the introduction of invasive species.

As colonization inland from these ports increased, "ballast" species were carried inland. For example, canals were constructed to move large amounts of people and goods to and from inland areas. The Erie Canal system in New York opened up a transportation route from the Great Lakes (Buffalo, New York) to New York City. Interestingly, the plant known as purple loosestrife that is native to Europe became established in ballast piles in seaport areas, and then spread inland along the canals. Now regarded as a common "weed" and pest of many New York wetlands, it is more competitive than many of the native wetland plants (cattails for example). Similarly, as trains replaced canals as the major transportation mode, railway lines became corridors for species dispersal. These days, it is the interstate highways that provide additional dispersal routes for species. Seeds are often blown down the highways by the passing vehicles. The common reed plant (*Phragmites australis*) uses this as a major mode of dispersal and now is common throughout the United States, especially in roadside ditches. It, too, is outcompeting our native wetland plants.

The twentieth century, especially after World War II, experienced not only a rapid increase in human population, but also a huge increase in the global traffic of people. One only has to look at an in-flight magazine on any major air carrier to see the extent to which large-scale travel is readily available. We can easily have breakfast on the European continent one day and eat dinner in Australia on the next. Air travel has made it possible to move people, goods, and unintended passengers to opposite ends of the globe in merely a few hours. Compounding any impact of human travel, bigger and faster planes, which will allow for more transport in shorter time frames, are still being produced. For example, the new Airbus A380 has a maximum passenger capacity of 840 and 40,000 cubic feet of cargo space. The International Air Transport Association (IATA) tracks domestic and international traffic of both passengers and freight. In October 2005, almost 180 billion revenue passenger kilometers[6] were booked on international flights. Similarly, almost 12 billion freight ton kilometers[7] were flown during that same period.

These figures mean that the potential for moving humans and their goods around the globe is unprecedented in history. This also means that intended and unintended species that humans bring along is at an all-time high.

Intentional Introductions

Introductions of plants and animals well beyond their natural borders have not been limited to "useful" agricultural species nor to accidental dispersal events as outlined above. Humans have a tradition of intentionally changing the natural environment to mimic or closely resemble what they remember from home. The colonial period saw the expansion of European empires. It also harbored, in the era of deliberate expansion, plants and animals for merely ornamental purposes. The Royal Botanical Gardens at Kew, founded in 1759, would often collect and transplant newly described species back in England. Likewise, colonialists often took their favorite ornamental plants with them when they established colonies along their trade routes. As early as 1698, an ornamental garden was established in Philadelphia by John Bartram. He set up an exchange of plants between England and New England (cited in Reichard and White 2001). The result is that the American landscape is now pocked with such species (e.g., barberry), and well over 50 percent of the naturalized plants of Australia are former ornamental plants (Kloot 1987).

The acclimatization societies of the nineteenth century were set on introducing (acclimatizing) European species throughout the colonies outside of Europe, such as the Americas, New Zealand, and Australia. Their goal was often to make the new landscapes resemble familiar (primarily) English landscapes. In a bizarre version of this, one such society was intent on introducing every species of bird mentioned in the works of William Shakespeare into North America. The common starling (European starling) was once considered a Palearctic species restricted to Europe and Siberia, down to the Mediterranean. It became a Holarctic species (found in both the Palearctic and Nearctic regions) because of its successful introduction to North America (Nearctic region). It became more or less pan-global as it was successfully introduced into South America, South Africa, New Zealand, and Australia. Birds captured from the wilds of exotic places were a favorite type of display animal back in Europe. Even today, you can obtain exotic species as pets without much trouble, although more regulations are now in place to prevent potential pest species from being transported as part of the pet trade.

Conclusions

Various disciplines define and study the implications of globalization through differing lens; however, the reduction or annihilation of borders and boundaries and the increasing social interconnectedness remain a common theme (e.g., Chong 2007). Modern globalization facilitates an unprecedented exchange of materials and ideas across space and time. Natural (nonhuman) systems worldwide also experience the effects of globalization. Natural boundaries that define species ranges are becoming increasingly porous, and there is unprecedented interconnectedness now among previously distinct ecological entities—the shrinking of space. Under natural time, natural borders shift over millennia. Human movements and behaviors that are the direct result of globalization patterns are causing these changes to occur on the scale of years to decades—the shrinking of time. The end effect of all of these intentional and accidental introductions of species by humans across natural borders is the homogenization of the world's flora and fauna. Globalization blurs the once distinct social features of human societies and the features of ecosystems. Based solely on the types of plants and animals in the specific environment, a biologist can no longer always identify the correct geobiographical setting.

The ecological effects of this homogenization are beginning to be realized. Each new species introduction has the potential to alter environmental conditions, which in turn increases the risk of further invasions—the so labeled "invasional meltdown" (Ricciardi 2001). For example, the zebra mussel has changed the architecture of the bottoms of the Great Lakes from a rather homogeneous, sandy bottom to one littered with dead and living mussel shells. These shells provide new habitats that the native species have trouble adapting to. However, other invasive species that would not have survived in the sandy bottoms, many of which are assumed to have been introduced but never survived, now find the altered habitat acceptable. In extreme cases, invasive species may cause the extinction of native species (Ricciardi 2004); in other cases, invasive species simply increase the diversity of an ecosystem as they use resources not exploited by native species (Sax and Gaines 2008). In either case, the rate of new introductions is much higher than it has ever been. The consequences for humans are also obvious. The United States spends hundreds of billions of dollars every year trying to control or prevent further dispersals of such species. One of the problems is that an established species becomes part of the natural ecosystem, making eradication difficult. Each successive generation of humans permanently alters the natural borders for the next generations.

Because human activities can be directly implicated in causing the ecological changes outlined in this chapter, factors affecting the movement of humans have bearing on these natural processes. The literature on globalization also needs to consider the changes we are intentionally or unintentionally imposing on natural processes.

Notes

1. In general, advances in technology, most often related to transportation, have caused increases in the number of successful species introductions. Paradoxically, technology may also cause a reversal of this trend. Telecommunication is certainly increasing globalization by compressing the space and time needed to transmit information. This may result in less necessary travel, which could, in turn, decrease the overall numbers of potentially invasive species in transport.
2. Spiders are some of the earliest species to arrive on new islands (Simberloff and Wilson 1969).
3. The hawthorn apple is the only similar species native to North America. Johnny Appleseed was a historic figure and did indeed play a significant role, dispersing apples beyond their cultivated range in North America.
4. See the map showing the timeline of recorded Bubonic Plague outbreaks along the Silk Route (http://www.brown.edu/Departments/Italian_Studies/dweb/images/plague/plague_routes.jpg).
5. Most recent density plots of shipping traffic are available at www.amver.com.
6. The term revenue passenger kilometer refers to the sum of the products obtained by multiplying the number of revenue passengers carried on each flight by the flight distance.
7. The term freight ton kilometers refers to the sum of the products obtained by multiplying the total number of tons of each category of revenue load carried on each sector of a flight by flight stage distance.

References

Anderson, Benedict. 1991. *Imagined Communities: Reflections on the Origin and Spread of Nationalism.* Revised edition. London and New York: Verso.

Burns, C. E., K. M. Johnston, and O. J. Schmitz. 2003. Global Climate Change and Mammalian Species Diversity in U.S. National Parks. *Proceedings of the National Academy of Sciences of the United States of America* 100(20): 11474–77.

Chong, T. 2007. Practicing Global Ethnography in Southeast Asia: Reconciling Area Studies with Theory. *Asian Studies Review* 31(3): 211–26.

Gabel, Medard, and Henry Bruner. 2003. *Globalinc.: An Atlas of the Multinational Corporation*. New York: New Press.

Glick, P. A. 1939. *The Distribution of Insects, Spiders, and Mites in the Air*. United States Department of Agriculture Technical Bulletin. 673.

Kloot, P. M. 1987. The Naturalized Flora of South Australia, 3: Its Origin, Introduction, Distribution, Growth Forms and Significance. *Journal of Adelaide Botanic Gardens* 10: 99–111.

König, W. 1978. *Dtv-Atlas zur Deutschen Sprache. Deutscher Taschenbuch*. Munich: Verlag GmbH and Co.

Lewellen, Ted C. 2002. *The Anthropology of Globalization: Cultural Anthropology Enters the 21st Century*. Westport, CT: Begin and Garvey.

Lloyds Register Fairplay. 2006. http://www.lrfairplay.com/Maritime_Data/Statistics. html (accessed in October 2007).

Norway Heritage. http://www.norwayheritage.com/ (accessed in March 2008).

Ogutu-Ohwayo, R. 1990. The Decline of the Native Fishes of Lakes Victoria and Kyogo (East Africa) and the Impact of Introduced Species, Especially the Nile Perch *Lates niloticus* and the Nile Tilapia *Oreochromios niloticus*. *Environmental Biology of Fishes* 27: 81–96.

Olson, D. M., E. Dinerstein, E. D. Wikramanayake, N. D. Burgess, G. V. N. Powell, E. C. Underwood, J. A. D'amico, I. Itoua, H. E. Strand, J. C. Morrison, C. J. Loucks, T. F. Allnutt, T. H. Ricketts, Y. Kura, J. F. Lamoreux, W. W. Wettengel, P. Hedao and K. R. Kassem. 2001. Terrestrial Ecoregions of the World: A New Map of Life on Earth. *Bioscience* 51(11): 933–38.

Porter, A. N., ed. 1991. *Atlas of British Overseas Expansion*. London: Routledge.

Pringle, R. M. 2005. The Origins of the Nile Perch in Lake Victoria. *BioScience* 55(9): 780–87.

Reichard, S. H., and P. White. 2001. Horticulture as a Pathway of Invasive Plant Introductions in the United States. *BioScience* 51: 103–13.

Ricciardi, A. 2001. Facilitative Interactions among Aquatic Invaders: Is an "Invasional Meltdown" Occurring in the Great Lakes? *Canadian Journal of Fisheries and Aquatic Sciences* 58: 2513–25.

———. 2004. Assessing Species Invasions as a Cause of Extinction. *Trends in Ecology and Evolution* 19: 619.

Ruiz, G. M., T. K. Rawlings, F. C. Dobbs, L. A. Drake, T. Mullady, A. Huq, and R. R. Colwell. 2000. Global Spread of Microorganisms by Ships. *Nature* 408(6808): 49–50.

Sax, D. F., and S. D. Gaines. 2008. Species Invasions and Extinction: The Future of Native Biodiversity on Islands. *Proceedings of the National Academy of Sciences of the United States of America* 105: 11490–97.

Simberloff, D. S., and E. O. Wilson. 1969. Experimental Zoogeography of Islands: The Colonization of Empty Islands. *Ecology* 50(2): 278–96.

Tackenberg, O., P. Poschlod, and S. Kahmen. 2003. Dandelion Seed Dispersal: The Horizontal Wind Speed Does Not Matter for Long-Distance Dispersal— It is the Updraft! *Plant Biology* 5: 451–54.

Wallace, Alfred R. 1876. *The Geographical Distribution of Animals; with a Study of the Relations of Living and Extinct Faunas as Elucidating the Past Changes of the Earth's Surface.* 2 volumes. London: Macmillan.

Echoes from the Past Reflections

Thomás Sakoulas

As I walked under the hot sun in Tinos, one of the marble-producing islands of Greece, I could not help but marvel at the stone carvings of local artisans, which appeared everywhere, over front doors, over windows, decorating church altars or bell towers, and even lining the streets upon which I stepped. The land had remained the host of the carvers' labor for over two millennia, and I was happy to put my own little sweat beads in this continuum by doing some carving on the island. Being a native of Greece, I felt a strong connection with what I consider to be my heritage, the ancient Greek carved masterpieces of art and architecture. Globalization can sweep you away but can also bring you back home. Upon returning to my studio in upstate New York, I began searching for ways to maintain the dialogue with the ancient past, and more specifically with the ancient decorative motifs I found myself studying intently. My ideas, my skill, and my chisels travel with me, but marble requires complex logistics even in this "globalized" world. For a while I thought that without Tinos marble I would have to abandon my latest line of work and even attempted to engage different ideas that would have been more fitting to my current environment, which is in the central area of New York State.

Having settled in the United States after being raised and schooled in Greece, I have become acutely aware of the similarities and differences between the cultural outputs of both countries, vis-a-vis the conceptual development of the plastic arts. No matter how great the influence of the West or the East, Greek art always gravitates toward the irresistible pull of its own historical precedents. On the other hand, art in the United States very often attempts to deny specific points of historical origin. Influenced by American art currents—the United States is a place where the weight of every world torrent finds a forum—I sought for years to shed the burden of history from

my work. But in the end, I always returned to the comfort and security of
the Greek cultural thread of which I feel I am an extension. I have been
fortunate enough to live in a world where the exchange of ideas is fluid, and
the ease of travel and communication is conducive to maintaining one's
identity, and I find myself consumed with the study and observation of
ancient Greek art styles, either through museum and site visits when I travel
to Greece, or through written sources when I return to the United States.

In the light of this, my body of work, which was exhibited as "Echoes
from the Past" (see it online at www.sakoulas.com/exhibitions/echoes.html),
was an amalgamation of American minimal lines, European expressionist
texture, and ancient Greek iconography and ideals. I emulated ancient
architectural decorative motifs I had studied in Greece, with clean minimal
lines that were in turn defined through the expressive marks of a very physical process. In the end, much of the artwork seemed to echo not only my
own historicity and aesthetic sensibilities, but also the process by which the
ancient artists themselves refined their original styles. The merging of styles
is evident everywhere in and around the Aegean region. One can trace
direct relationships between Mycenaean and Minoan art, between Minoan
and Cycladic work, between Minoan and Egyptian, or between Egyptian
and Archaic sculpture. As I looked at the ancient artifacts in museums and
archaeological sites in Greece, I always pondered the ancient artists and
artisans. How did they come to establish their styles and motifs? How did
they learn about the art of other artists from the past or from other cultures
of the ancient world? Did Minoan artists go to Egypt to see the artwork?
Did they travel to Mycenae to produce the palace frescoes? Did they only
see the products of commerce that came from abroad? Or were they immigrants themselves who found a way to make a living with their art, and in
the process, did they help define the cultural signature of the Cretans?

An artist is mainly concerned with producing art, and his/her focus
always revolves around what this knowledge produces in terms of artwork.
While dedicated study can make one a good historian, in order to achieve
effective merging of stylistic and conceptual approaches it is not enough for
one to desire emulation or to study the stylistic approaches from different
eras. Such convergence comes from immersion in the ideals of one or more
particular traditions. It does not come from mere thinking, but from deep
immersion in cultures. My artwork series that revolved around a "Lotus"
image was more the result of trying to understand the process of repeating
simple geometric patterns to achieve a large whole, than an attempt to recreate an icon that has been ubiquitous in a number of cultures from ancient
to modern times (see the cover of the book and the "Lotus" series at www.
sakoulas.com/exhibitions/echoes.html).

The repetition of a simple arc in space is something with which I have worked for more than fifteen years in various forms, but it was only in this work that it resulted in a clean, visual connection to ancient Greek iconography. In the "Lotus" series, the simple repetition of an entity—an arc—defines a larger and more wondrous whole as it moves in space and becomes transformed in a different context. In a way it becomes a metaphor for the artist's own movement in time and space. This simple weaving of the arc in time and space produces other, more complex, independent forms free from their source but without ever denying their origin. Cropped from the circle, and moving like chorus lines in an ancient tragedy, a simple arc became a "Lotus" without ever refuting the circle. The arc stitched time through the fabric of space, and the process raised both to a new level of understanding. Additionally, the variation in materials adds another dimension and defines the concepts as they materialize in different dimensions. Relief carving on stone describes a different object than pigment on plastic, and both define a different reality than a steel sculpture in the round. The materials themselves add their own cultural connotations to the work since they lend themselves to connotations from different eras and cultures, and add to the meaning of the shape as they decode it with their presence. We tend to associate stone sculpture with antiquity, steel with modernity, and plastic with contemporary culture.

As I drove around upstate New York and compared the gray hills, filled with vegetation, to the barren Tinos hills, where veins of marble expose themselves to the sunlight on the surface, I thought of the local artisans of Greece who for eons used not only what came to them via global trade, but mostly what was familiar and readily available to them. This simple thought was enough to change my entire view of the scene. It was not a landscape barren of the objects and ideas I desired any longer, but a rich landscape made of rock that I could make part of my own cultural continuum. And so, I spent a few months carving the upstate New York "bluestone," the characteristic local variety of grey-bluish sandstone, which proved to me that even though it does not encompass the qualities of marble, it possesses a unique character and aesthetic qualities very suitable for the more expressive iconography for which I was yearning. In the process, the two stones from two different places of the globe, along with the motifs and techniques of a different era, taught me a bit more about myself and my environment by building the bridge from my daily landscape to the signs of a different era and a faraway place I also call my own.

Notes on the Contributors

Joseph F. Chiang is Professor of Chemistry and Biochemistry at the State University of New York (SUNY) College at Oneonta. Chiang received his MS and PhD degrees from Cornell University. With over fifty research papers and book chapters published, he is currently the editor of the book entitled *Recent Research and Development in Solar Cells*, to be published by Tsinghua University Press-Springer. He is also the associate editor of the journal *The Frontiers of Environmental Science and Engineering in China*. He has delivered many lectures and papers in China as an invited lecturer.

Shiao-Yun Chiang, PhD in Communication and Sociology, State University of New York at Albany, is an Associate Professor of Communication Studies at SUNY College at Oneonta. His main research interests include social semiotics, intercultural pragmatics, and instructional interaction within and across cultural boundaries. His recent publications in international journals are "Reformulation as a Strategy for Managing 'Understanding Uncertainty' in Office Hour Interactions" in *Intercultural Education* 19, no. 3 (2008); "Mutual Understanding as a Procedural Achievement in Intercultural Interaction" in *Intercultural Pragmatics*, vol. 6, no. 3 (2009); and "Personal Power and Positional Power in the Discourse of Doctoral Supervision" in *Discourse & Communication*, vol. 3, no. 3 (2009).

Robert Compton is Associate Professor of Political Science at SUNY College at Oneonta. Compton's research interests focus on political development in East Asia and Southern Africa. In addition to journal publications, he is the editor of and contributor to *Transforming East Asian Domestic and International Politics* (Ashgate: 2002) and the author of *East Asian Democratization: Impact of Globalization, Culture, and Economy* (Praeger: 2000). A 2008 U.S. Fulbright Scholar to Zimbabwe, he taught at the University of Zimbabwe and was also a Visiting Scholar at the Center for Civil Society (CCS), University of KwaZulu-Natal, Durban, South Africa, in 2007.

Brian D. Haley, Associate Professor and Chair of Anthropology at the SUNY College at Oneonta, is author of "Anthropology and the Making of Chumash Tradition" (*Current Anthropology* 1997), "How Spaniards Become Chumash and Other Tales of Ethnogenesis" (*American Anthropologist* 2005), and *Reimagining the Immigrant: The Accommodation of Mexican Immigrants in Rural America* (Palgrave Macmillan, forthcoming).

Matthew Hendley, Associate Professor of History at SUNY College at Oneonta, has published articles in the *Canadian Journal of History, Albion, Journal of the Canadian Historical Association,* as well as a book chapter in *The Culture of Fascism: Visions of the Far Right in Britain*, coedited by Julie Gottlieb and Thomas Linehan (London: I. B. Tauris, 2004). His dissertation, "Patriotic Leagues and the Evolution of Popular Patriotism and Imperialism in Great Britain 1914–32," received Honorable Mention for the John Bullen Prize (for the best doctoral dissertation accepted at a Canadian university). Dr. Hendley received a Research and Scholarship Award for excellence in scholarship from the Research Foundation of SUNY in 2007 and the Richard Siegfried Prize for Academic Excellence from SUNY Oneonta in 2003.

Thomas Horvath is Associate Professor of Biology and Director of Environmental Sciences at SUNY College at Oneonta. His research focuses on the dispersal of aquatic invasive species in freshwater, especially zebra mussels and crayfish. He is the author of "Economically Viable Strategy for Prevention of Invasive Species Introduction: Case Study of Otsego Lake, New York," which was published in *Aquatic Invasions* in 2008.

Raymond Lau accepted a position with an innovative structural engineering firm in London, and later was invited to join the world-renowned Zaha Hadid Architects, UK, in 2007, after completing his master's degree at the Architectural Association, London, UK. Besides earning awards in numerous international competitions, Lau has been a project architect and project manager during his second employment, handling large-scale projects in Dubai, UAE, and in Chengdu and Beijing, China. He is researching the relationship between ethno-cultural identity and architecture with Ho Hon Leung, and they are working on research projects in China, Hong Kong, Macau, Canada, Greece, and the United States. His article "Visionary Development Plan of Macau and Zhuhai" has been published in *The Proceedings of The Fourth Symposium on Sustainable Development: Cooperation among Hong Kong, Macau, and Guandong, 2008.*

Orlando Legname is an Associate Professor of Music at SUNY College at Oneonta, as well as a composer, conductor, musical theorist, and Digidesign

Certified "Pro Tools Expert." He also currently holds the position of Director of the Audio Arts Production Program at SUNY College at Oneonta. Legname has received the State University's prestigious Chancellors Award for Excellence in Scholarship and Creative Activities and numerous other awards. His compositions have been widely performed and recorded in the United States and Europe. Dr. Legname's composition "Septet" received the Walsum Award, and his work "Event Horizon III" was released as "Cigar Smoke," a compact disc (CD) by INNOVA Records. He has published two textbooks and several articles, and has produced CD recordings, theater music, jingles, and commercials.

Ho Hon Leung is Associate Professor of Sociology and Chair of the Steering Committee of the Center for Social Science Research at SUNY College at Oneonta. His research interests include ethnic relations, immigrants, ethnic aging, and globalization. He has developed a new research interest in ethno-cultural identity and architecture with Raymond Lau. They are writing a book on the intertwining relationship between ethno-cultural identity and architecture. Dr. Leung is the coeditor of and contributor to *Investigating Diversity: Race, Ethnicity, and Beyond* (Linton Atlantic Books: 2008). He is also the author of "The Road Less Taken: Settlement of Chinese Immigrants in Small Towns," *Asian and Pacific Migration Journal* 16, no.1 (2007).

Walter Little, Associate Professor at SUNY at Albany, is a cultural anthropologist who studies cultural identity politics, political economy, and tourism in Antigua, Guatemala. He is the codirector of Tulane University's Oxlajuj Aj: Kaqchikel Maya Language and Culture Course. Some of his major publications include the books *Mayas in the Marketplace: Tourism, Globalization, and Cultural Identity* (University of Texas Press: 2004), *La utz awach? Introduction to the Kaqchikel Maya Language* (University of Texas Press: 2006) with Judith Maxwell and Robert M. Brown, and *Mayas in Post-War Guatemala: Harvest of Violence Revisited* (University of Alabama Press: 2009) with Timothy J. Smith, as well as numerous articles.

Hanfu Mi, PhD, is Associate Professor and Coordinator of Literacy Education in the Department of Elementary Education and Reading at SUNY College at Oneonta. His main research interests include language acquisition and literacy development, with an emphasis on sociocultural linguistic factors. His most recent publications include a journal article, "Reformulation as a Strategy for Managing 'Understanding Uncertainty' in Office Hour Interactions," *Intercultural Education,* vol. 19, no. 3 (2008), and a book chapter, "A White Horse is Not a Horse!—Vocabulary

Development through Conceptual Understanding and Sociocultural Experience" in *The Lives of Young Children, Research and Public Policy,* edited by Judith McConnel-Farmer (Linton Atlantic Books: 2009).

Maria Cristina Montoya, born in Colombia, is Lecturer of Foreign Language at SUNY College at Oneonta, and teaches language courses in grammar, conversation, and phonetics, in addition to courses with a cultural component, such as Spanish for native speakers and Spanish and Latin American film. She is currently ABD in Linguistics from SUNY Albany, pending the completion of her dissertation titled "Expression of Possession in Spanish in Contact with English: A Sociolinguistic Study across Two Generations in New York." Her research area focuses on heritage language maintenance and language and gender.

Joshua M. Rosenthal, Associate Professor of the Department of History and Non-Western Cultures at Western Connecticut State University, is a student of Mestre Caxias of Grupo Capoeira Brazil. He has organized panels about and presented papers on capoeira at the Annual Meeting of the American Historical Association, as well as at other conferences and seminars. He has written reviews and review essays on capoeira that have appeared in the *Latin American Research Review* and the *Hispanic American Historical Review.* He has commented on capoeira for Wisconsin Public Radio. He also researches issues of state formation and political culture in nineteenth-century Colombia, working mainly with material held in the Archivo General de la Nación in Bogotá. He is the editor for reviews in History and Social Sciences of the *Revista de Estudios Colombianos* and a member of the Asociación de Colombianistas, the Colombia section of the Latin American Studies Association, and the Conference on Latin American History.

Thomas Sakoulasis is an artist who was born in Greece and now resides in Oneonta, New York. He received his master's degree in Fine Arts from the Maryland Institute College of Art, Rinehart School of Sculpture, in 1994, and his work has been exhibited and collected nationally. His art in stone, metal, drawing, and digital media reflects his interest and investigation of elemental geometry, ancient Greek art, and the transformation of visual signs as they become fragmented and detached from their original context. He is Associate Professor of the Department of Art, and teaches sculpture and computer art at SUNY College at Oneonta.

Xu Xi (www.xuxiwriter.com) is the author of seven books of fiction and essays. Recent titles include *Evanescent Isles* (2008, essays), *The Unwalled City* (2001, novel), and *Overleaf Hong Kong* (2004, stories and essays). Her novel

Habit of a Foreign Sky (2007) was shortlisted for the inaugural Man Asian Literary Prize, and will be published in 2010. She has also edited several anthologies of Hong Kong writing in English, including *Fifty-Fifty* (2008) and *City Voices* (2003), and is regional editor of Routledge's *Encyclopedia of Post-Colonial Literature* (2nd ed., 2005). She is currently faculty chair of the MFA in Writing program at Vermont College of Fine Arts, and also teaches graduate and undergraduate creative writing workshops at various international universities. In 2009, she was the Bedell Distinguished Visiting Writer at the University of Iowa's Nonfiction Writing Program.

Index